THE ILLUSTRATED HISTORY OF·
RAILWAYS
IN BRITAIN
·Geoffrey Freeman Allen·

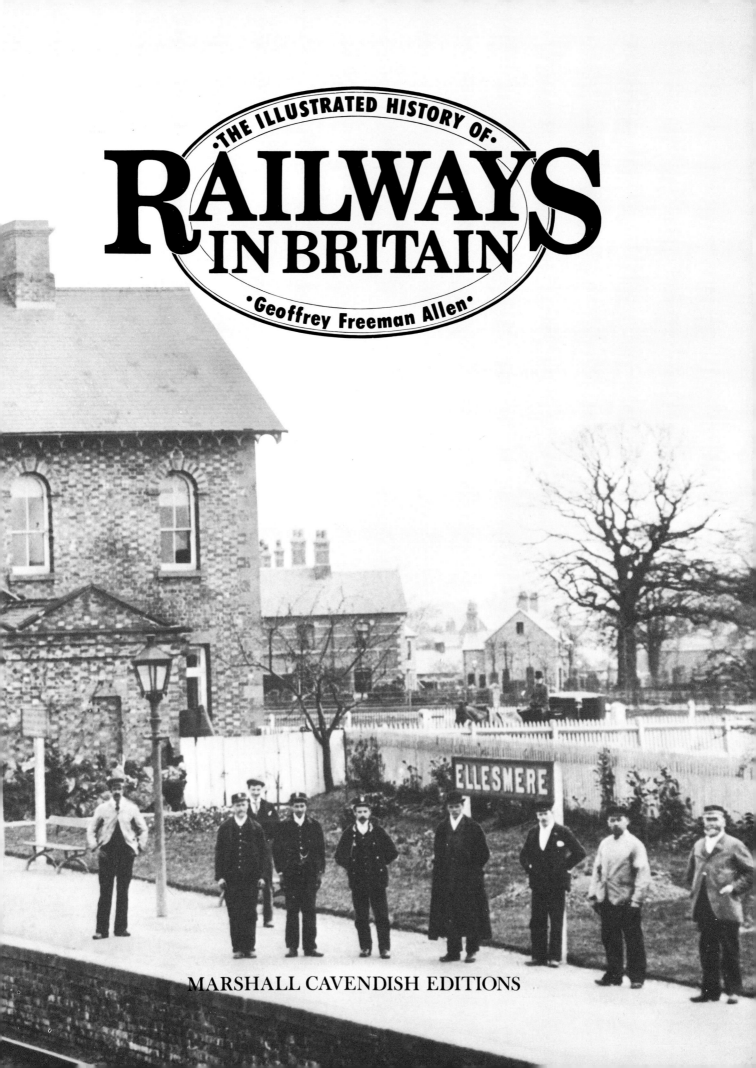

THE ILLUSTRATED HISTORY OF
RAILWAYS
IN BRITAIN
Geoffrey Freeman Allen

ELLESMERE

MARSHALL CAVENDISH EDITIONS

Front endpapers: *A classic railway scene; the crossover at the east end of Newcastle Central Station on a winter's day in the 1930s, with A3 No. 2570* Sunstar *pulling away on an Edinburgh express. The A3s were the mainstay of the East Coast route at this time.*

Back endpapers: *Part of life for a century, never to be seen again.*

First page: *Dowles Bridge, the highlight of the Tenbury and Bewdley Railway, is shown to good effect by a carefully posed train shortly after its opening in 1864. The engine, No. 1A* Great Western *was built the same year.*

Previous pages: *The days when a small country station could support a staff of nine! Ellesmere, a junction on the Cambrian Railways, in 1895 – thirty years after it was built.*

This page: *The last days of the broad gauge; a Paddington-bound express rushes through Uphill Junction on the dual-gauge main line in the late 1880s.*

Contributors
Peter Semmens
Basil Cooper
John Clay
Geoffrey Freeman Allen

Photographs selected by Phil Soar
House editors: Sarah Parr, Anne Wilson
Designers: Pedro Pra-Lopez, Jim Bamber, Eddie Pitcher
Picture research: John Adams

Prepared in association with
Colourviews Limited, Birmingham

Published by Marshall Cavendish Books Limited
58 Old Compton Street
London W1V 5 PA

© Marshall Cavendish Limited 1979, 1982

First printing 1979
Second printing 1982
Typesetting by Clerkenwell Graphics
Reproduction by Monographics
Printed in Hong Kong
ISBN 0 85685 714 9

FOREWORD

A HOARY APHORISM HAS it that if the Stephensons had perfected the internal combustion engine instead of the steam locomotive, no-one would have needed to evolve the railway. I doubt it. The first question to answer is whether motor vehicles would have so perfectly matched the needs of the Industrial Revolution as the railway. Without the railway's crucial asset of cheap and reasonably swift movement of industry's raw materials in bulk – coal especially – development might surely have taken a slower and perhaps different course.

Lacking the train's cheap mass movement capability I wonder, too, whether travel would have been popularized so quickly. One tends to forget that within just 20 years of the opening of the Liverpool and Manchester as many as 80 million passenger journeys a year had been generated. Many industrial towns and seaside resorts mushroomed from a hamlet purely as a result of the new railway's imput of traffic. Not that the railway's effect in this context has been all gain, however. The teeming dormitories of North-East London, for instance, were born of the Great Eastern's steam suburban enterprise.

The railways had it too good for their own comfort in the nineteenth century, though. The feverish and fierce cut-and-thrust of their geographical development makes exciting reading, but apart from the refinement of operational discipline and safety provisions one looks hard for significant technological improvement until the last decade or so. Then, with the eager pursuit of mainline speed and passenger comfort and, with growing benefit of electric traction which brought the emergence of the modern commuter systems, British railways crossed a watershed into their second age. It has only just ended.

The railway's romance tends to be its competitive drawback in modern times. Its fascination – apart from the emotional impact of its now vanished steam power – is the intricate, interdependent organization it needs to run its strictly controlled service on a reserved right of way with speed and safety. But because it is so ramified, method is not easily changed, and when change becomes inescapable the upheaval is traumatic. Such a drastic revision of commercial and operating method was forced on British railways by the mid-twentieth century destruction of its few remaining monopolistic advantages. Consequently the last 20 years or so of its history have been as full of incident and advance as any since the very first 20.

No doubt about it, the railways of Britain have just stepped into their third age. To my mind it is as full of promise – within a more limited sphere, granted – as the first unveiled over 150 years ago by the Stockton and Darlington and Liverpool and Manchester.

GEOFFREY FREEMAN ALLEN

CONTENTS

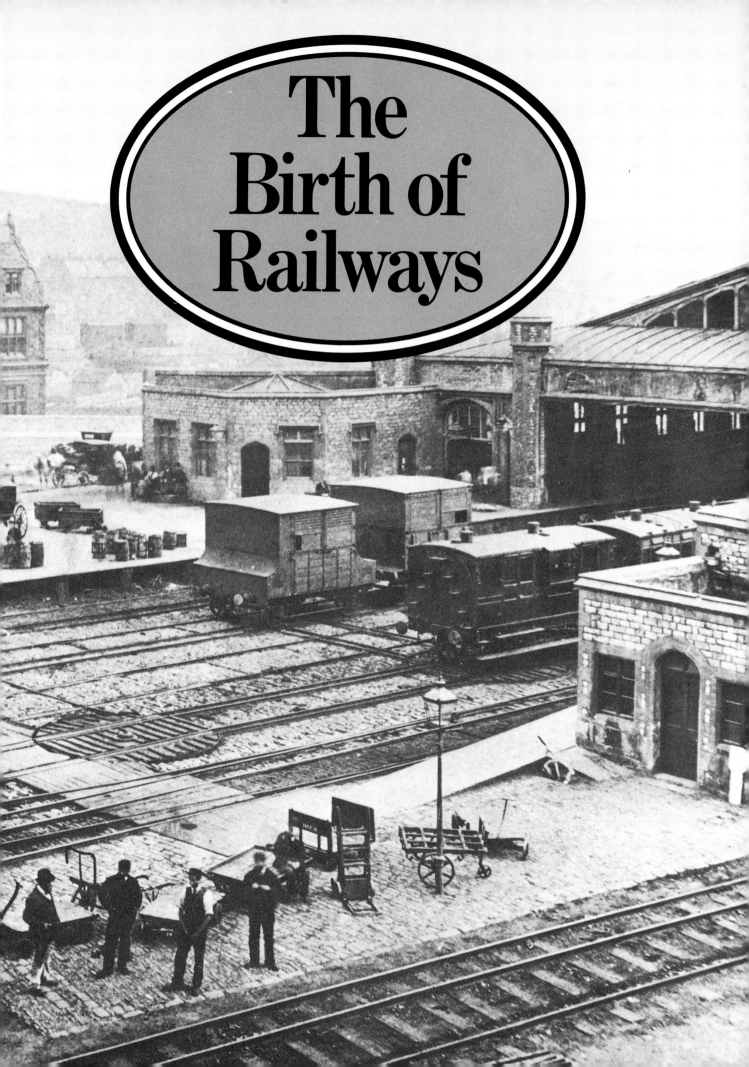

The Birth of Railways

Chapter 1

Steam and Stephenson

Above: The burly Richard Trevithick – the Cornish steam pumping engineer who was the first to sense the potential of steam power in alliance with late-eighteeth-century wagonways.

Previous pages: Brunel's original Bristol station in the 1880s. Note the coach on the flatcar (far left); the mixed gauge and also the turntables and lateral tracks used to manoeuvre vehicles from one line to another.
This picture is particularly notable for having been taken before the new Temple Meads was built. The London and Bristol terminus is on the right; the Bristol and Exeter at right angles to it behind the refreshment rooms. Until the new curve was built goods had to be transhipped from one terminus to the other. For many years the GWR was, not unreasonably, known as the Great Way Round and the Bristol cut-off – through Westbury and Frone – was not actually built until the early years of this century.

I N THESE DAYS of great personal mobility, with Inter-City 125 trains making 125 mph in regular service every day and a ratio of three road vehicles to every four British households, it is extremely hard to appreciate what travelling conditions were like for our ancestors two centuries ago. One can get some impression from a writer of 1756 who complained that the Mile End Road, only a mile east of Aldgate in what is now the heart of the City of London, was just a stagnant lake of deep mud that made it 'hard work for four horses pulling a light chaise to go faster than a foot pace'. In fact British roads at that time were in a worse state than they had been under the Romans.

But the Industrial Revolution was beginning to touch much of the country. One of its early economic effects was to increase the demand for overland goods transport. Until then the sea and the country's many navigable rivers had been an adequate if rather risky means of transporting most heavy loads. It was the Severn, for instance, which encouraged the development of coal, iron and other industries in the south-west well before such activity had taken root in the north; in 1750 no fewer than 200 firms were operating barges or 'trows' for freight movement on the river. Now industrial activity was growing in areas without suitable natural waterways. The primitive road systems were not an alternative, since in winter they often became impassable, even for pack animals which could usually pick their way around morasses that bogged down wheeled transport.

The first solution was to increase the availability of waterborne transport. Construction of artificial waterways goes back to the Exeter Canal of the mid-1500s, but it was not until two centuries later, in 1761, that the first part of the famous Bridgwater Canal, from the collieries at Worsley to the suburbs of Manchester, was opened. The commercial success of this venture led to the great age of canal-building, and Britain's increasing prosperity during the remainder of the eighteenth century provided the very considerable capital required.

A canal-based transport system, however, is only feasible economically when the area to be served is relatively flat; otherwise the requirements for locks and their water supply present increasingly complex problems, and seriously slow down the movement of goods. In many places the mineral wealth being won from mines and quarries could not easily be moved by the main natural waterways or by canal. As a result, transport techniques first adopted for use in mines began to develop into the earliest tramway and railway systems.

There were two vital differences between a railway and the early roads. First, the rails provided a bearing surface which did not degenerate into an impassable swamp when rain fell on them, and second, a mechanical guidance system enabled 'trains' of vehicles to follow each other. Within the confines of an underground mine, all the disadvantages caused by the low bearing capacity of wet earth had long been known, and since the fourteenth century, the mines on the mainland of Europe had used a wooden truck called a *Hund*. The wheels of a *Hund* ran on two parallel wooden planks, and by the sixteenth century a vertical pin had been added to the underside of the vehicle so that it protruded into a slot between the planks and provided guidance. A model at the National Railway Museum, York, shows a mine with many *Hund*s in operation, while the Swiss Transport Museum at Lucerne has a beautifully preserved example dating from 1785. These mining systems, however, rarely emerged into the open air, and even then only far enough to enable the wagon's contents to be tipped on to a heap for subsequent removal by other means, since the ordinary hand barrow or cart provided a satisfactory means of transport away from the adit or underground gallery.

When surface railways developed, they used very different means of guidance, because the *Hund* system provided only for narrow vehicles which, although admirable for underground use, were of no economic advantage out in the open. There were a few early European guide-wheel railways, in which horizontal rollers operated on the wooden track in addition to the carrying wheels, but the development of flanged wheels took place in England from the early years of the seventeenth century. Wooden wagonways using

flanged wheels were built very extensively to transport coal to the waterways in the Tyneside coalfield.

Underground, the relatively primitive transport methods were revolutionized by John Curr's invention of the L-section iron plate rail in 1787. Its use in mines spread quickly and it was very rapidly adopted for surface operation throughout Britain, except on Tyneside. Earlier, in 1767, Coalbrookdale had seen the first use of iron plates to provide a more durable surface to the wooden rails. This development led to the discovery that an iron wheel on an iron rail was very free-running; as a result, heavier loads could be handled, and a horse could now haul more than a single vehicle. A flanged metal wheel running on the top surface of a metal rail produced better economies and was to supersede all other forms of construction.

By the end of the eighteenth century, mining was being carried out on a large scale in several parts of the country. Some of the most important of the various enterprises were the metal mines of Cornwall and the collieries of Durham and Northumberland, both of which were to make a significant contribution to the development of the steam railway. For nearly a century already, many of these mines had been utilizing fire – or,

more correctly steam – engines to pump water from their depths. However the materials and techniques of construction available severely limited the maximum steam pressure which could be employed, and indeed, the Newcomen engine used its steam solely as a means of producing a vacuum, against which the pressure of the atmosphere moved the piston. As a result the engines were enormous in size and very slow-acting. Watt went slightly better, but it was a Cornishman, Trevithick, who developed the concept of the high-pressure steam engine in which the exhaust from the cylinder was discharged into the atmosphere rather than condensed. This enabled far greater power to be produced by a cylinder of a given size, and so the way now lay open to construct a successful steam *locomotive* engine – in other words, one capable of load haulage.

The first locomotive

Although Cugnot in Paris had succeeded in operating his steam trucks, intended for artillery haulage, in the late 1760s, they had not proved to be a practical proposition. However, in 1804 Trevithick's steam locomotive, operating on the Pen-y-Darren Tramway in South Wales, success-

Below: Forerunner of the steam railway – a typical horse-operated tramroad of the kind laid to convey material between pit or factory and the nearest navigable waterway. The first British examples were built in the mid-seventeenth century.

fully hauled a ten-ton load, covering the nine and a half miles in just over four hours. But even on this trial trip, which was to win a wager of 500 guineas, its weight broke the track. Consequently it only had a short life as a locomotive before it took up its originally intended function as a stationary engine driving a hammer at the ironworks. The same fate awaited a similar locomotive built for Blackett of Wylam, near Newcastle. The technical problem of supporting the weight of the locomotive was to remain unsolved for several years to come.

The early railways had cast iron rails, and, even after the adoption of a fish-bellied shape, could not support any great weight. The designer of a steam locomotive was faced with a dilemma – he had to ensure that his machine was not too heavy to damage the track, but also that it still carried enough weight to produce the necessary grip between iron wheels and iron rails and prevent slipping. Horse-worked tramways and railways had often been built with steep gradients, which made adhesion difficult. For years there was widespread conviction that this problem was insoluble, so engineers busied themselves with devices to supplement the grip of wheel on rail. John Blenkinsop combined an

ingenious rack with running rails to produce the first successful colliery locomotive for the Middleton Railway in 1812. Other, less effective, ideas that were tried included a machine which pushed itself along the line by means of two 'feet' at its back.

Eventually it was William Hedley who showed by means of some very cleverly designed experiments, that it was possible to obtain enough adhesion for transmission of power via the carrying wheels. His *Puffing Billy* and *Wylam Dilly* were both put into service in 1813. Even so, they were too heavy for the early track and had to be rebuilt to run on eight wheels rather than the original four, but later, when stronger rails had been installed, they were re-converted. In spite of all these changes, and the temporary adaptation of one of them to provide motive power for a steam tug, both had a long working life. *Wylam Dilly* continued in use until 1866, and is now on public exhibition at the Royal Scottish Museum in Edinburgh, while *Puffing Billy* is similarly accorded a place of honour in the Science Museum at South Kensington in London.

Much of this activity in the north-east was noted by George Stephenson, who was born in a

Below: Richard Trevithick built this locomotive – the first to haul a load successfully over rails, at Pen-y-Darren ironworks near Merthyr Tydfil, South Wales, on 13 February 1804. The engine was soon retired because it was too heavy for the light track.

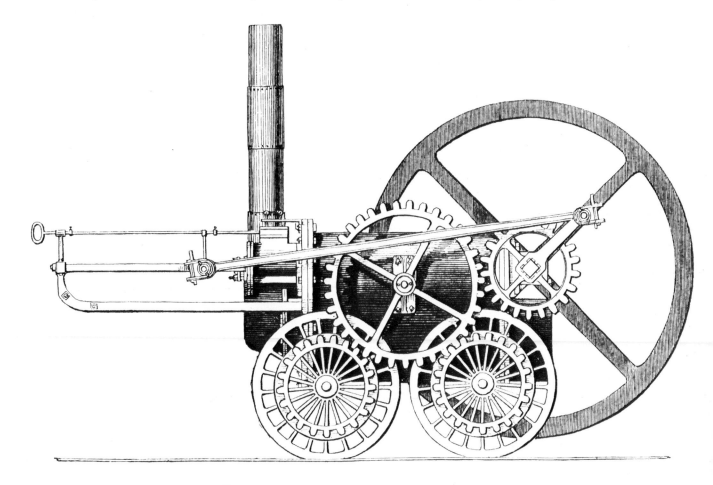

cottage alongside the Wylam Waggonway in 1781. His first direct involvement with steam engines was as assistant fireman at one of the collieries. He quickly developed a great interest in their operation, and in his early thirties he was appointed enginewright for a group of collieries around Killingworth. It was here that he developed his steam locomotives and at the same time worked out his principles of railway construction and operation, which were later to find such widespread application.

Stephenson had numerous design problems with these early locomotives. Although the solutions he first worked out made the result rather ungainly by subsequent standards, there was logical thought in the various features. For instance, Trevithick's use of high-pressure steam meant that there must be no condensation of the steam either in the cylinders (the Newcomen principle) or in a separate condenser (Watt). To ensure that efficiency was not lost by condensation taking place inadvertently, Stephenson mounted the cylinders inside the boiler itself, as indeed Trevithick had done. However, Stephenson put his in the top of the boiler, rather than at one end, which simplified the problem of transmitting their thrust to the driving wheels.

Cross-beams on the tops of long piston rods resulted in relatively small side thrusts during each revolution of the wheels, keeping them within the limits that could be withstood by the primitive slide bars or parallel motion arrangements. At the same time, springing of a sort was possible to minimize the shocks which the locomotive had to withstand from the irregularities in the rough permanent way, and to ensure that maximum adhesion was always obtained. This springing also reduced the shock loads on the track, which prevented breakages.

In the years during which his development work was being carried out at Killingworth, Stephenson's reputation as an engineer spread. At the same time it was becoming apparent that railways and steam locomotives offered economic advantages for collieries away from navigable waterways. As a result, Stephenson's services were sought to build locomotives for elsewhere, even as far afield as the Kilmarnock and Troon line in Scotland. More significant, however, were the plans he produced for a complete railway system to provide an outlet for the coal from Hetton colliery, south-west of Sunderland in County Durham. These were based on three principles, which he worked out in conjunction

Below: Perhaps the oldest existing picture of a working engine shows William Hedley's Puffing Billy *of 1813 built for the tramway of the Wylam Colliery near Newcastle, where he was Superintendent. It was the first locomotive with more than one axle powered, which Hedley achieved by gearing.*

with Nicholas Wood, the head viewer at Killingworth:

1. On the level or nearly level gradients, horses or locomotive engines were proposed to be used, a rule being laid down that, if practicable, the gradients ascending with the load should not be more than 1 in 300.
2. In gradients descending with the load, when more than 1 in 30, the use of self-acting planes.
3. In ascending gradients with the load, where the gradients did not admit of the use of horses or locomotive engines, then fixed engines with rope.

These enabled maximum advantage to be taken of the low rolling resistance of an iron wheel on an iron rail, but at the same time kept the tractive effort required within the limits set by the adhesion weight of the heaviest locomotives which the track could withstand. Thus, when the Hetton Colliery Railway was opened in November 1822, the stationary steam engines, self-acting inclines and steam locomotives were all to be seen in operation. One of the locomotives is still preserved at Beamish Open Air Museum, having operated in steam at the head of the procession in 1925 to mark the centenary of the opening of the Stockton and Darlington Railway.

The Stockton and Darlington was opened in

Right: The flat-rimmed wheels of eighteenth-century horse-drawn wagons were prone to slide off iron rails. To keep them aligned, colliery manager John Curr and James Outram's foundry at Ripley, Derbyshire, in 1775 devised L-shaped rails, here seen on the Little Eaton wagonway, near Derby.

Right: The first Stockton and Darlington trains were preceded by a rider brandishing a red flag. The practice was re-enacted at the line's 1925 Centenary display, where Stephenson's Locomotion No. 1 naturally starred. A hidden petrol engine provided the power: burning oily waste made a show of smoke from the chimney.

1825, and was an even more ambitious under-taking, designed to provide a better outlet for the collieries in the Auckland Coalfield than had the inadequate Coal Road. The idea of such an enterprise had first been suggested publicly in 1810 and its feasibility had been the subject of fierce debate. On the day that the necessary Act of Parliament, based on a survey by Overton, was obtained in 1822, George Stephenson met the Quaker Edward Pease in Darlington. This led to Stephenson's appointment as engineer of the line. He made a number of improvements to the original plans which greatly facilitated the railway's subsequent operation; it was at his

suggestion, too, that the company sought parliamentary sanction to use steam locomotives.

So it was that the inaugural Stockton and Darlington train was steam-hauled to Stockton by *Locomotion* on 27 September 1825. George Stephenson's 'improved locomotive engine' had steamed the 21 miles from Shildon, hauling up to 600 passengers on 38 wagons, and had achieved speeds of 15 mph. By the end of the following November the improved transportation had brought coal prices in Stockton down by a third, and within 18 months they had been more than halved. Moreover, the railway was making a profit for its promoters.

Chapter 2

The first steam passenger railway

Above: George Stephenson (1781-1848), the Northumbrian colliery enginewright who created the Stockton and Darlington.

Aᴛᴛᴇʀ ɪᴛs ᴛʀɪᴜᴍᴘʜᴀɴᴛ opening day, the Stockton and Darlington Railway's normal operations at first relied very considerably on horse traction, although after two years the operators could see that steam locomotives, in spite of their unreliability, were 30 per cent cheaper than horses for freight traffic. For the first eight years all the passengers were hauled by horses – in fact the whole of this traffic was in the hands of contractors who had their own vehicles and merely paid tolls for the use of the line. In this sense the operation of the railway approximated more to that of a toll road or turnpike, whose owners maintained the route, which anyone could use for the appropriate payment. Indeed, the original Stockton and Darlington Act specified that landowners adjoining the line were entitled to build their own lines and connect them to those of the Company. However, it was soon discovered that the disciplines necessary to operate a successful railway enterprise, with all the complications resulting from a reserved route incorporating a mechanical guidance system, were impossible unless the total operation was under the company's control. So the idea of a public railway disappeared for good. Continuous fencing of railway property became a feature of British railway lines, and was made mandatory by the Railway Clauses Act of 1845.

The stimulus of the Stockton and Darlington Railway set off a traffic explosion, and within a few years exceptional means had to be employed to stop the system choking itself. In 1831-2 the line east of Brusselton was relaid with heavier rail, and also doubled, while numerous improvements were applied to the motive power. *Locomotion* and her three sisters were not the

most reliable machines, in spite of being the most developed versions of Stephenson's colliery locomotive design. Nevertheless they were a lot better than the fifth locomotive the railway obtained – nicknamed the *Chittaprat* from the noise it made – which soon had to be laid aside. However the boiler shell of this engine was incorporated in Timothy Hackworth's 0-6-0 *Royal George*, which entered service in November 1827 and quickly established an excellent reputation. It was the first of Hackworth's double-tender locomotives which were to become such a characteristic feature of the Stockton and Darlington Railway. Two of the later engines to this general design are *Derwent*, now at Darlington North Road Museum, and *Samson* in New Glasgow, Nova Scotia.

Nevertheless, in spite of the successful appearance of *Royal George*, an important technical breakthrough that occurred on the motive power front in 1828 had nothing to do with steam locomotives. By the simple expedient of letting the horses ride on the downhill sections in the dandy-cart attached to the rear of the train, the Stockton and Darlington Railway increased the useful work achieved by each animal by no less than 40 per cent, to 240 miles per week. The normal load for a horse on the railway was four chaldron wagons, carrying approximately 12 tons of coal, a considerable improvement on the maximum of a few hundredweight which could be managed by a single pack animal; on an ordinary road of those days the heaviest rate load that could be managed reliably was only about a ton.

Given the new markets for coal in Darlington and north Yorkshire which the railway had opened up, there was naturally a dramatic increase of mining activity in the Auckland area. The fortunes of the railway prospered too. Edward Pease had forecast a modest five per cent interest on the capital invested, and this was achieved in the first full year of operation; a decade later the dividend was as high as 14 per cent. With the Stockton and Darlington Railway becoming such a successful enterprise, the rest of the country – and indeed the industrialized world – was soon beating a path to the Stockton and Darlington Railway to learn how to build and operate its own railways.

The Liverpool and Manchester Railway

One of the early approaches to the Stockton and Darlington was made by the directors of the embryo Liverpool and Manchester Railway.

Below: The Middles-brough extension of the Stockton and Darlington opened on 27 December 1830. It crossed the Tees on the first railway suspension bridge, designed by a naval engineer, Captain Samuel Brown. An inadequate load-bearer, it was replaced by an iron girder bridge in 1841.

They were told that they should make whatever arrangement they wished direct with George Stephenson, who thus found himself appointed the engineer of an even bigger enterprise. For the first time all the basic essentials of inter-city steam railways were to be incorporated in a single undertaking which connected two major industrial areas and centres of trade. Both cities were growing dramatically, the population of each more than doubling during the three decades up to 1821, while the tonnage of shipping using the port of Liverpool had increased by over 170 per cent in less than a quarter of a century. This was the area where canal and river navigation companies had developed an extensive waterborne transport system, and were paying annual dividends as high as 50 per cent.

The costs of transport by canal were less than half those by road, and the newest canals had produced some very impressive engineering, such as Thomas Telford's Pont-y-Cysyllte aqueduct which carried the Ellesmere Canal a distance of 1007 ft over the valley of the Dee, near Llangollen, at a maximum height of 127 ft. Unless they had a special Act of Parliament, the canal companies were unable to act as carriers, and merely provided the route in the same way as the turnpike trusts. This was intended to prevent the creation of a transport monopoly, but where all the available systems were operating to capacity there was little incentive for anyone to try and undercut a rival, or to offer a faster journey. So bales of cotton were taking longer to cover the 30 miles from Liverpool to Manchester than they had to cross the Atlantic aboard a sailing ship.

The idea of a railway between the two cities had been talked about for many years. With the appointment of George Stephenson as engineer in May 1825, route surveying was launched in earnest as a vital prelude to the presentation of the parliamentary bill. There had been problems over delineation of the Stockton and Darlington route, but in that case the only serious antagonists had been the local landowners. In Lancashire the surveyors had also to contend with the canal interests, who did their best to prevent the survey taking place, as well as cutting their waterborne transport rates by 25 per cent. In spite of all this, and his continuing work on the Stockton and Darlington Railway, George Stephenson completed his survey by the end of 1824, and the Bill was duly presented to Parliament. But the survey had been too rushed. In the long sessions at Westminster some damaging gaps in the information available were revealed, and the bill was defeated. A year later the railway company, this time using a new survey and buying off much of the opposition, got its Act.

Stephenson now went back to the north-west as an engineer. The success of the Liverpool and Manchester Railway, as of the Stockton and Darlington, was, in time, to depend on the basic principles which he had already outlined and was able to carry through. Even a casual comparison on the map of Stephenson's fine Stockton and Darlington Railway route with that of Overton's survey shows clearly how the line, as built, was laid out to make it the most economic route to operate; the same applied in Lancashire. If there were natural obstacles in the way they were overcome by the manual efforts of thousands of 'navvies', a name derived from those who had built the river navigations during the previous century. The variety of the engineering work was enormous: the 70-ft deep Olive Mount cutting was hewn out of solid stone, while at other extremes the line had to be laid across the semi-liquid morass of Chat Moss and carried over the Sankey Valley on a magnificent nine-arch viaduct.

The railway was built as double track from the beginning, with the same distance (4 ft 8½ ins) between the inner rails of the two lines as there was between the rails of each track. This feature was meant to enable out-of-gauge loads to be carried by wagons running on the centre pair of rails, but the narrowness of the resulting gap was to have fatal consequences. Apart from those sections where it was intended to use stationary engines, gradients were negligible, and gentle curves connected the long straight stretches.

Below: The Stephensons' 0-4-0 Invicta *for the Canterbury and Whitstable Railway, which was opened on 3 May 1830 to give Canterbury access to a navigable waterway. The engine worked only a short coastal section of the line; steep grades inland demanded use of rope haulage and stationary power.*

Although many steam locomotives had been built since the opening of the Stockton and Darlington Railway, their overall performance was by no means as good as railway companies would have liked. With this in mind, the directors of the Liverpool and Manchester decided to hold a competition in October 1829 to determine the best type of locomotive available. Various stringent requirements had to be met by the contestants. Each of them had to travel 75 miles, which they achieved by moving backwards and forwards with their load over the one-and-three-quarter-mile course on Rainhill Level. Great interest was aroused

by this event, and some 15,000 sightseers turned up to watch on the first day alone.

The very conclusive winner of the £500 prize was Stephenson's *Rocket*. This was a vastly improved locomotive compared with *Locomotion* of four years earlier. Having successfully completed the requirements laid down, it went on to show that its capabilities were greatly in advance of what had been stipulated in both speed and haulage capacity. Gone were the cumbersome overhead beams of the colliery-type locomotive; *Rocket's* leading wheels were driven by short connecting rods, braced to the outside cylinders by simple slide bars. This arrange-

Above: The Liverpool and Manchester Railway's entry into Manchester, seen from Water Street in one of a famous series of views of the line published by Ackermann in 1831. The original Liverpool Road terminus, the oldest station in the world, is to the right.

Below: The Liverpool and Manchester's Sankey Viaduct – another Ackermann impression of 1831.

ment enabled more efficient use to be made of the steam, which was produced in a multi-tubular boiler fitted with an external, water-jacketed firebox. For the first time all the features required for a successful steam locomotive had been combined in one machine. As one contemporary observer put it, 'It is so much superior to all the old locomotives in use, as to entitle Mr Stephenson to the most marked and liberal consideration for the skill and ingenuity displayed in its construction.'

The opening of the Liverpool and Manchester Railway on 15 September 1830 was planned as an elaborate gala event. Several locomotives of the same general type as the *Rocket* joined in the task of hauling the eight special trains from Liverpool to Manchester. The guest of honour was the prime minister, the Duke of Wellington. On route, while the Duke's train was standing at Parkside to take water, William Huskisson, a Liverpool MP who was President of the Board of Trade, was caught between the premier's carriage and the *Rocket* which was hauling a train on the other track. That night, in Eccles, he became the first man to die from injuries sustained in a railway accident,

after being hurried there at an average speed of 35 mph by George Stephenson himself driving the locomotive, *Northumbria*. That was not the only unpleasantness of the day. When the Duke's train arrived in Manchester, it was met by mobs yelling for political reform, and the Prime Minister considered it wiser not to alight from his carriage before returning to Liverpool.

Nevertheless, in spite of these setbacks, the line rapidly became a commercial success. While the Stockton and Darlington was still using horses for much of its coal traffic, and its contractors were hauling all the passenger coaches by the same means, every train on the Liverpool and Manchester Railway was from the outset worked by steam locomotives. Freight and passengers were quickly attracted to the new line, to the detriment of alternative modes of transport.

Within three months over half the stage-coaches which had plied between the two cities were off the road, and by the end of 1830 the Liverpool and Manchester Railway was reporting a net profit on three and a half months' operations of £14,432. The railway age proper had begun.

Below: Robert Stephenson himself is believed to be the figure by the tender of the famous Rocket. *The Liverpool and Manchester sold the engine in 1839 to a Carlisle colliery owner and he in turn handed it to the Robert Stephenson works for preservation early in 1851.*

Chapter 3

The main lines are laid

BY 1830 THE RAILWAY'S status was changing. No longer regarded just as a short-haul means of transportation serving the extraction industries, it was now visualized as a main artery for the movement of people and goods between pairs of major cities. The prosperity of the first enterprises, moreover, provided a strong commercial incentive to realize the dream.

But construction of a railway from, say, London to Birmingham was a very different proposition from building a line of only 30 miles from Manchester to Liverpool. Nearly four times the distance was involved and the difficulties increased commensurately. Selection of the best route, in particular, was much more complicated. Just as Darlington interests had insisted on a lengthy detour of the Stockton and Darlington Railway to ensure that Darlington was properly served, so every substantial industrial community within reach of a projected railway now campaigned for the route to be deviated their way.

Conversely, many powerful interests mistrusted the railway as a threat to their way of life, and fought to keep the railway builders away from their doorstep with virtually the same arguments as those deployed by the opponents of new motorways in the 1970s. They had

plenty of precedent, for the tradition of opposing the passage of minerals was a good two centuries old; records of disputes over wayleaves for coal wains go back to the sixteenth century, and in the seventeenth century litigation over the Tyneside wagonways kept many lawyers busy. On the longer-distance routes, too, the terrain exerted a much greater influence on the siting and construction of the line, especially when railways came to be built through the hills and across the valleys of the more rugged areas of the country.

Branch lines

Concurrently with the main-line undertakings, there was great activity on a smaller scale in the construction of short branch lines and quite separate railways, which were still being built to connect mines and other industrial enterprises with the sea or a navigable waterway. In time many of these would be intersected by a trunk route, but it was rarely a foregone conclusion that they would become feeders to a main line. A case of splendid isolation for all time was that of the Plymouth and Dartmoor Tramway, although it must be admitted that it originally chose an unfortunate gauge of 4 ft 6 ins. Opened in 1823, it was crossed a quarter of a century later by the South Devon Railway, yet the two lines were never connected and the flat crossing at Laira Junction, Plymouth, survived for over a century to be battered by the wheels of British Rail's diesels before it was finally removed in 1960. Similarly the last self-acting inclines in County Durham, which take National Coal Board traffic down to Seaham Harbour, are unable to feed traffic into the British Rail line along the coast, because the connecting incline at Swine Lodge, Dawdon, was taken out some years ago. The trunk routes fulfilled a very different purpose from that of the local mineral lines. Later still more marked differences would materialize between the character and operating practices of the main routes and country branch lines.

The early financial success of many lines generated intense competition and feverish

Below: Opening day ticket of the Leicester and Swannington Railway. The first railway tickets were of paper, torn from a book as they had been by stagecoachmen – hence the later designation of ticket offices as 'booking offices'.

OPENING

OF

The Leicester and Swannington

RAILWAY,

Tuesday, 17th July, 1832.

The Bearer of this Ticket is entitled to Seat, No. *III* in Carriage No. *4* Entered *John Eles*

COCKSHAW, PRINTER.

Right: The northern terminus of the London and Birmingham was Curzon Street Station, Birmingham, shown in 1840, before the erection of an adjoining hotel. The monumental portico symbolized the railway's ambition to be regarded, like the city gates of old, as the modern entrance to the world beyond. The entrance still survives.

building of many rival routes. The course adopted for the Stockton and Darlington Railway through Darlington had put considerable additional mileage on the journey from the Auckland coalfield to the River Tees at Stockton, so in 1833 the Clarence Railway opened their line from Simpasture on the Stockton and Darlington Railway to Stockton, which was only 11½ miles long compared with 17½ miles by the original route. Furthermore, the Clarence had planned access to the Tees appreciably nearer the sea than Stockton, at Samphire Batts,

which was to become, in due course, Port Clarence.

This threat provoked the Stockton and Darlington to extend its line in 1830 from Stockton across the Tees to a site further downstream on the opposite bank. Here the Stockton and Darlington built some elaborate loading facilities at Port Darlington, where previously 'the silence and solitude of this part of the Tees were only broken by the presence of a few grey-bearded seals and a few shrimping women'. In spite of this, Stockton and Darling-

on coal traffic suffered from the activities of the rival line; so it resorted to commercial and operating pressures. The Clarence traffic had to use the earlier Stockton and Darlington line for the first mile or so eastwards from Shildon, so by juggling with the freight rates and such devices as making the Clarence drivers weigh their wagons while its own were merely counted, the Stockton and Darlington eventually forced its rival into bankruptcy. Not for the last time in the history of Britain's railways did it prove that the longer of two routes was in fact to be the survivor.

Masterpieces of engineering

The advantages of the low rolling resistance of the iron wheel on the iron rail were by this stage clearly apparent, and the engineers were consequently anxious to minimize the gradients on the main lines so that locomotives could haul heavier loads or attain higher speeds. To achieve this, vast civil engineering works were required, as exemplified by the one-and-a-half-mile cutting at Roade on the London and Birmingham Railway and the embankments of Joseph Locke's London and Southampton Railway. However, more than that was needed to achieve the easy alignments required, so cuttings gave way to tunnels, and embankments led out on to vast viaducts. The trains of the Liverpool and Manchester had in 1830 disappeared down a rope-worked tunnel at Edge Hill. Now there were to be bores carrying steam trains more than a mile underground, while the

Liverpool and Manchester's Sankey Viaduct was soon to be surpassed by much larger structures, culminating in such masterpieces as the 28 arches of the Royal Border Bridge across the Tweed at Berwick, or the Ballochmyle Viaduct in Ayrshire, the 181 ft main span of which was, at the time of its opening, the widest masonry arch in the world.

The building of the trunk routes utilized the services of a handful of men who made an enormous contribution to the transformation of Britain from a farming community to the industrial centre of an empire. George Stephenson had seen to it that his son Robert had a good formal education, which was then supplemented by practical experience, first alongside his father on the Stockton and Darlington Railway, and then in America. Robert was to prove perhaps the most influential of all the railway engineers; his Britannia Tubular Bridge over the Menai Straits has been described by L. T. C. Rolt as 'the greatest and boldest Civil Engineering feat of the early Victorian era'. He became a Member of Parliament, and such was his national esteem that his funeral procession in London was accorded the rare privilege of passage through Hyde Park; business and trade throughout Newcastle ceased for the day. Amongst many lines, he was responsible for the London and Birmingham. This was opened in 1838, just over a year after the Grand Junction Rail Way, the first trunk route in the world, had been opened between Birmingham and Liverpool, so that the two lines connected the main industrial centres of

Above: Robert Stephenson (1803-1859) son of George and generally acclaimed the greatest engineer of the Victorian era. At his death he was given virtually a State funeral.

Below: The Royal Border Bridge at Berwick, one of the two great bridges of Robert Stephenson's design which completed a direct east coast Anglo-Scottish route in 1850. It carries the railway 126 ft above the river bed on 28 arches each of which has a 61½ ft span.

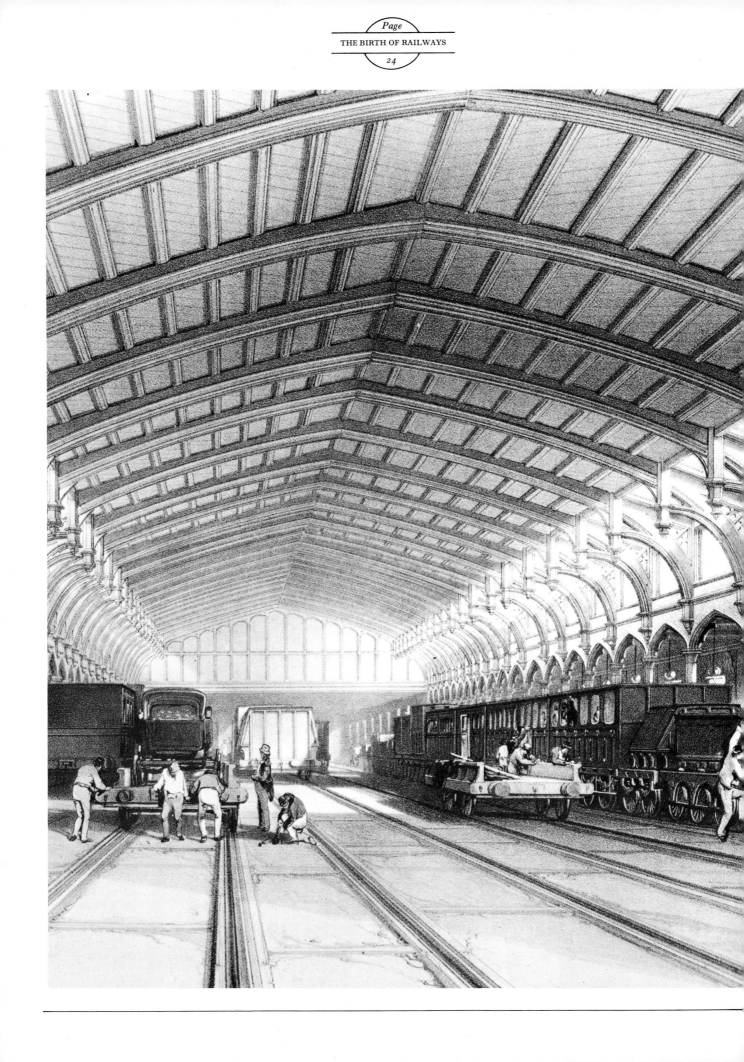

England – Liverpool, Manchester and Birmingham – with each other and with the capital.

Early railways in the south

In the south of England it was the ports rather than the industrial centres which stimulated the construction of trunk routes. Bristol was still the second city in the kingdom up to the 1820s, and had long sought a better connection with London. The first proposal for a railway between the two was put forward in the autumn of 1824, and a company was set up, while a more modest rival scheme for a 'proposed Rail-Road from Bristol to Bath' was also raised in the same year. The opening paragraphs of the Bristol to Bath prospectus are as remarkable for their punctuation and syntax as for their optimistic faith in the railway's abilities to overcome the contemporary economic problems of overland transport, bearing in mind that the Stockton and Darlington Railway still had ten months to go to its opening.

The elevated and distinguished Position of this Country, was probably never more visible than at the present Period. The Commercial Prosperity of almost every Town and District in the Kingdom, and the Plans now in Contemplation to facilitate and increase Trade and Manufacturers, must be so apparent to every Observer, that to Particularize, is unnecessary.

Among the most important is, that Grand Improvement, the LOCOMOTIVE STEAM ENGINE, for the Conveyance of Passengers and Merchandise on a Rail-Road; by Means of this Power, a Company will be enabled to transport the heaviest Goods with Certainty and Security, by Day and Night, at all Times of the Year; – in Periods of Frost or of Drought, at the Rate of at least Eight Miles an Hour, and Passengers at the Rate of Twelve.

Left: The concept of an overall train-shed at stations is as old as the Liverpool and Manchester Railway, which built one at its Crown Street station in Liverpool. On the GWR Brunel fashioned his of wood in ornate Tudor style. Shown in Bourne's famous illustration, this at Bristol was his first.

Below: Brunel's original Bristol train-shed remained in use by LMS route trains alongside the new Temple Meads station until BR re-signalling of the area at the end of the 1960s. In this 1963 view, LMS 2-6-0 No. 42707 heads the 6.3 pm stopping train to Birmingham.

Right: Isambard King-dom Brunel (1806-1859) pictured at Millwall (back row, extreme right) just before the calamitous first attempt to launch his ship Great Eastern in November 1857.

Below: Construction of the London and Birming-ham Railway between Euston and Camden in 1836. From the line's opening in 1837 until 1844 trains were worked up and down the steep bank be-tween Euston and Camden by an endless rope under the power of stationary winding engines.

Neither of these proposals came to anything, in common with countless other schemes of the time. Nine more years were to elapse before, in July 1833, a public meeting in the Guildhall at Bristol firmly resolved that

a Company should be formed for establishment of Rail-way communication between Bristol and London, and for that purpose a body of Directors for Bristol be appointed, who, in conjunction with a similar body to be appointed in London, shall constitute a General Board of Management for securing sub-scriptions and obtaining an Act of Parliament for effecting the same object.

The two committees attacked their brief with great vigour. Within three weeks they had held their first joint meeting, and adopted the title of 'Great Western Railway', thus setting up a company which was to remain operative under the same name for more than a century, out-living all its contemporaries by many years.

The engineer for the line was Isambard Kingdom Brunel, another of those giant characters who strode across the early Victorian engineering scene. The son of a famous immigrant engineer, Marc Brunel, he was 27 years old in 1833. Isambard had had miraculous escapes from drowning during the construction

of his father's Thames Tunnel (today used by Metropolitan Line trains) and was now engineer of the Clifton Suspension Bridge at Bristol, construction of which had ground to a halt following the Reform Bill riots of 1831 in that city; he was also engineer to the city's Docks Company. His energy was immense. Over the next few years he was to cover the countryside at a prodigious speed in his specially built carriage – nicknamed the 'Flying Hearse' – surveying and building the railway.

The problems of trunk route construction were by no means confined to the stages of surveying the line and obtaining parliamentary approval. For the physical tasks of the actual construction, men, horses and what primitive equipment was available had to be organized on a scale never seen before, and it was discovered that many of the contractors and their traditional practices were not up to the demands of the railway age. On the Grand Junction Railway, however, Joseph Locke developed a system of estimating which worked well in conjunction with a small force of skilled constructors.

An important name among these early firms of railway contractors was that of Thomas Brassey. When Locke was building the London and Southampton Railway, Brassey secured contracts to build no less than 118 miles of line, worth £4.3 million, in this one scheme alone.

Europe and America

At one time Brassey's total labour force was 45,000. Some of his men were employed on the mainland of Europe, since Locke went on to engineer lines abroad, notably those from Paris to Rouen, Le Havre, Nantes and Cherbourg in France, as well as some in Holland and Spain. Robert Stephenson was also active abroad, in Belgium and Sweden, while Brunel surveyed the Italian lines between Florence and Pistoia, and from Genoa to Alessandria.

While railway construction in Britain was left entirely to private enterprise, in other countries the driving force for a railway system was often the state itself. In Belgium, for example, in 1830, after the country had become fully independent of Austria, a strategic network of railways was planned, starting with a route from Ostend to Germany, to be crossed at Mechelen (Malines) by a Brussels–Antwerp line. The plans were signed by the king himself. The first order for rails was placed with a Welsh ironworks, and the three locomotives employed on the opening day were built by

Robert Stephenson and Company. Britain was also responsible for the first locomotives used by the Dutch and German railways, and replicas of the pioneer engines from each country, *De Arend* and *Adler*, can be seen at the railway museums in Utrecht and Nurnberg respectively. Both names mean *Eagle*. The Dutch locomotive was actually the second one to reach that country, the first being *Snelheid* (*Speed*), one of four in an initial order built by Longridge of Bedlington; *Adler* was a Stephenson product. Earlier still, steam locomotives had been built in Britain for use across the Atlantic. One of the most interesting was the *Stourbridge Lion*, sister engine of Foster Raistrick's 1829 *Agenoria*, now in Britain's National Railway Museum, which became the first locomotive to run on edge rails in North America.

Above: Thomas Brassey the pre-eminent railway contractor. A phenomenal organizer and leader of men, he undertook the building of 1700 route-miles of British railway and a further 2800 elsewhere, as far afield as Canada.

The navvies

The armies of workmen employed in the building of the early railways had to be housed near their place of work since the only way they could reach the sites was on foot. Most of the vast labour force required for a specific project had to be brought into an area specially, and since their stay was likely to last only a few years, temporary accommodation was all that most of them received in the shanty towns which sprang up miles from anywhere. Even in the town houses and farm cottages used by the working classes there were not many comforts, and few buildings could boast solid floors. The shanties were even more primitive than this; many were constructed entirely of mud and turf. As late as 1887, the best a contractor could offer his men in the way of accommodation was some old naval hulks towed up the nearby river.

It is not surprising that disease and death were rife in such conditions. The 1832 burial ground opposite the mighty station at York is a reminder that cholera outbreaks were not unknown in England at that time, and the shanty towns were an easy prey to such epidemics. Many other workmen were maimed or killed at work. Not only were there major disasters when tunnels flooded or collapsed, but fatalities occurred in relatively simple operations – for instance, when a boy working in Sonning Cutting on Brunel's London–Bristol line slipped in the mud and a horse stepped on his head. The navvies themselves were often fearless, and took great risks to show off their prowess and skill. After the fortnightly pay day an orgy of drinking often made the men foolhardy or,

Right: A hovel typical of the makeshift shanty towns erected on or near the sites of railway construction for the 'navvies'. These men were a hard-living, pugnacious and mainly Irish force, but the energy which piece-work pay rates extracted from them was formidable. Each man was reckoned to hump as much as six tons of spoil a day up a height of six feet. This picture was taken in 1898 in the ruins of the old Nottingham Workhouse, which had been pulled down to make way for the Great Central's extension to London.

worse still, aggressive towards their fellows or the local inhabitants who had to suffer this sudden massive intrusion into their lives.

The shanty towns also attracted those who sought to profit from the high wages earned by the navvies. Some contractors set up their own sources of supply for the essentials needed by their workmen in isolated areas. An admirable system in theory, it quickly became abused, with some contractors earning less from the work itself than from sales to their workmen, who were paid in goods or tickets which were only valid at the company's stores. Although the Truck Act of 1831 made this abuse illegal in factories, it did not apply to railway construction sites, and navvies continued to pay high prices for short weight throughout the railway-building era. Parliament never extended to them the protection of this legislation because, it was said, of the many and varied railway interests of MPs.

Passenger travel

With the opening of the railways it soon became apparent that the new means of travel had great advantages over road transport, even for those who had their own private road vehicles. Not only were the railways quick to enable those who wished to ride in their own road carriages loaded on to a flat wagon (a facility denied to today's Motorail passengers), but the early railway coaches were very similar in structure to those used on the roads. At least, that was the case for those able to pay the first-class fare; the luckless second- and third-class passengers rode in open wagons with or without seats, exposed to the vicissitudes of the British climate and the rain of cinders and smuts from the locomotive. The first class was plushy, even if not over-endowed with head-room, as can be seen from the Liverpool and Manchester replica vehicles constructed in 1930, one of which is normally on exhibition at the National Railway Museum. Above all, of course, the railway was faster than road transport.

With the opening of the trunk routes, royalty took notice of rail travel – to the pleasure of the railway companies, naturally. In 1839 Prince Albert rode on the Great Western Railway from Slough to Paddington after visiting Queen Victoria at Windsor shortly before their wedding. The following year Queen Adelaide, the widow of William IV, became the first queen to travel by rail in Britain, and two years later Queen Victoria herself was persuaded to take the train

for a Windsor–London journey. The splendid Swindon-built saloon coach first used by Queen Adelaide was marshalled in the train which embarked the royal party at Slough at mid-day on 13 June 1842, and Brunel himself rode on the footplate of the locomotive *Phlegethon* for the 25-minute journey to London. When the train reached Paddington, wrote one onlooker, the young queen was greeted 'with the most deafening demonstrations of loyalty and affection we have ever experienced'.

By the time of the queen's journey, the railways had already been used to convey the Royal Mail for more than a decade. The Post Office had begun to send mails on the Liverpool and Manchester Railway in 1830, and in 1838 a special Act of Parliament had regulated this particular traffic. By then the zenith of the coaching era on the roads was over; in 1835 700 mail coaches and some 3300 stagecoaches had been operating on British roads requiring more than 150,000 horses. All this took place, it must be remembered, before the introduction of the Penny Post and stamps by Rowland Hill in May 1840. When that happened, the railways were poised to carry, and profit from, the enormous increase in postal business which followed. Such has been the dependence of the postal system on the railways ever since that, even in 1978, overnight delays to mail trains caused by tunnel reconstructions on the East Coast main line could only be overcome by using aircraft to fly mails between London and Yorkshire. The railways were also extensively used by the military during the Chartist disturbances of 1839 and 1842, and it is generally held by historians that the existence of railways, enabling troops to be moved extremely rapidly, prevented the Chartists becoming the equivalent of the 1848 revolutionary movements which existed throughout Continental Europe.

By 1842 there were nearly 2000 miles of railway in operation throughout the country. Passengers were using the lines to an extent never dreamed of in the days of stagecoaches, while freight was being syphoned off the canals and new traffic generated. The railways were moreover profitable, with an annual revenue of some £4 million, so that, with the core of the trunk system already in operation, the stage was set for an extravaganza of railway construction and speculation never since equalled.

Above: Sketch of a London and Southampton Railway Royal carriage of 1844. The compartment scheme derived from the early builders' idea of fashioning bodies like a terrace of stage-coach superstructures.

Below: In the early days the railways would convey the gentry's own coaches on flatcars.

Chapter 4

Brunel and the broad gauge

OUTSTANDING AMONG THE early trunk routes was the main line of the Great Western Railway from London to Bristol. Not only was this laid out superbly, with the minimum of curvature and gradients, but a unique track gauge was used, of no less than 7 ft $0\frac{1}{4}$ ins between the two rails. According to one's viewpoint, Brunel's adoption of the broad gauge was to be either a magnificent example of his refusal to be bound by existing practices, or a maverick aberration in the logical development of the steam railway system based on Stephenson's precepts!

Tradition has it that George Stephenson fixed the gauge of the Stockton and Darlington at 4 ft 8 ins by making a survey of carts on the roads, but in fact this gauge was already firmly established on the wagonways of north-east England. It was specifically the Willington system, the first section of which was completed in the 1760s, which pioneered this gauge. To it were connected the Killingworth lines, on which George Stephenson carried out his early experiments with steam locomotives. It was natural, therefore, that he should use this gauge on the Hetton colliery line, and on the Stockton and Darlington and the Liverpool and Manchester railways.

The extra half inch crept in some time later to give extra clearance between the backs of the

flanges and check rails, although one wonders how accurate the gauging of these early lines was in practice. With the limited equipment available, they were undoubtedly less precise than they were at the end of the steam era, by which time speeds of 90 mph had become common. The track irregularities of some of the pre-Beeching branch lines were often apparent to the eye, while the present lines that are engineered for Inter-City 125s running normally have to be within about 1 mm of today's metric gauge of 1432 mm, which is in fact equivalent to 4 ft 8⅜ ins. The loss of the eighth of an inch has come about in the interests of reducing the susceptibility of bogies to 'hunt' or oscillate laterally at high speeds.

Brunel's broad gauge

This puny gauge was no good for Brunel. Although traceable back to the Willington wagonway, and indeed further to the rut-ways of the Romans, the dimension was probably dictated by the maximum length of axle which

Above: Meeting of the gauges at Uphill Junction, south-west of Bristol. On the mixed-gauge main line a broad-gauge express heads for Devon while to the left a standard-gauge goods on the Weston loop waits to follow it.

Left: The West of England was the last stronghold of broad gauge; the Paddington-Plymouth main line was not converted to exclusive standard gauge until May 1892. A characteristic GWR broad-gauge 4-2-2 skirts the sea wall at Teignmouth beside the famous vantage point in the late 1880s.

Above: The Punch *cartoon of 4 June 1892 marking the end of Brunel's broad gauge after the Paddington-Plymouth conversion of the previous month.*

partly to provide a clear passage for the horses, but also because of weight considerations. However, stone sleeper blocks only supported the ends of each rail and, even with the use of the fish-bellied rail shape to add strength, there was a limit to the maximum weight that could be carried on each axle which the track could sustain. Brunel had carefully noted the practices and achievements of the railways before deciding on his 'Baulk Road', in which each rail was continuously supported. By these means he was able to achieve first-cost economies in both iron and timber compared with a track of I- or T-section rails laid on cross sleepers; and in use his longitudinal broad gauge track proved slightly cheaper to maintain than the orthodox narrow gauge variety.

Brunel's permanent way, then, consisted of a massive timber framework. The up and down lines were supported by four longitudinal pine timbers some 6 ins deep by 13 ins wide. On top of these was a hardwood bearing surface to which the bridge rails were fastened. The main wooden members were 30 ft long, with massive cross-timbering at each joint, and intermediately. Each of these cross-members was firmly located by a 10 in. diameter pile under each track, and ballast was consolidated right up to the bottom of the rails themselves. Originally the timbers were all treated with a mercury salt as a preservative, but this highly hazardous process was soon replaced by the use of creosote. Unfortunately the rigidity of Brunel's permanent way created a very rough ride for the passengers, and it was soon realized that some vertical resilience in the track was needed to supplement the springing on the carriages.

The interaction between track and vehicle is very complex, and only in the last ten years or so have all the factors at work been fully understood. Modern vehicle suspension systems allow the track to be built even more rigidly than Brunel's, as witness the recent development of a continuously-cast concrete slab to support the rails. Nowadays, the calculations taken into account in designing a carriage for passenger comfort even allow for the resilience of the seat springs, as can be discovered from the apparent deterioration of the ride on one of British Rail's Inter-City 125 sets when one leans on the bar rather than reclines in a seat! The 'Baulk Road' nevertheless lasted until the end of the broad gauge. Indeed, it considerably assisted in the great changeover of May 1892, when 171 miles of broad gauge track were converted to narrow in two days, an event marked by a *Punch* cartoon in which the ghost

could readily be handled by one man. Since the Industrial Revolution was now making mechanical aids available, there was no need for human limitations to dictate the gauge of the railway line; and it was obvious that greater stability and speed could be obtained by using something wider.

Another significant feature of Brunel's broad gauge track was its use of continuous beams to support the rails. The earliest lines had been built with separate lines of blocks to carry the ends of each rail. On the Stockton and Darlington Railway the western half of the line had stone blocks from local quarries, while at the Stockton end oak had been used instead. When the line had to be relaid and doubled in the early 1830s, larger stone blocks were used throughout. These were much heavier than the original ones, and could only have been economically transported from the quarries by rail – a clear example of how the coming of the railways enabled heavier loads to be carried at an acceptable cost. The blocks were still separate from each other,

Left: Trans-shipment of goods from Great Western broad to standard gauge. Most notorious of these transfer points was Gloucester, astride the busy Birmingham-Bristol route, where long delays and loss of packages were an infuriating common-place in the 1840s. When the matter was investigated by Parliament the narrow gauge companies deliber-ately created far more chaos than was usual in an attempt to force gauge standardization.

of Brunel looked down on the burial of a broad gauge locomotive, with accompanying verses by Edwin Milliken which concluded:

Slowly and sadly we laid him down,
He had filled a great chapter in story;
We sang not a dirge, we raised not a stone,
But we left the Broad Gauge to his glory.

Such were the emotions that the broad gauge could arouse, even at its demise.

The gauge war

The whole problem with the broad gauge was that it was just not compatible with the railways already constructed or being built everywhere else in the country. MacDermot, that eminent chronicler of the Great Western's history, has a chapter called 'The Gauge War', which he considered to be a much more fitting description than 'Battle of the Gauges', since there was a span of ten years from the time when the rival gauges first met until 'the Broad Gauge forces were at last defeated by the mere multitude of their enemies'.

The first and most notorious point of contact was Gloucester. Here the Bristol and Gloucester Railway met the Birmingham and Gloucester. When the Bristol and Gloucester decided to adopt the Great Western's broad gauge, its engineer had justified the choice with an assurance that 'a very simple arrangement may

effect the transfer of the entire load of goods from the wagon of one company to that of the other.' However, as traffic increased, the sheer scale of the operations rapidly outstripped the facilities available, and goods were subjected to intolerable delays.

Parliament was concerned with the gauge problem and set up the Gauge Commission to investigate the pros and cons of the two systems. When the Commissioners visited Gloucester to see the transhipping operation at first-hand, the narrow gauge management stage-managed a special performance by unloading two trains which had already been dealt with, thus ag-gravating the usual muddle to a chaos which was duly noted by the Commissioners.

However, if the GWR lost the freight-transfer battle, it was much more successful when it persuaded the Gauge Commission to compare the performance of the locomotives on the different gauges. There were no specific re-quirements for these trials, unlike those at Rainhill, and various dodges were adopted by the narrow gauge parties (as the GWR called them) to try and score an advantage. Their main contender was a locomotive specially built for the Great North of England Railway. It was known simply as 'A' but nicknamed the 'Great A', and was a rather ungainly 4-2-2 which, with the benefit of pre-heated water in the tender, succeeded in averaging nearly 48 mph between Darlington and York. The North Midland

Above: Typical of Brunel's iconoclastic genius was his decision, having kept his London-Bristol main line near level most of the way, to dive through the hills to Bath on an unprecedented slope of 1 in 100 in Box Tunnel instead of taking an easier, more circuitous course. The entrances were built unnecessarily large to attempt to reassure passengers entering them in the open carriages of early days. On a clear day it is possible to see right through it and, on 9 April each year, looking from west to east, the sun can be seen rising, before it has risen over the hill. That date happens to be Brunel's birthday, a fact which is thought to be not entirely coincidental.

Railway's participant was less impressive, as it became derailed halfway along the route.

The Gauge Commissioners pronounced very clearly in favour of the broad gauge engine's performance, adding that, 'We feel it a duty to observe here that the public are mainly indebted for the present rate of speed and the increased accommodation of the railway carriages to the genius of Mr Brunel and the liberality of the Great Western Railway Company.'

In spite of this accolade, the broad gauge came badly out of the Commission's report, which recommended that all future public railways should use 4ft 8½in track. But in the event, GWR opposition kept the Gauge Act of 1846 less restrictive than at one time had been threatened. It remained possible for any new railway Act to specify exemption from the need to use standard gauge, and broad gauge could still be adopted for future lines built in the areas covered by the GWR and its allies.

Warfare continued, with both parties achieving varying success. By the mid-1850s the GWR had its first narrow gauge track, which it was forbidden to widen, and considerable lengths of mixed gauge lines had been laid. The high-water mark for the broad gauge came in the mid-1860s, when 1040 miles of broad gauge and 387 miles of mixed gauge track stretched from London to Weymouth, Penzance, Milford Haven and Wolverhampton. Its hard-won territory was, however, deeply penetrated by narrow gauge lines, while the periphery festered with more than 30 breaks of gauge.

During the gauge trials the GWR locomotive averaged nearly 55 mph, but the following year saw its new 2-2-2 *Great Western* travel from Paddington to Didcot at an average speed of 67 mph, and achieve a running average of over 55 mph for the round trip from Paddington to Exeter via Bristol. By 1848 the GWR was consistently covering the 53 miles from London to Didcot in 48–50 minutes with the morning express from Paddington. This was all the more memorable because, at the time the first section of the line was opened in 1838, the locomotives available were, with one notable exception, distinctly unpromising.

When ordering the first batches of engines, Brunel had made certain stipulations regarding their weight and piston speeds which had resulted in the construction of a series of freaks – one of them, *Thunderer*, even had its boiler and cylinders on separate frames. Daniel Gooch had been appointed Locomotive Superintendent in 1837, just before his twenty-first birthday, and arrived on the scene before any of the locomotives. He was unimpressed with the design of his future charges, the first of which, *Vulcan*, ran a short distance along the line on 28 December 1837. This engine and her two sisters from the Vulcan Foundry at Newton-le-Willows

were delivered by sea to London docks, and the first of the Stephenson locomotives ordered by the GWR arrived at Maidenhead by barge five days later. The use of waterborne transport is a reminder of the difficulties of overland freight movement in those days, but the transport of locomotives by coastal shipping was not without its perils; on occasions they sank, to provide treasure trove for divers a century and a half later.

This voyage – from Newcastle to Maidenhead – for the two Stephenson locomotives, *North Star* and *Morning Star*, was much shorter than the one originally intended for them, since they

Below: One of Daniel Gooch's 2-2-2s is moved on to the traverser in the early engine house at Swindon in another of Bourne's famous prints. The works built its first locomotive, Gooch's 2-2-2 Great Western, *in the first 13 weeks of 1846.*

Above: Daniel Gooch was only 21 when, a graduate of the Robert Stephenson works in Newcastle, Brunel appointed him GWR Locomotive Superintendent. Eventually knighted, Gooch became the GWR's Chairman in 1865.

Below: The Croydon Railway tried to relieve its congested main line by building a single track with atmospheric traction between New Cross and Croydon. Opened in October 1845 it kept clear of the main line on a flyover at Norwood. Technical trouble forced abandonment of the atmospheric traction system in May 1847.

had been ordered by the 5ft-6in. gauge New Orleans Railway which had had to renege on the contract. Converted to run on the GWR, they provided Gooch with his only reliable locomotives at the start, and a further ten similar engines were promptly ordered, all carrying Star names. *North Star* itself worked the first directors' special in May 1838, as befitted the best and most reliable engine on the line.

The Stars had the 2-2-2 wheel arrangement and were of fairly standard Stephenson design. Further locomotives of the same general layout were ordered from other manufacturers while engines of the 2-4-0 and 0-6-0 wheel arrangements were built later for freight working, and some of the early 2-2-2s were converted to 4-2-2 tanks for use on branch lines. The last of these externally built locomotives was delivered in 1842. No more engines were then added to GWR stock for three and a half years, until the first to be built by the company itself appeared from its new works at Swindon.

The manufacture of steam locomotives by various companies in the north of England had quickly become established after the success of the pioneering railways, but the GWR realized that the works it was planning to construct for the repair of its rolling stock could also be used for the construction of its own locomotives. Gooch, after inspecting various places, decided in favour of various green fields in rural Wiltshire, at the junction of the Cheltenham branch, some two miles from the borough of Swindon. The works, on the north side of the line, were opened in January 1843 and consisted of a running shed, an Engine House for light repairs,

and an erecting house for major overhauls and new construction. *Great Western*, the first locomotive to be built there, was completed in 1846 at a time when considerable expansion of the facilities was taking place. To provide accommodation for its workers the company constructed a new town, south of the railway line, and the ordered layout of the streets is still apparent today, thanks to the conservation policies of Thamesdown District Council who are rebuilding the houses to modern standards. The company donated £3000 in 1853 to found the New Swindon Improvement Society, which provided a building to house that vital centre of Victorian 'improvement', the Mechanics Institute, as well as other amenities like public baths. Another early building, the model lodging house, was never needed in its planned form, and became instead a Wesleyan Chapel. After ninety years as a place of worship it was sold to the borough of Swindon and became the Great Western Railway Museum, housing many items from the National Collection, including five locomotives – though, alas, *North Star* is only a replica. The old and new towns continued to expand until they were combined into a new municipality in 1900, with G. J. Churchward, then the Assistant Locomotive Superintendent, becoming the first mayor. Such was the genesis of the first of the railway towns, which established a railway engineering tradition that had few equals anywhere in the world.

Brunel was not content with pioneering the extensive use of a new rail gauge and type of track, but later adopted a very novel method of propulsion when the railway was being extended

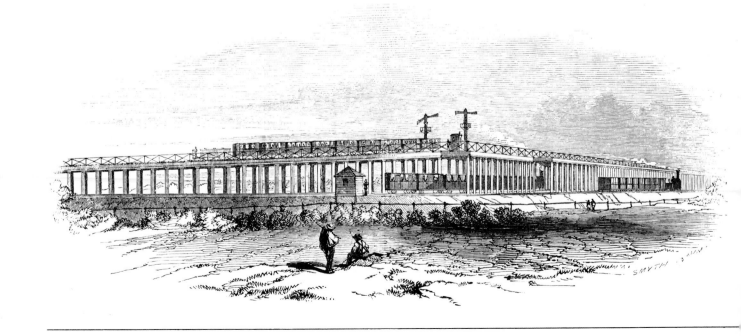

through South Devon. Like the various continuations of the broad gauge west of Bristol, this line was built by a separate company, the South Devon Railway. However, the GWR had an appreciable financial interest in it, both as a shareholder and as part-owner of the Bristol and Exeter Railway, and Brunel was the engineer.

The atmospheric system

Shortly after the Act of Parliament was passed in 1844, the South Devon company agreed to the adoption of the 'Atmospheric System' which, it was thought, would make it easier to work over steep gradients and so cut engineering costs on the slopes of Dartmoor. This means of propulsion had been patented five years earlier by Clegg and Samuda, and installed on the Dublin and Kingstown Railway and the line between Croydon and Epsom. In its South Devon form, a 15-in. diameter pipe was fixed between the rails, and through a slot in the top a piston was attached to the leading vehicle. A continuous flap closed the slot in front of the piston, thus enabling the air to be exhausted from the pipe by stationary pumping engines built at intervals along the line. Atmospheric pressure entering the pipe behind the piston forced it along, and with it the train. The stationary engines took a long time to build, so that when the line was complete, steam locomotive-hauled trains started running in 1846 as far as Newton Abbot. In February 1847 the first trials of the Atmospheric System commenced, and in September it was in public use as far as Teignmouth.

Except when occasional mishaps caused delay, the new mode of traction was almost universally approved of. The motion of the train, relieved of the impulsive action of the locomotive, was singularly smooth and agreeable; passengers were freed from the annoyance of coke dust and the sulphurous smell from the engine chimney.

So wrote one contemporary traveller. There were complications in getting trains in and out of the stations, and level crossings presented another problem. These difficulties, however, were trivial compared with the problem that soon occurred in the continuous leather seal. Atmospheric conditions made the leather porous and it then got saturated with water or even frozen in the winter, while corrosion set in between the tannin in the leather and the fastenings. Rats, eating the leather, were also found to be a problem. By June 1848 the valve was found to be disintegrating all the way from Exeter to Newton Abbot.

So, after less than eighteen months' service, repairs costing £25,000 were needed. Moreover, the system was proving very much more expensive to operate than estimated. Clearly it was not a viable proposition and at the end of August the Atmospheric System ceased operation; the subsequent sale of the plant raised nearly £43,000, a mere tenth of the capital expended, and George Stephenson's dismissal of it as 'a great humbug' had been amply vindicated. Steam returned to the South Devon Railway, a line burdened to this day with steep gradients that are a permanent memorial to the 'Atmospheric Caper.'

Below: From The Illustrated London News *of 1845, a close-up of the vacuum traction tube in the Clegg and Samuda atmospheric system; (a) is the piston; (b) the apparatus to connect it to the train's leading vehicle; (c) one of the wheels which raised the sliding valve (d), and (e) the wheel that closed the sliding valve after passage of the connecting apparatus.*

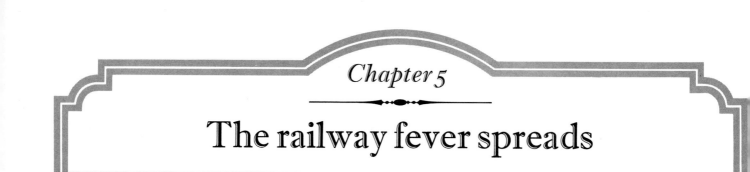

Chapter 5

The railway fever spreads

Above: William Ewart Gladstone, who was Vice President and President of the Board of Trade between 1841 and 1845. His clear objective was to exercise more direct government control over the spread and operation of railways.

THE STOCKTON AND DARLINGTON's first Act of 1821 was the twenty-first railway Act to be passed by Parliament since the beginning of the century. For nearly 27 miles of new construction this company's authorized capital had been just over £100,000, but in the event the pioneering line cost somewhat more. By the mid-1840s the sums needed for railway construction had risen considerably. The total authorized capital for the whole country had soared to about £76 million, covering a route mileage of just over 4000, although at the beginning of 1845 only 2150 miles were actually open to traffic. Not only were the costs per mile very much higher, but the total investment, given the state of the country at that time, was already large.

However, these figures paled into insignificance compared with the score of new proposals which were tabled in the next three years. By April 1846 no fewer than 519 railway bills were actually under consideration by Parliament. They involved a total share capital of some £230 million, exclusive of loans, which, if all of them had come to fruition, would have more than quadrupled the country's railway investment. This was the era of 'railway mania'.

It was really the financial success of some of the early railways which stimulated the whole industry. Within a decade of its opening the Stockton and Darlington was paying a dividend of 14 per cent compared with Edward Pease's modest promise of 5 per cent. The Liverpool and Manchester, initially relying primarily on passengers rather than freight, paid an average dividend of 9½ per cent from 1831 to 1845, and was probably inhibited from doling out more to its shareholders by the clause in its Act which stipulated that freight rates had to be cut if the dividend exceeded 10 per cent. The mere

existence of a railway, however, was no guarantee of financial success; the Eastern Counties Railway, with its main line from London to Norwich, was soon in dire trouble because it was badly run and its shareholders and directors were in conflict. In these early days of large-scale finance, the half-yearly meetings of shareholders were a trial of fortitude for all concerned; no one with an appreciable stake in the company risked missing it, and directors could easily find themselves thrown out of office.

Railway law

It must be remembered that at the beginning of Queen Victoria's reign the whole system of company law was very different from present-day statutes. In fact it was the development of the railways, more than anything else, which changed things, because they were the largest single influence in the evolution of a capital investment market. The eighteenth century was notorious for its love of gambling, and after the scandal of the South Sea Bubble, Parliament passed an Act in 1720 forbidding joint stock companies except where they were covered by their own specific legislation; this Act was not repealed until 1825. As a result, most enterprises were owned by individuals, by members of a family or a partnership, and they did not, in consequence, enjoy the protection of limited liability. If the enterprises failed, those to whom it owed money could exact repayment from the owners individually. If the owners were unable to pay, they stood the risk of being sent to a debtors' prison, a fate that was to befall even the 'Railway King' himself, George Hudson.

Hudson was first and foremost a speculator and it is not unknown for them to come unstuck, but even Robert Stephenson lost a considerable sum of money when the Stanhope and Tyne Railway became bankrupt in 1840. He had accepted shares in the company, when it was built, in exchange for his services as an engineer, but it had not been constructed under an Act of Parliament, and the liabilities of its shareholders were, in consequence, not limited. Hasty steps had therefore to be taken to salvage the situation, by settling the most pressing debts and transferring the physical assets to a new company, the Pontop and South Shields Railway, authorized by Parliament two years later.

Although limited liability could be obtained by registration from 1825 onwards, railways still continued to obtain their own Acts, since this permitted them, among other things, to acquire by compulsory purchase the land they needed. Most railway companies were thus statutory

Below: The definitive railway town, Crewe, in 1865, looking south from the locomotive works to the station. To the left of the locomotives clustered in the foreground is the west coast main line to the north; on the right is the line to Chester.

companies, and did not use the word 'Limited' in their title; this is still the case today with the handful of private companies that remain, such as the Derwent Valley and the Festiniog. Company accountancy was also an undeveloped profession in the 1840s. At best, the railways were required to account financially only to their shareholders rather than to Parliament, the Board of Trade or the public at large.

Before the Act of Parliament required for incorporation of a new railway company was granted, the proposal was examined by a Private Bill Committee. At this period fears were felt that a powerful railway company would exercise a monopoly of transport, so the committees tended to look favourably on small competing schemes in the belief that, with plenty of these in existence, all companies would be kept on their toes. Little regard was paid to the orderly build-up of the system as a whole.

In 1844 a Select Committee was set up under the chairmanship of Mr Gladstone, then President of the Board of Trade, to review the situation. Its report commented that:

in the future proceedings of Parliament railway schemes ought not to be regarded as merely projects of local improvement . . . each new line should be viewed as a member of a great system of communication, binding together the various districts of the country with a closeness and intimacy of relation in many respects heretofore unknown.

It was recommended that in future all railway bills should be reported on by the Board of Trade before coming before Parliament; one advantage of this system was seen to be 'very beneficial effects in deterring parties from attempting to entrap the public by dishonest projects'. Gladstone's clear objective was to exercise more direct government control over the spread and operation of railways (some other European countries were pointing the way), but in this he was to be defeated. He did, however, obtain powers to enable the nation, if it wished, to purchase any new railway company after a period of twenty-one years – a provision which was to lie dormant for more than a century, until 1948.

A special department of the Board of Trade was set up to implement the Gladstone Committee's proposals, and at the end of the year it announced the bills it was prepared to recommend. In the booming state of the railway share market this provoked a tumultuous outcry from disappointed promoters. Restraint may be prudent, but often it is politically inexpedient, and that was evidently the feeling in the 1840s. In the next parliamentary session Prime Minister Sir Robert Peel conceded that the old procedure of leaving the endorsement of railway bills to the judgment of Private Bill Committees would be resumed.

Parliament was later to regulate the railways, and their accountancy methods, still further. Some idea of the extent to which nineteenth-century speculation in railways demanded special checks can be gained from the fact that in the 1970s the auditors of the independent Derwent Valley Railway were still compelled formally to qualify their annual certificate with the words: 'This Company, being a statutory undertaking, the Accounts are prepared in accordance with the Railway Companies Act 1911 . . . which prevents compliance with the Standards of Accountancy Practice in current use.'

Unscrupulous entrepreneurs like George Hudson had a simple way of evading such controls as there were in the mania years. So long as a company had a capital account oper

Right: The early British railways usually let their own engineers build their station train-sheds, leaving only the frontal buildings to commissioned architects. The Ipswich and Bury's, however, let Ipswich architect Frederick Barnes design this remarkable combination of Tudor buildings and Renaissance-style train-shed for Bury St Edmunds in 1846.

for new construction, any expenditure which it did not want revealed in revenue accounts could be conveniently lost under the heading of capital; this increased the apparent profitability of the operations and, where necessary, enabled dividends to be paid out of capital. In short, it was not very difficult in the 1840s to improve the financial appearance of a dubious railway company enough to maintain the support of the shareholders or to attract more investment – both, in the end, aimed at increasing the directors' power and personal influence.

There were still many areas of the country not yet served by railways, and a lot of personal prestige and gain were potentially to be had by launching a new company successfully. Competition was rife among standard gauge lines. It could even erupt into physical confrontation when 'running powers' were granted, which permitted one railway to operate its trains over the tracks of another. The owning company's usual counter to this arrangement was to schedule a slow train just before the other company wanted to run one of its expresses. Endless battles broke out all over the country as competing companies tried to extend their areas

of influence. These engagements started first with the promotion of various rival proposals, each of which tried to obtain sufficient promise of support to enable the combatants to move on to the next stage – the parliamentary engagement.

As already mentioned, the cachet of parliamentary approval was necessary for virtually every railway scheme to succeed. In order to ensure that only *bona fide* applications came before MPs, various standing orders were laid down, with which each company had to comply. Parliament changed the rules too from time to time, with the aim of limiting valuable committee time in the House itself to the more worthwhile bills. Any bill gave the Opposition the opportunity to protest that it would damage their own interests; they would go to great lengths to find loopholes in the technical or commercial arguments put forward, in the same way that airlines today argue over route licences. Nor did the battles necessarily stop when the Act had been passed, since at this stage the company usually had yet to find a high proportion of the capital required, and at times this could be difficult – or made to be so. When

Above: The first stations often handled goods and passenger traffic on the same premises. Dundee and Newtyle Railway's Dundee station, shown here in an astonishingly early photograph taken in 1839, is one example. The goods depot is on the left, the passenger platform on the right.

Right: A share certificate for the Wear Valley Railway. The company was incorporated in 1845 and opened from Wear Valley Junction, near Bishop Auckland to Frosterley two years later. In 1858 it was amalgamated with the Stockton and Darlington.

Opposite, above, Huyton station, Lancashire, seen about 1850. From its beginnings, railway architecture was eclectic. Some designers favoured adoption of dominant styles in the area of the station.

Opposite, below: An impression of Liverpool's Edge Hill station in 1848. Following the example of the city's first station, Liverpool Crown Sreet, the overall trainshed was a near standard feature of early stations large and small, but it later fell into disrepute because it trapped engine smoke. Early artists found it very difficult to get the perspective of railways – tending to exaggerate the width of engines and track.

construction actually started it sometimes proved possible to find ways to delay the work, even if it meant resorting to violence. There were many physical skirmishes of one sort or another around the country, incidents that may now seem funny, but which at the time were deadly serious and occasionally caused bloodshed. Local feelings often ran high. If the success of a parliamentary bill sometimes set off jubilant ringing of church bells, there were ways of harnessing local sentiment to protest with equal clamour and vigour.

In the early days of railway construction shares in a company had been relatively expensive, but the price dropped as the years progressed, enabling ordinary people to invest in the companies fairly easily. The cost of a share in the Liverpool and Manchester Railway had originally been fixed as £100, but by the 1840s shares could be as small as £10, or even less. Furthermore, it was customary for subscribers to be called on initially for only a portion, usually 10 per cent. This system of part payment is, of course, still known with new issues on the Stock Exchange today, but

purchasers have a clear indication of when further instalments will fall due and can plan their commitments accordingly. In the railway construction era, Parliament would usually insist on the raising of a proportion of the capital, customarily 10 per cent, before it would start the legislative procedures. This relatively modest requirement encouraged the early purchase of shares in the quantities needed to launch the enterprise. However, timing the calls for further instalments of committed money depended on the progress of construction. During the intervening period the state of the national economy, as well as the subscriber's purse, could deteriorate. Directors always had to be careful in deciding when to make a call and how large it should be. If too many shareholders failed to pay up, and thus forfeited their holding, the company would be left short. not only of this contribution, but of all subsequent ones from the same source. When shares were only partly paid, even a small premium represented a high percentage increase in their value, so that it was not very difficult to rig the market by artificially pushing the price of shares up or down, depending on whether one wished to sell or buy. The use of inside information to the directors' or their friends' advantage was common; there was a notorious example when Hudson's friends were able to buy shares in the Leeds and Selby Railway and obtain 6 per cent interest on the remaining call, knowing that they would not have to subscribe it for the next 18 months.

Since a railway company could be floated for a fraction of the capital required to build the line, undoubtedly some schemes were brought forward which the promoters never intended should succeed. Once the initial subscriptions had been acquired, and possibly even the Act itself, the company could be traded off against some other scheme or quietly allowed to die, the money subscribed being absorbed in the costs of a leisurely liquidation. At times the whole business degenerated into farce. Four separate schemes were put forward in the 1836 parliamentary session for lines between London and Brighton, and, all having been unsuccessful, they were followed in the next session by no fewer than six more!

Right: An optimistic railway promoter deposits plans with the Parliamentary offices in 1845. That was the first of the 'mania' years, 1845-7, in which 815 separate Bills for new railways were laid before Parliament.

Railway mania of the 1840s

In 1833–7 the country had had its 'railway boom'. This was the second period in the first half of the nineteenth century when railway proposals and investment suddenly rose to a peak. The first had been in 1825–6, and was very modest compared with the second, though both were completely overshadowed by the 'mania' of 1845–7. These gaps of about a decade each were dictated by various factors. With increasing industrialization, the trade cycle of economic activity had replaced a successful harvest as the main contribution to the immediate apparent prosperity of the country, although it must be admitted that important effects were felt from bad harvests at this time, notably in Ireland. These cyclic booms and recessions undoubtedly affected the drafting of railway schemes, but another important influence was the time required for a successful railway company to construct its line, bring that line into operation, and then earn enough return on its capital to enable it to plan equally promising investments elsewhere. Nor must it be forgotten that there had been a similar boom in canal construction in the 1790s; knowing how others had prospered half a century earlier, people were anxious to emulate them in fortune making.

Statistics can show the magnitude but cannot re-create the railway fever which infected all classes of society in the mid-1840s. A few years later Tennyson pilloried the spirit of the time in his dramatic monologue *Maud*, which he himself described as 'a little Hamlet, the history of a morbid, poetic soul under the blighting influence of a recklessly speculative age'. The hero's father has been found dead: 'Did he fling himself down? Who knows? For a vast speculation has failed.' Later on in the piece this nineteenth-century angry young man enquires, 'Why do we prate of the blessings of Peace? We have made them a curse, pickpockets, each hand lusting for all that is not its own.'

In 1843 new railway promotion had followed a normal sedate course, with twenty-four Acts for new lines passed. In successive parliamentary sessions the number of bills presented rose to thirty-seven, then leaped to 248 and finally peaked at 815. Some of this huge number were never considered for technical reasons, or because deposits were not paid, but over 700 reached the Private Bills Office. The route mileage actually sanctioned by Parliament was 2700 in 1845 and 4538 in 1846, followed by a drop to 1354 in 1847. All this meant that 8592 miles had been sanctioned in three parliamentary sessions. They were not all built; 3560 miles were abandoned by the normal procedure and 2000 miles were quietly forgotten by their promoters.

The human side of the mania was eloquently described by John Francis in his *History of the English Railway*, in which he relates how eventually 'there was scarcely a family in England which was not directly or indirectly involved in the fortunes of the rail'. As already mentioned there were far too many bogus enterprises, so it was fairly easy to issue a prospectus for a railway company with a high-sounding title and adorn it with the names of distinguished personalities quite unsuspecting of the honour done them. Subscriptions for shares were invited, dividends

of 10 per cent or more promised, and the money of the credulous gratefully accepted. In *Our Iron Roads* Francis Williams quotes a contemporary writer:

The directors and secretaries bragged to the newspaper writers; surveyors composed epics on the capabilities of the lines and shareholders listened to the lay, with the swelling, dreamy delight of opium eaters under the influence of their drug; all counted upon the share in the plunder which they had in imagination allotted to themselves, being as sure as if they already held it in gold.

The outcome for many was disaster. Sermonizing on the vice of speculation, another commentator wrote:

Every day brings us some new instance of its hateful effects upon private happiness and public character. Now we are told of shameful disclosures affecting the honour of men in office . . . Now we are called to deplore the utter ruin of a household dashed down from decent competency into beggary and disgrace in the frantic pursuit of sudden wealth. The next moment we hear of a pious defaulter for hundreds of thousands; and, turning from him in disgust, we stumble on the body of a suicide!

Certain towns were a focus of speculative activity. Among them was Southampton, where there was considerable dissatisfaction with the service provided at the time by the London and Southampton Railway, and at the company's blocking of a scheme to build a branch from Basingstoke to Newbury and so improve communication with the industrial Midlands. Between 1845 and 1847 some twenty-five companies applied to Parliament for powers to build lines affecting Southampton in one way or another. Many of them had little prospect of approval for their schemes, but were sustained by the hope that other groups with similar aspirations would buy them off. Some sought new routes to London, others an extension to the West Country, and others again a rail link to the Midlands and the North.

Only the westward extension was translated into reality in the shape of the Southampton and Dorchester Railway. Of the others, the one coming nearest to fruition was the Manchester and Southampton Railway. Its bill was rejected twice, first on the grounds that the case for such a line was not proven, and the second time because of errors in the surveys. By that time railway mania had passed its climax, the money market was in disarray, and the Manchester and Southampton faded from the scene. The line has been classed among the 'bubbles' of the mania period – perhaps unfairly, for there were surely strong arguments for a direct link between the port and the industrial North. Yet the later experience of the Midland and South Western Junction Railway, which completed a new link between Southampton and Manchester in 1873, when the trade of the port had multiplied many times, suggests that the traffic prospects for the Manchester and Southampton were not as bright as they seemed.

Left: Newlay station, north-west of Leeds, in Victorian times. The double-armed station signal, one arm for each direction, was characteristic of the mid-nineteenth-century style. The first known semaphore signals were installed on the London and Croydon Railway in 1841.

The Network Spreads

Chapter 6

The social impact of railways

Previous pages: An LNWR *Precedent class 2-4-0, No. 2189* Avon*, climbs to Shap summit with a northbound west coast route express in 1899. As yet trains were not vestibuled throughout.*

BY THE YEAR 1658 stagecoach services were being advertised from London to places as far afield as Exeter and Wakefield. Both were shown as four-day journeys costing 40 shillings, but forecasts of journey times were sometimes optimistic and operators often added the prudent caveat 'if God wills'. For the traveller to Durham the duration was unspecified. He paid his 55 shillings and resigned himself to whatever might be in store. Years later people were still saying that a man might drown in the ruts on the Great North Road after heavy rain, and stagecoach guards carried blunderbusses as a deterrent – often ineffective – to highwaymen.

The Turnpike Act of 1751 marked the beginning of a period of road improvements in which the stagecoach was to reach its prime, culminating in what has been called 'the brief interval of

highway glory between Waterloo and the railways'. G. M. Trevelyan attributed the increase in social, commercial and intellectual contact during the age of Doctor Johnson largely to improved traffic conditions. Boswell writes of the formidable Doctor accompanying him by stage to Harwich, and astonishing their fellow travellers first with a spirited defence of the Inquisition and then with a justification of the use of torture in the judicial processes of Holland. At Colchester he reproved Boswell for over-tipping the coachman. A tip proportional to distance was expected at every stage, and coachmen failed to live up to their later genial Christmas card image if they thought they had been underpaid!

In the 1770s Arthur Young in his *Farmer's Letters* contrasted the time when 'a stage coach was four or five days in creeping an hundred miles' with the transport then available. 'A country fellow one hundred miles from London', he wrote, 'jumps on a coach box in the morning and for eight or ten shillings gets to London by night.' In due course he would no doubt return to his home with fine tales of the capital for the ears of 'country fools' who would then be induced to 'quit their healthy clean fields for a region of dirt, stink and noise'.

The advantages of mobility were understood by the time the railways came, but travel by stagecoach was expensive for any distance involving overnight halts, while the frequency of services varied greatly. Few roads were like the Brighton road, by which coaches left the town every few minutes at some times of day. On less frequented routes the intending traveller might have to wait for a long time before a seat was available, particularly if he joined the coach at an intermediate point.

An already burgeoning passenger travel market existed for the railways. It had been created by the Industrial Revolution which greatly increased the number of businessmen, salesmen and so on who needed to move about the country. The same industrial activity also required freight transport – as we have already seen, passengers were a secondary consideration for the Stockton and Darlington – but the

Right: An advertisement from Drake's 1838 Road Book *of the Grand Junction Railway in 1838. Inns were the passenger assembly and ticket issue points of the stagecoaches and until stations were built the early railways used them in a similar way.*

V.   **R.**

ROYAL HOTEL,
MAIL AND COACH OFFICE.

———

FROM THIS OFFICE,

DEPART ALL

HER MAJESTY'S ROYAL MAILS,

(Except the Burnley Mail);

ALSO, A GREAT NUMBER OF

FIRST-RATE,

FAST, FOUR-HORSE COACHES:

THUS AFFORDING

OPPORTUNITIES FOR TRAVELLING

By Superior Conveyances, to the

NORTH, INTO YORKSHIRE, AND TO ALL PARTS OF THE KINGDOM,

ALMOST HOURLY.

LACY AND ALLEN,

PROPRIETORS.

canals, navigable rivers and coastal trades were less immediately affected than the road passenger carriers. Early horse-worked lines were often feeders to water transport, and the Stockton and Darlington itself took coal to the River Tees for shipment.

The social impact of the first railways

The railway age is generally accepted as beginning with the opening of the Liverpool and Manchester Railway on 17 September 1830. Here passenger transport between the two cities was the primary objective and goods traffic did not begin until the following December. At first the idea of travel by train at unheard-of speeds was greeted with a nervousness akin to that aroused in a later generation by the aeroplane, but the railways were soon accepted. Guidebooks with helpful advice and notes on what the traveller would see on his journey were produced in large quantities. This was an age when self-improvement was taken seriously and writers were not slow to expound the natural sciences. The purchaser of a guide to the Brighton line, for instance, was told of the varieties of clay, chalk and greensand over, through and under which he would pass *en*

Left: A plaque on an A5 road bridge marks the location of the one-time Denbigh Hall Inn, north of Bletchley, whence road coaches conveyed London and Birmingham passengers to Rugby between April and September 1838, before the completion of the Kilsby Tunnel.

Below: A Victorian scene at Clitheroe station on the Lancashire and Yorkshire Railway, as farmers wait to load their churns on to the Manchester milk train. The railways had revolutionized local farming habits.

route, and if he read diligently he would arrive well informed on the history and architecture of a broad tract of Surrey and Sussex. One gets hints from this guide, too, of the new mobility people were enjoying. Cuckfield, 'a short two miles from the station' (Haywards Heath), is described as a place to which 'Brighton residents resort for a change of air and scene', while the view from the train between New Cross and Forest Hill afforded 'numerous signs of tea gardens, bowling greens and other temptations for the Londoner to come into a fresher atmosphere'.

The impact of the railways on the coaches was immediate. Some services survived for a time as feeders or as extensions of lines still under construction, while others provided cross-country links, but as the railway network spread these fringe operations were withdrawn one by one. Direct competition seemed insuperable. When the London and Southampton Railway was opened in 1838, an old coachman is reported to have said, 'Hang up my old whip over the fireplace; I shan't want it never no more.' Some found work driving vehicles between stations and surrounding villages or became 'cabbies'

waiting for hire in station forecourts, but others joined the railway service in various capacities. As early as 1851 the railways were carrying 80 million passengers a year.

It was the same with road freight traffic, but here some carriers were more resilient and adapted themselves to the new conditions. A classic case was Pickfords, whose principal partner, Joseph Baxendale, had by 1838 built up a widespread distribution network using roads and canals. He began sending goods by the Liverpool and Manchester Railway at the end of 1830, but the close involvement of his firm with the railways started with the establishment of a trunk route linking London, Manchester and Liverpool at the opening of the Grand Junction and London and Birmingham Railways in 1837–8.

The canals in turn succumbed to railway competition, although as late as 1844 the Select Committee on Railways noted that there was nothing like the same railway monopoly in freight as in passenger transport, 'since railways are, in many cases, exposed to effective competition from canals, and since the saving of time does not give such a decided superiority over the old modes of conveyance'. For a time

Below: Awaiting the train at Bingley, on the Midland Railway. In the background is the Leeds and Liverpool canal climbing a set of locks. Previously the most important route for transporting goods across the Pennines, it quickly fell out of use with the coming of the railways – symbolizing perhaps the most immediate social impact of the iron road. The advertisement seen on the further platform for Bradford's Midland Hotel is a reminder that the Midland was one of the chief railway entrepreneurs in this field, with 12 hotels.

Above: A sparkling, brand new Buckie station, on the Great North of Scotland Railway, which opened the first section of its 334-mile network in 1854.

he principal effect of the railways on the canals was to make the canal operators reduce their charges, and they continued to carry bulky loads for which speed was relatively unimportant. By 1850, however, the railway had become the normal method of transporting heavy loads and many canals ceased business. Some were bought out by railway companies.

In some countries the industrial revolution was started by the railways, but in Britain they accelerated and expanded a movement that was already under way. In social life, too, the railways were conveniently at hand to cater for the new pattern of holidays which superseded the somewhat haphazard profusion of saints' days, fair days and so on that had relieved the tedium of the daily round for agricultural communities.

In some places the steamboat anticipated the railways in catering for the holidaymaker. Trips were run from London to Gravesend, Southend, Ramsgate and Margate; from Liverpool to the Wirral and Rhyl; from Glasgow to the Clyde coast resorts. In due course both the London and Blackwall and the Glasgow, Paisley and Greenock Railways tried to persuade the steamboat companies to connect with their trains at the Blackwall and Greenock piers so that excursionists could make the first stage of their journey more quickly by rail, but they met with little success. On the Thames, for example, trippers bound for a day out at Gravesend still preferred

to join the boats at London Bridge and it was not until the railways reached out to the Kent coast resorts that they won the traffic.

Cheap return tickets were offered by the railways at an early period, resulting in trains of mammoth length, which were frequently overcrowded. The special excursion train was a natural development. Sometimes it was chartered by other organizations, such as Thomas Cook's pioneer Leicester to Loughborough excursion for a party of 1000 temperance reformers on 5 July 1841. Occasionally firms chartered trains for their employees' annual outings. Old local newspapers tell of these exciting occasions, when the excursionists might be met on arrival by the town band and conducted to their pleasures with drums beating and trumpets sounding, the whole proceedings to be concluded with buns, milk and tea, and three cheers for the management. Somebody seems to have tampered with the milk and tea for a Sunday School outing from Winchmore Hill soon after the branch to Enfield was opened, for a local vicar is recorded to have resolved 'never to allow such a dissipation under the name of a treat to happen again'. This sinister development had evidently not been foreseen by the factory inspectors, who in 1845 noted with approval that 'railway carriages may be as easily hired as steamboats are chartered for summer excursions', and recommended the practice to employers.

By rail to the seaside

Until the late eighteenth century the seaside was often regarded simply as a place where dry land ended, but royal patronage of Brighton and Weymouth opened society's eyes to the pleasures of the strand. Brighton was already a resort when the London and Brighton Railway was opened on 21 September 1841, making it accessible to the masses, who were soon being attracted by cheap fares. In one summer week of 1859 the visitors decanted at Brighton by train outnumbered the town's residents.

Further along the Sussex coast, Eastbourne was little more than a straggling village with a row of apartment houses on the seashore. When two branch lines were opened from Polegate in 1849, one to the inland country town of Hailsham and the other to Eastbourne, the Hailsham branch was at first considered the more important. This was soon to change as Terminus Road, running from Eastbourne station to the sea, became lined with lodging houses. Happily the Duke of Devonshire, the principal local landowner, stepped in to arrest haphazard development; as a result 'a straggling series of hamlets' was converted into 'a handsome well laid-out town with miles of streets ornamented by noble terraces and stately mansions'.

Bournemouth was even more obscure than Eastbourne before the railway came, and when the extension was built from Southampton to Dorchester the line swung inland after Brockenhurst to serve Ringwood, not returning to the coast before the shores of Poole Harbour. A branch from Ringwood reached Christchurch in 1862. When it was extended to Bournemouth on 14 March 1870 the history of the town as a major health and pleasure resort began, but the direct route from Brockenhurst to Bournemouth

Left: The end of the road: Kyle of Lochalsh, terminus of the scenically splendid Highland Railway line in the Western Highlands, at the turn of the century. The mountains of Skye, for which Kyle was and still is the principal departure point, loom across the water. At the platform is a Jones 'Skye Bogie' 4-4-0.

Below: The Hammersmith Junction Railway linking the District Railway with the LSWR was opened in 1877 and thereafter District trains began through working from Mansion House, in the City of London, to Richmond. One of the District's first Beyer Peacock 4-4-0Ts of 1871 is seen at Richmond.

via Christchurch was not opened until 5 March 1888.

There were ferry services to the Isle of Wight before the first railway in the island, from Cowes to Newport, was opened on 1 July 1862. The string of resorts from Ryde to Ventnor were interconnected by railway lines between 1864 and 1866, but trains could not run to and from the pierhead at Ryde for direct connection with the steamers until 12 July 1880, when the two mainland railways interested in the Isle of Wight holiday traffic – the London and South Western and the London, Brighton and South Coast – opened a new pier and a rail link with the former terminus at Ryde St John's Road.

Other resorts grew to meet the holiday needs of the industrial areas in the Midlands and north. Workers in Lancashire were taking holidays in Blackpool even before the railway age, sometimes walking the forty miles from Manchester, although they often hired carts. The Chester and Holyhead Railway reached Rhyl in 1849, no doubt to the disappointment of the operators of the Liverpool steamboats. At one time the company was interested in taking a 50 per cent share in an hotel at the resort but later it withdrew from the project, seeing it as incompatible with the terms of its Act. As the line continued towards its goal along

the North Wales coast, place names once familiar only to the natives, and sometimes barely pronounceable by others, found their way into the guidebooks and holiday literature; and so it continued all round the coasts of the British Isles.

Thomas Cook began organizing continental holidays in 1855, so that something approximating to the Grand Tour was no longer the prerogative of the wealthy and leisured classes, although cheap tickets to single continental destinations had been offered by the South Eastern Railway as early as 1848. Cook was not alone in the package tour business. Advertisements of other agencies can be found in the newspapers of the 1840s, one of them in 1849 offering first-class travel to Paris, full board and lodging for a week, and free entry to places of amusement and theatres 'under the guidance of intelligent cicerones speaking English', all for the sum of £8. The holiday abroad was now within the grasp of 'middle management' at least.

The popular literature of the Victorian age reflects a lively interest in information of all kinds – crowds flocked to the Great Exhibition of Works of Industry of all Nations held in the Crystal Palace in Hyde Park in 1851. Without railways to transport materials the Crystal

Below: Railways came to the Isle of Wight with the opening of the Cowes and Newport Railway in July 1862 and the Isle of Wight Railway from Ryde to Shanklin in August 1864, the latter extending to Ventnor in September 1866. The 2-4-0 tank Ryde *stands at Ryde St John's Road in about 1865, a year after the line opened.*

Palace could hardly have been conceived on its impressive scale, nor could such a range of exhibits have been assembled in time. Only the railways could convey the six million visitors from all over the country who saw the exhibition during the six months it was open, when excursion fares as low as five shillings return were on offer from Manchester or Leeds to London. The age of 'improving the mind' had begun. Paris joined in with International Exhibitions in 1855 and 1867, and for the 1867 one Thomas Cook arranged excursions to Paris for working men at the cost of 34 shillings for a four-day trip. The Crystal Palace was removed from Hyde Park after the Exhibition and re-erected at Sydenham, where it continued to be a centre for shows and entertainments of various kinds until destroyed by fire in 1936. A branch line was built to its new site. In 1873 the competitive Alexandra Palace was opened at Muswell Hill in north London and it, too, was served by a new branch.

The first commuters

The readiness with which the railways granted fare concessions at this period contrasts strongly with their attitude to third-class passengers in earlier days, and the ill grace with which they

Midland and North Eastern Railways.

GARIBALDI

DEMONSTRATION
AT THE CRYSTAL PALACE,

On SATURDAY, APRIL 16,
A Cheap Excursion Train will leave

HULL, SELBY, YORK
And the undermentioned Stations for

LONDON
(KING'S CROSS STATION)

FARES THERE AND BACK AND TIMES OF STARTING.

Stations			a.m.	FIRST CLASS. s. d.	COVERED CARR. s. d.
Hull	-	-	dep. 6. 0	**25 0**	**12 6**
Howden	-	,,	6.54		
Selby	-	,,	7.20		
York	-	,,	7.15	**21 0**	**10 6**
Church Fenton	-	,,	7.43		
Milford	-	,,	8. 2		

LONDON (KING'S CROSS) ARRIVE ABOUT 4.45 P.M.

Children under Three years of Age, Free; above Three and under Twelve, Half-fares.

The Return Train will leave the King's Cross Station,
London, on Wednesday, April 20th, at 10.15 a.m.

Tickets are not transferable, and will be available for returning by this Train only.

Luggage must be conveyed under the Passengers' own care, as the Company will not be responsible.

Ten Minutes will be allowed at Trent Station for Refreshments both in going and returning.

Derby, April 1864.   BY ORDER.

Bemrose and Sons, Printers by Steam Power, Derby.

Left: An excursion train poster of 1864. Note the journey time from York to Kings Cross – 9½ hours!

Below: Barred by the LB&SCR from using running powers over its lines to serve Crystal Palace, the LCDR built its own branch, opened in 1865 and terminating in this monumental station. An ornate tiled subway led direct to the Palace (which had been moved from its original site in Hyde Park) from the station, which had its own refreshment rooms.

Above and right: From
The Illustrated London
News *of 1844, an artist's*
impressions of, repective-
ly, first- and second-
class passengers. Early
rail passengers needed
rugs and greatcoats in
winter – travelling could
be an austere business.

received Gladstone's Act of 1844 requiring them to run 'Parliamentary trains' at a penny a mile with proper seating and protection against the weather for third-class travellers. Once they overcame their reluctance, the railways found that the policy was commercially sound, for by 1850 third-class receipts accounted for nearly 30 per cent of the total and by 1860 they exceeded those from second and first class.

Trains took men to their daily work as well as in pursuit of pleasure and instruction. When lines penetrated into the heart of towns and cities, much housing was demolished and workmen who had once lived near their jobs had to move further away and travel daily by train. When the London, Chatham and Dover Railway built its Metropolitan extension lines from Herne Hill to Blackfriars, opened in 1864, there was considerable public sympathy for the families who had to find new homes further from their work. The company therefore volunteered to run special cheap-fare trains for 'the exclusive accommodation of artisans, mechanics and daily labourers, both male and female, going to their work or returning from work to their houses'. Times and fares were laid down in the Act of Parliament sanctioning the Herne Hill – Blackfriars line. Similar

Below: Swindon,
Brunel's railway
town, as it looked to an
artist in 1845, with the
first buildings of the
GWR's *locomotive and*
carriage works appearing
in the previously
pastoral landscape.

Left: Swindon, a century later, in the last decade of its steam locomotive construction activity. The erecting shop is seen in 1951, with the frames of a new BR *Class 4 4-6-0 assembled in the foreground.*

facilities were provided by other companies as time went on, and workmens' tickets survived long after special workmen's trains were discontinued.

Railway towns

Workers employed on the construction and maintenance of railway rolling stock and locomotives often found themselves provided with accommodation close to their work, in the 'railway towns' which developed at various places on the main lines where the companies found it convenient to set up manufacturing facilities. Some of them, such as Swindon and Ashford, were already small market towns because of good road communications with the surrounding district. Others were barely known before they became railway junctions and were chosen as sites for works on that account. Crewe and Bishopstoke (later Eastleigh) were in that category. Wolverton was not an important junction but was chosen for a locomotive works by the London and Birmingham Railway because of its convenient position at approximately the mid-point of the line, and for its proximity to the Grand Junction Canal.

At Swindon a new estate for Great Western employees was built about a mile outside the town and the first 300 workmen were moved there in 1843. Two years earlier the population of Swindon had been 2459; ten years later it was 4876, and by 1881 had risen to 19,904. According to the 1851 census, 92 per cent of employed persons in 'New Swindon' were at the railway work shops; at Wolverton it was 85 per cent.

Other towns grew for traffic reasons from virtually nothing; Middlesbrough, for example, was a small farming community until, in the 1840s, it was developed for shipment of coal brought by an extension of the Stockton and Darlington Railway, built because Middlesbrough was downstream of the shallow which had to be negotiated by ships sailing from Stockton Wharf. But Middlesbrough also had ironstone deposits on its doorstep, and soon the local ore and the coal brought to the town by railway became the foundation of a thriving iron and steel industry.

Rail travel was mass travel, but it left its mark on the individual who found himself competing with large numbers of his fellows for a seat in the carriage or something to eat in the refreshment room. For this he had to develop new patterns of behaviour. *The Railway Traveller's Handy Book*, published in 1863, was designed to help those who did not adapt by instinct. Here was wise counsel on 'disposing of ladies and children' during the 'noise, bustle and confusion inseparably attendant on the arrival of a train'; on 'treatment of unpleasant travelling companions'; and on 'how to act in cases of threatened accident'. The Victorian traveller standing at the refreshment room counter and crying out 'ale', 'soup', or some other monosyllable (never mind 'a basin of' if you simply want soup, advised the *Handy Book*) was an exponent of lifemanship.

Chapter 7

George Hudson, the 'Railway King'

Above: George Hudson, the York draper who manoeuvred himself into control of more than 1000 route-miles of railway and was acclaimed the 'Railway King'. He was lionized by London society until his financial skullduggery was unmasked and he was voted out of all his company chairmanships.

THROUGHOUT THE MANIA years responsible railway building was making steady progress. The ultimate goal was Scotland. The Liverpool and Manchester had made a tentative northward thrust by opening its Wigan branch in 1832, and on 28 October 1838 the Northern Union Railway provided an extension with its line from Wigan to Preston. Next came the Lancaster and Preston Railway on 26 June 1840, and from this time road mail coach services began running from Lancaster to Carlisle, Edinburgh and Glasgow in connection with the trains. There was an alternative route to Scotland by the day mail trains between London and Liverpool, which connected with a steamer sailing between Liverpool and Ardossan. On 12 August 1840 Ardrossan was connected with Glasgow by the opening of the first section of the future Glasgow and South Western Railway.

Also in 1840 through trains were instituted from London (Euston) to York. They followed the London and Birmingham Railway to Rugby, branching there on to the Midland Counties Railway to Derby. From Derby to Altofts Junction, beyond Normanton, the route was over the North Midland. Travellers this way were passing through the territories of George Hudson, the Railway King, chairman of many railway companies and architect of much of the railway system in the Midlands and north, until he over-reached himself.

To return to the western side of the country, the opening of the Preston and Wyre Railway on 16 July 1840 connected Preston with the new port of Fleetwood, and henceforth the Ardrossan steamship service operated from there. Meanwhile the forging of the all-rail route to Scotland continued. Beyond the existing northern terminus of the route at Lancaster, the fells of Westmorland challenged both the civil and the locomotive engineer aiming for the border at Carlisle. George Stephenson had suggested a route via Ulverston, Millom and Whitehaven, crossing Morecambe Bay on an embankment stretching from Hest Bank to Kent's Bank, but he was cautious about gradients and had once offered to eat his hat if 'Joe Locke' took a railway across the Pennines from Sheffield to Manchester. Stephenson avoided the hills enclosing Sheffield (though it was the most important town in the region) when building the North Midland Railway, and left it to citizens to build their own branch along the Don Valley to connect with his line at Rotherham.

Right: A characteristic Midland Railway station scene, thought to be Chesterfield, photographed in 1867. The engine is a 'Jenny Lind' 2-2-2 of 1855 build, No. 728.

Left: The double-deck High Level Bridge over the Tyne at Newcastle, completed in 1849, was one of Robert Stephenson's design masterpieces. Trains go over the top, other traffic underneath. This and Stephenson's Royal Border Bridge at Berwick, opened in 1850, forged the first East Coast Anglo Scottish rail route.

But faith in the steam locomotive and the adhesion of the steel wheel on a steel rail was growing. Locke did build his railway from Manchester to Sheffield, and when he surveyed a route from Lancaster to Carlisle he chose to go across Shap Fell at an altitude of 914 ft. At one time he considered tunnelling under the summit, but his earlier work on the Grand Junction Railway had impressed him with the importance which boardrooms attach to economy, and so over the top he went. In doing so he left a permanent reminder of himself to subsequent generations of designers of motive power. Even today, when electric locomotives and power cars sail at 1 in 75 up the final four miles to the summit from the south with apparent unconcern, and drivers have to notch back their controls to keep within the 75 mph speed limit at the top, in the world of slide rules and calculators where modern motive power has its origin, Shap must still be considered in terms of temperature rise in traction motors and cubic feet of cooling air per minute.

The Lancaster and Carlisle Railway was opened from Lancaster to Oxenholme in September 1846, coinciding with the opening of the Kendal and Windermere Railway from Oxenholme to the lake. For a time Lancaster and Carlisle trains ran through to Kendal to connect there with coaches to Scotland, but in December the section over Shap was com-

pleted and Carlisle became the point of transfer.

Railway building was also afoot in Scotland. The Caledonian Railway opened from Beattock to Carlisle on 10 September 1847, and on 15 February 1848 completed its lines from Beattock to Glasgow and Edinburgh. This forged the first unbroken chain of rail communication between London and the two Scottish cities. The most important variation of the route after that time was the opening of the Trent Valley line from Rugby to Stafford on 26 June 1847 for goods traffic, and on 1 December of the same year for passengers. London–Scotland services from Euston took the Trent Valley route until a daytime Euston–Inverness service – the 'Clansman' – was scheduled to travel via Birmingham and Wolverhampton in 1976.

The year 1850 saw an East Coast route to Scotland completed by Robert Stephenson's High Level Bridge at Newcastle (finished in 1849) and the Royal Border Bridge at Berwick, although a temporary bridge over the Tyne had been erected by October 1848. At this time the East Coast trains still ran to and from Euston via Rugby and the various elements of George Hudson's railway ran north from there. The Great North of England Railway had been opened for passenger traffic between York and Darlington on 30 March 1841. A line from Darlington to Gateshead was completed in 1844, and on 1 July 1847 the Newcastle and Berwick

Railway was completed. By that time Hudson was in control of all lines between Rugby and the Tweed.

The formation of railway companies, and the construction of lines, needed the drive of individuals, and the 1840s saw the emergence of the first of the railway barons. Their easiest way to power was to gain the support of the shareholders. A higher proportion of average shareholders was at that time active than in any concern today; the 'Liverpool interest' was always particularly strong – much of the early railway capital had been contributed by people from that area. It was this route to the top that was exploited *par excellence* by George Hudson.

George Hudson

Hudson was a native of York. He began his business life with a draper's shop in the city and in later life used to say that his misfortune was to have been left a legacy of £30,000. Thus armed, he was able to enter the world of railway finance at a time of great activity and much opportunity. The doors of boardrooms were opened to him and he earned a reputation for putting right the affairs of ailing companies. From seats on the board he proceeded to chairmanships; in 1837 he became Lord Mayor of York and in 1845 was elected Member of Parliament for Sunderland.

Frederick Williams quotes an eye-witness account of Hudson at the height of his fame and social prestige. The scene was a conversazione at which the Prince Consort was present:

They looked like rival monarchs each with his obsequious courtiers around him . . . suddenly there was a movement and a gentleman was seen to pass from the Prince Consort's followers and to make his way to the little court which hemmed in the Railway King. It was like a plenipotentiary carrying a message between neighbouring potentates. 'The Prince has asked to be introduced to Mr Hudson.'

In his later years Hudson liked to recall that

Sydney Smith, sir, the Rev. Sydney Smith, the great wit, first called me the Railway King; and I remember well that he made a very pretty speech about it saying that while some monarchs had won their title to fame by bloodshed and by the misery they inflicted on their fellow creatures, I had come to my throne by my own peaceful exertions, and by a course of probity and enterprize.

Hudson had become Chairman of the York and North Midland Railway when it was formed

Below: The delightful curved present-day station at York dates from completion of a direct Doncaster-Selby-York route in 1871. Previously through trains had reversed in a dead-end station to the south-east of the new one.

o connect York with the London–Leeds lines t Altofts Junction, north of Normanton. That was straightforward railway promotion, but in the following year, 1840, the machiavellian character of the man was revealed when he eased the Leeds and Selby Railway so that he ould promptly shut most of it to passenger raffic and force its travellers to make a longer ourney via his own York and North Midland. It was one way of compensating for his failure to get Stephenson to agree to 'Mak' all t' railways um t' York.'

With control of traffic flowing between the West Riding and both York and Humber secure, Hudson attacked to the north, promoting chemes which would extend the Great North of England Railway from Darlington to Newcastle. He could make no accommodation with the Stockton and Darlington, which lay at right angles to his path, so he simply drove through it; the resultant flat crossing of the two lines at Darlington survived in the East Coast main line well into the twentieth century. For a year and a half the Stockton and Darlington Railway advertised its own 'through service' from Darlington to the Tyne, but unsuspecting travellers who tried it found themselves ejected from the train after less than a dozen miles' progress at South Church, Bishop Auckland, and forced to take a horse bus to the next railhead at Rainton Meadows.

Hudson was also instrumental in securing the North British Railway's construction of a line from Edinburgh to Berwick. After that it only needed bridges across the Tyne and Tweed to forge another rail link between London and Scotland. Edinburgh to Berwick, the first main line of the North British Railway, was inaugurated on 18 June 1846; permanent bridges across the Tyne and Tweed, replacing the temporary structures of 1848, were opened in 1849 and 1850 respectively.

Meanwhile, Hudson had been stretching his empire south-westwards. Back in 1842 he had made his first successful appeal to shareholders other than those of his own York and North Midland, and won the chairmanship of the North Midland Railway itself – whereupon he immediately started cutting the wages of the various grades of employees. When some enginemen protested, they were paid off on Christmas Eve and the drivers' jobs filled by such unlikely replacements as a stonemason, a platelayer, a fireman, two unemployed drivers

Below: Ambergate's strange triangular station, photographed in 1911, was built in 1876 after the Midland line over the Peak had branched away from the original North Midland line from Derby to Sheffield. The gabled stone building of the previous station is seen in the right background, in the fork of the junction.

Above: Derby locomotive works and station, the heart of the Midland Railway, seen from the North Stafford sidings circa 1885. In the middle distance is Johnson 4-4-0 No. 1320, built in 1877.

sacked for drunkenness and another who had overturned thirty wagons down the side of an embankment! Hudson's railways were certainly not notable for their safety or their efficiency.

So far, Hudson had only spread his influence by becoming associated with a number of different companies, but in 1844 he brought about the formation of the Midland Railway by amalgamation of the North Midland, the Midland Counties and the Birmingham and Derby Junction. All of these met at Derby, and the competition between the last two companies had, by 1843, reduced the fare for through passengers to London to as little as one shilling for the 38 miles from Derby to Hampton. By repeated appeals to the shareholders at half-yearly meetings, and other means, Hudson succeeded in bringing about the amalgamation, a business *coup* of previously unknown magnitude. He now ruled a railway route, or its projected extensions, all the way from Bristol in the south-west and Rugby in the south to Edinburgh in the north.

There was already considerable pressure for a

direct rail route from York to London. Hudson was bitterly opposed to anything of the sort, for although the existing route depended on the goodwill of the authorities at Euston for access to the capital, most of it was under his own control. By 1846, however, the Great Northern Railway had obtained its Act and proceeded to build a line from Askern, north of Doncaster, to London by way of Retford, Lincoln, Boston and Peterborough. The route from Askern to York was over the Lancashire and Yorkshire Railway to a junction with the York and North Midland near Knottingley. A temporary London terminus was opened at Maiden Lane on 8 August 1850. Kings Cross was brought into use in October 1852 after the opening of the direct line from Peterborough to Retford – avoiding the original detour via Lincoln – in August.

It may seem surprising that the Great Northern first reached York over a Hudson line – the York and North Midland – but by this time Hudson's star was fading. When railway share prices tumbled after the railway mania had passed its climax, pertinent questions about his management of finances were raised at company meetings. Once the questioner would have been ⸺ered for his lack of faith; now the once un⸺thinkable happened, and at a meeting of the ⸺astern Counties Railway in March 1849 Hud⸺on was hissed and hooted. It emerged that ⸺rices of shares in his railway empire had been ⸺ept artificially high by paying dividends out of ⸺apital rather than profits, and with this ⸺evelation confidence in Hudson collapsed. A ⸺onth later he resigned his chairmanship of the ⸺idland Railway Company. A committee of ⸺nquiry found that Hudson had 'abused the ⸺onfidence that was placed in him by wielding ⸺he power he obtained to forward his own ⸺nterest'.

In the end Hudson over-reached himself. ⸺hether he rose to power by the path of ⸺robity and enterprise as defined by a strict ⸺oralist may be debatable, but it was probably ⸺n line with the rough-and-tumble of the com⸺ercial practice of his day. His contribution to ⸺he railway system is beyond dispute and he has ⸺is memorial in Hudson House, now the York ⸺eadquarters of British Rail's Eastern Region.

Amalgamations

⸺espite the preference of Parliament for a large ⸺umber of competing companies, amalgama⸺ions of those with a common interest were ⸺eginning in the 1840s. Hudson's formation of

Left: The Midland Railway's coat of arms.

the Midland Railway has already been noted. In 1845 the Grand Junction took over the Liverpool and Manchester, and on 16 July 1846 the London and North Western Railway – destined to become the world's largest joint stock company – was formed by the amalgamation of the London and Birmingham, Grand Junction, and Manchester and Birmingham. The last of these was opened between Manchester and Crewe on 10 August 1842, and its trains reached Birmingham over the Grand Junction. It formed the third side of a triangle of which the other two sides were the Grand Junction line from Birmingham to the London and Manchester at Earlestown, and the section of the London and

Below: Heeley, on the Midland Railway's 1870 extension from Chesterfield to Sheffield, the core of Hudson's great empire. This appears to be a contractor's train suitably garlanded for the opening.

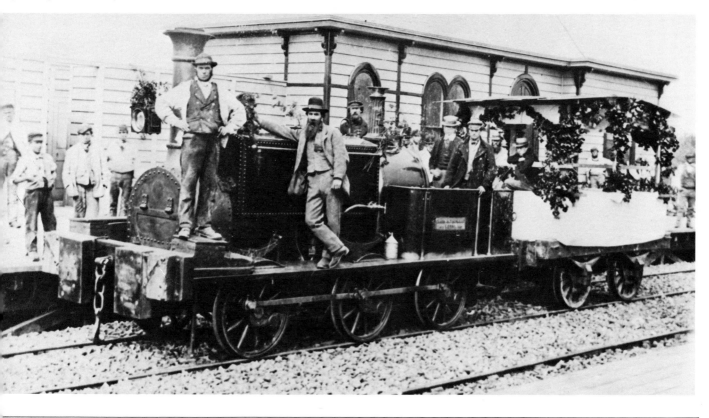

Manchester between there and Manchester. Thus it shortened the route from the south and the Midlands to Manchester, compared with the original one via Earlestown. Some of the constituents of the West Coast route north of the London and Manchester line had already been merged with the Grand Junction and came into the LNWR in that way. The Lancaster and Preston Junction and the Lancaster and Carlisle Railways were leased to the LNWR in 1859 and vested in that company in 1879. The Lancashire and Yorkshire and the Manchester, Sheffield and Lincolnshire were each a combination of five smaller companies.

On the other side of the country the various lines that had formed the East Coast route north of York, together with the Leeds Northern, were merged into the North Eastern Railway in 1854. In most cases the major companies concerned in the amalgamations had already absorbed a number of smaller concerns.

Formation of a new company by amalgamation required an Act of Parliament and the consequences of the arrangement were closely scrutinized. There was some uneasiness at the size of the London and North Western giant, and when a few years later the Midland sought amalgamation with the LNWR as a means of gaining access to London the proposal was turned down. The Midland then reached agreement with the Great Northern Railway for its trains to run into Kings Cross from Bedford via Hitchin, and in due course a Midland–Great Northern merger was mooted, but public opinion as reflected in Parliament was unfavourable and the idea was dropped. Nevertheless there was a flurry of amalgamations and absorptions on a smaller scale throughout the 1850s and 1860s, so that in those years the railway system assumed the form it was to retain almost unchanged until the railway grouping after the First World War.

The formation of these large companies was to bring about the emergence of more great railway personalities, not engineers like the Stephensons and Brunel, or entrepreneurs like Hudson, but managers. These were the people who welded together the increasingly complex organizations necessary to operate a rapidly expanding commercial enterprise which stretched continuously across the countryside for up to several hundred miles. Foremost amongst these was Captain Mark Huish, who for more than a decade ruled the newly formed London and North Western as an autocratic dictator, while as an aggressive frontiersman he extended its tracks and influence ever further from Euston.

Another contemporary railway character of great importance was Edmund Denison, chairman of the Great Northern Railway. Not only was his line the largest so far ever authorized by a single Act, but the fight to get their bill passed was the greatest railway battle ever argued out in Parliament. Lasting for two sessions in 1845 and 1846, it set the company back well over £400,000 while the costs to its opponents, notably George Hudson's interests, were also large. The antagonists failed to defeat the project and merely delayed a route which was to shorten the distance between York and London by 30 miles. Inside two decades railway transport had escalated from being simply an adjunct to mining enterprises to being the first known example of big business.

Below: Present-day BR *has taken care to blend its modern travel centre in the forecourt of Kings Cross, seen in the lower picture, with the original 1852 facade. The architect of the Great Northern terminus was Lewis Cubitt. Note the vertical exaggeration of the facade in the artist's drawing.*

Chapter 8

Early steam locomotives

THE CHARACTERISTIC OUTLINE of the *Rocket*, with its high-pitched and steeply inclined cylinders, was not perpetuated. In the next batch of otherwise similar locomotives the cylinders were lowered and nearly horizontal, for the original arrangement had contributed to a rather unsteady motion.

In October 1830, only a month after the opening of the Liverpool and Manchester Railway, Robert Stephenson's works at Newcastle delivered the locomotive *Planet*. In this machine the cylinders were placed for the first time between the frames and below the smoke-box, ahead of the driving wheels instead of behind them. With one pair of leading carrying wheels and one pair of drivers, *Planet* was 2-2-0.

Another early variant of the four-wheeled locomotive was the 0-4-0 (two coupled driving axles), but as the power and weight of the locomotives increased it became desirable to distribute the load over more axles. Stephenson achieved this in the 2-2-2 *Patentee* locomotive of 1834 with one driving axle behind two carrying axles. It was a pattern to be followed for many years by different builders, and the

basis upon which future development took place.

Edward Bury, Superintendent of the Locomotive Department of the London and Birmingham Railway, remained faithful to four-wheeled locomotives, 2-2-0 or 0-4-0, until 1845. Osbourne's *London and Birmingham Railway Guide* assured its readers that the Bury locomotive hauling their train was 'of the most improved character' and went on to make the bold assertion that 'steam locomotion on railways has now perhaps nearly attained the highest pitch of perfection'. After his four-wheeled types had shown a tendency to leave the rails, Bury began building six-wheeled engines.

Gooch's engines

In the meantime the 7 ft $0\frac{1}{4}$ in. gauge Great Western Railway was pursuing a policy of locomotive construction which was to become widespread. Elsewhere railways had been looking through manufacturers' literature and ordering what seemed suited to their needs. Discontented with the unreliable machines ordered prior to his appointment, Daniel Gooch, the GWR's Locomotive Superintendent, decided to state exactly what *he* wanted, and to provide

Below: London and Birmingham Railway No. 1. Edward Bury, the L&BR's locomotive Superintendent was the Stephensons' only significant design competitor in the 1830s. His engines were characterized by their round-top or 'haycock' firebox.

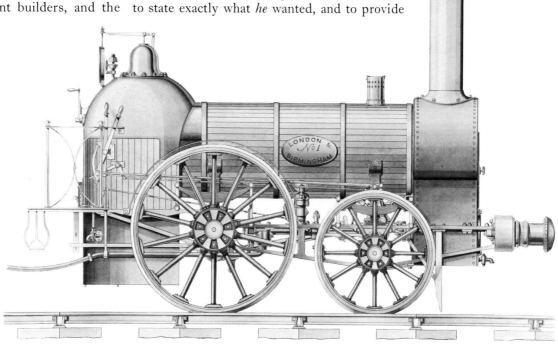

builders with a detailed specification. Gooch's first engines were built by contractors (he himself came from Stephenson's at Newcastle); most of these engines were of the 2-2-2 Fire Fly class. A new era opened in the spring of 1846 when the 2-2-2 *Great Western* to Gooch's design was the first product of the GWR's recently established Swindon works. A few more 2-2-2 engines followed, then in 1847 came the first of Gooch's 4-2-2s, the Iron Dukes. By later standards the Gooch 4-2-2s were relatively crude machines, but their large boilers and fireboxes, in combination with driving wheels of 8 ft diameter, short piston strokes and a weight of 53 tons with a loaded tender, made them eminently suitable for light train haulage at high speeds. For that kind of work they had the benefit of Brunel's superbly engineered London –Bristol main line, with its easy gradients and freedom from all but gentle curves most of the way. By the mid-nineteenth century Gooch's engines and Brunel's broad gauge in combination had opened up previously inconceivable speed horizons and laid the foundations for much higher inter-city rail speed in the twentieth century.

On a test run in 1847 one of the Gooch 4-2-2s attained 78 mph on a falling gradient of 1 in 100. That was probably a world record for any form of transport at the time. However, a performance of much greater merit was implied by the claim that, on 11 May 1847, the engine *Great Western*, hauling a load of approximately 60 tons, ran the 53 miles from Paddington to Didcot in $47\frac{1}{2}$ minutes start to stop. This run was so remarkable for the period that doubts were cast on its accuracy by experts such as Charles Rous Marten, the leading nineteenth-century authority on locomotive performance who suspected a carelessly kept guard's journal and by E. L. Ahrons, an engineering writer who had served his time as an apprentice at Swindon and who had experience of the Gooch 'Eight-footers' in their later days. Ahrons throught that the run was technically just possible, but that the evidence was far from convincing.

In February 1940, however, powerful support for the authenticity of the claim came from a scholarly examination of the evidence of two professional engineers of repute, J. T. Turner and M. Grehan, who published their findings in *The Railway Magazine*. They pointed out that

Below: The broad-gauge Bristol and Exeter Railway had some remarkable 4-2-4 well and back tank engines with 8ft 10 in. or 9 ft driving wheels built for its Exeter expresses by Rothwell & Co between 1853 and 1873. One is here seen as GWR No. 2002.

the run was mentioned in a paper delivered by Daniel Gooch to the Institution of Civil Engineers. It is inconceivable that Gooch would have deliberately misled a learned society, especially at a time when the battle of the gauges was raging fiercely and when the advocates of the narrow 4 ft 8½in. gauge would have relished any opportunity to discredit him. In more recent times, in the magazine *Railway World*, Group Captain J. N. C. Law, who has made a special study of locomotive and train resistance, has estimated that an indicated horsepower of 500–550 would make the timing credible. This accords with Gooch's figures of water consumption; moreover, the train's power/weight ratio of around 4½ hp/ton was similar to that which produced comparable speeds half a century later.

Designs for speed and safety

Gooch's design vindicated Brunel's claims for the speed and safety of travel on his broad gauge, but not in time to influence the findings of the Gauge Commission, as described in a previous chapter. Nonetheless, despite new construction on the standard gauge and the addition of a third rail to create numerous mixed-gauge sections, broad gauge did not disappear until 20 May 1892 – the culmination

of an extraordinary operation that dealt with the whole of the Paddington–Plymouth main line and numerous West Country branches in a conversion programme of less than a fortnight. It should be added that the GWR did not generally exploit the speed potential shown by the Gooch engines in regular daily service. As time went on, in fact, broad gauge expresses became heavier and slower. When the end of broad gauge came in 1892 other standard gauge lines were running faster trains.

Back in the 1840s, the standard gauge railways strove to match the speeds attained on the broad gauge with their own, smaller engines, and evolved a number of ingenious but largely impractical designs to achieve this. Their engineers were continually worried that the risk of overturning at high speed increased with the narrower wheel spacing of a standard gauge line. To lower the centre of gravity, therefore, they thought up different ways of matching a relatively low-slung boiler to large driving wheels. One such idea was the brainchild of an engineer working amid the broad gauge theorists of Swindon. He was Thomas Russell Crampton, who patented a locomotive with a particularly low centre of gravity achieved by locating its driving axle and large diameter driving wheels at the extreme rear; carrying axles only were beneath the boiler. Crampton's design had

Above: GWR *broad-gauge 4-2-2* Lord of the Isles, *one of the 29-strong 'Iron Duke' class with 8 ft driving wheels built at Swindon to Gooch's design between 1847 and 1855. The engine is here decorated to work a special for the Sultan of Turkey.*

Above: A 'Convertible' 2-4-0 approaches Teignmouth with the down 'Cornishman' on 20 May 1892, only days before the conversion of the surviving broad-gauge stronghold west of Exeter. The sleepers between the rails have already been trimmed in preparation for the conversion. This photograph is taken from the same spot as the one on page 31, but looking north.

Top: Mixed gauge in Sonning Cutting, near Reading, in the last May 1892 days of broad-gauge working from Paddington to Plymouth. The engine is a Gooch 4-2-2.

considerable success on the Continent, but not in high-speed running. Stable they may have been, but the 'Cramptons' were hard on the track. A Crampton engine, tested on the LNWR, ran the forty-one miles from Wolverton to Coventry in 42 minutes, probably the nearest that the narrow gauge came to GWR standards by 1847.

Another variation was the Stephenson 'long boiler' locomotive. Here the aim was also to increase thermal efficiency. Better use was made of the fuel, it was argued, because of the increased heating surface gained from the longer tubes in the boiler, and the fact that they suppressed the emission of hot cinders. But the wheelbase had to be short for operating reasons and so all the wheels were in front of the firebox. The resultant overhang at the rear made the engines sway at speed and caused accidents.

In both these types there was a return to outside cylinders although in some of the 'long boilers' they were inside.

In 1847, at Crewe works, Francis Trevithick built his famous engine *Cornwall* for the LNWR. In order to use driving wheels 8 ft 6 in. in diameter, the largest ever employed on the standard gauge, he slung the boiler below the driving axle. The latter passed through a channel recessed in the top of the boiler, while the rear carrying axle was threaded through the firebox in a transverse tube. There is no evidence of any exceptional performance by this engine; certainly it did nothing likely to worry broad gauge supporters, and in 1858 *Cornwall* was completely rebuilt from a 4-2-2 to a conventional 2-2-2 with its boiler above the driving axle. In this form it did better work, though it achieved nothing that could not have been matched by the ordinary LNWR 2-2-2s with 7 ft 6in. wheels. For many years it hauled the chief mechanical engineer's inspection coach.

Among the variations on the 2-2-2 formula, the design of E. B. Wilson and Company of Leeds pointed the way to further development of this wheel arrangement. Wilson's designer, David Joy, produced his 2-2-2 in 1846 for the London, Brighton and South Coast Railway, then in dire need of passenger motive power. He did not subscribe to the view that a low centre of gravity was necessary for stability in a standard gauge locomotive intended for fast running, but he provided a fairly long wheelbase with the 6 ft diameter driving wheels outside the frames and the carrying wheels inside. He also used a boiler pressure of 120 lb/in², which was high for its day. The first

engine was named *Jenny Lind* after a Swedish soprano, and its numerous successors were referred to collectively in the same way.

Two of the Jenny Linds went to the London and North Western Railway where they suggested a new line of development to J. E. McConnell, Locomotive Superintendent of the LNWR's Southern Division, which still retained its own locomotive works at Wolverton.

McConnell's first 2-2-2s appeared in 1851. He retained a fairly long wheelbase as in the Jenny Linds but all wheels were outside the frames. The complete exposure of the 7 ft drivers in his locomotives earned them the nickname 'Bloomers' from a contemporary attempt to reform women's dress, which revealed the fact that they owed their mobility to the possession of two legs. It was no less a personage than a President of the Institution of Mechanical Engineers who is reported to have complained that 'McConnell cleared away the decent skirting of an outside frame and exhibited the whole of his wheels to the gaze of the traveller.' The Bloomers, of which there were several series with driving wheels of various diameters, outdid the Jenny Linds with a boiler pressure of 150 lb/in^2. They had a long and successful career in fast passenger traffic on the LNWR.

McConnell was a progressive engineer and another of his products to attract attention was his Patent class 2-2-2 with 7 ft 6 in. driving wheels, built in response to the call of the LNWR directors in the early 1850s for trains to connect London and Birmingham in two hours. The Patent 2-2-2s were criticized in some quarters for their high centre of gravity, but in hindsight their weakest feature was the complicated boiler with an unprecedented size of fire-grate, which

Above: A Robert Stephenson long-boiler 4-2-0 of the 1840s. The long boiler achieved Stephenson's objective of greater thermal efficiency, but the rear overhang made a long-boiler single-driver unstable as an express engine. In Britain the idea had a future only in 0-6-0 goods engine form.

Right: The first Crampton engine, the 6-2-0 Liverpool of 1848 for the LNWR. It was reputed to have reached 78 mph, but it did heavy damage to the track.

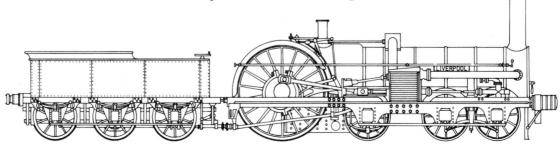

Above: One of the Midland Railways's first engines, a 'Jenny Lind' 2-2-2 built by E. B. Wilson in 1848.

Below: No. 127 Peel, one of Ramsbottom's 'Problem' or 'Lady of the Lake' 2-2-2s built for the LNWR between 1859 and 1865.

McConnell devised to burn coal instead of the more expensive coke that until then had been the preferred fuel. A simple answer was eventually to prove the most effective – the insertion in the firebox of a brick arch and deflector plate – of that more in a moment.

McConnell was a believer in high boiler pressures. In his day 120 lb/in² was the ratio generally preferred, but in the Patent type and in three larger 2-2-2s he built just before his retirement McConnell went up to 150 lb/in².

Another to adopt this ratio was A. Sturrock of the Great Northern Railway ('The finest gun is no good without plenty of powder,' he once remarked). The GNR management, too, was after speed and envisaged East Coast route trains reaching Edinburgh within eight hours of leaving London; over the GNR part of the journey the target was a non-stop trip to Grantham, $105\frac{1}{2}$ miles, in two hours. To serve their purpose, and to rival McConnell's LNWR engines, Sturrock built an experimental 4-2-2 which strongly resembled the Gooch broad gauge single-drivers, though its driving wheels were of 7 ft 6 in. diameter; no records of exceptional performance by this solitary machine have survived. Nevertheless, while it was 1905 before the LNWR was running two-hour trains to Birmingham in daily service, the GNR was making Grantham in just under two hours from Kings Cross by 1884.

In all the locomotives mentioned so far the axles, both driving and carrying, were mounted in the main frames. Allowance was made for some sideways movement as well as the vertical movements due to the spring suspension. Given the relatively short wheelbases, this was suf-

ficient free play to negotiate the curves of British lines. The practice of mounting the leading carrying axles in a 'truck' or bogie which could swivel relative to the centre line of the locomotive originated in the United States, where curves were often much sharper and the track uneven. A locomotive with a leading four-wheel bogie and single driving axle was designed and built by John B. Jervis at the West Point Foundry as early as 1831, and this type of construction soon became characteristic of US practice. After the 4-2-0 came the 4-4-0 and the latter wheel arrangement became so widespread in the United States that it was called the 'American'. It did not become established in the British Isles until much later; the first examples were seen in the early 1860s.

The leading bogie contributed to stability as well as helping in the negotiation of curves. With this arrangement the locomotive had a three-point support with the configuration of a three-legged stool. Two of the points were the bearings of the driving axle in the main frames; the third was on the centre line of the locomotive where the weight of the leading end was taken by bearing surfaces on the bogie transom.

As early as 1839 the US builder William Norris exported some 4-2-2 locomotives of his own design to the Birmingham and Gloucester Railway. The Birmingham and Gloucester was then looking for motive power suitable for a

main line which climbed over the Lickey Hills near Bromsgrove with a gradient of 1 in 37; it had been unable to obtain from home manu-facturers all the locomotives it required in time for opening in 1840. The Norris locomotives had outside cylinders, placed fairly high on the outside of the smokebox and at an angle to the track, with all the valvegear mounted externally as well. There was, therefore, clear space under the smokebox to allow support of the leading end of the locomotive on the leading bogie.

Developments in steam

While plenty of thought was being given to mechanical design in the interests of safety at speed and good adhesion, engineers were also concerned with efficiency in the generation and distribution of steam. The basic principle of a boiler with a number of small tubes providing a large heating surface throughout its length had been an article of faith from the days of the *Rocket*. There was little scope for drastic change, but unlimited opportunity for juggling with the proportions of tube and firebox heating surfaces, and grate area. One improvement was made not much later, in 1850, when a brick arch was built in the firebox, which in conjunction with a downward-sloping deflector plate inside the firebox door ensured that air entering through the grate or through the firedoor followed a

Above: A typical Edward Bury locomotive with round-topped 'haycock' firebox. Built for the London and Birmingham Railway, No. 15A was photographed after acquisition by the North London Railway, which was created in 1846 to link the LNWR at Camden with Poplar Docks via Highbury, Hackney and Bow.

course which kept it in contact with the fire for as long as possible before reaching the boiler tubes. Matthew Kirtley, Mechanical Engineer of the Midland Railway, initiated the experiments which led to the adoption of this modification. The experiments were conducted by his assistant, Charles Markham, and by 1859 the efficacy of the principle was proved. From then on the brick arch and the deflector plate were an essential part of the combustion system of any steam locomotive.

A break through in the distribution of steam to the cylinders had been achieved in 1841 when Robert Stephenson announced: 'One of our people has hit on a plan that beats all other valve motions.' In the arrangement to which he referred a reciprocating movement was imparted to the valve spindle by means of a rocking link, to which the spindle was connected by a block sliding in a slot in the link. The block could be raised or lowered in the link and in this way the travel of the valve·could be varied. Varying the valve travel altered the proportion of the piston stroke during which steam was admitted to the cylinders. For maximum efficiency the admission period was kept short so that steam already in

the cylinder when the valve closed continued to work by expansion.

The arrangement devised at Stephenson's works was called 'Stephenson's link motion', and it gave the driver finely graduated control of his engine. Other valve gears followed, notably Walschaerts' valve gear in 1849; this was a familiar feature of the steam locomotive until its last days, and was easily recognizable by its pattern of cranks and rods applied to outside cylinders. But here, too, there was a rocking link as in Stephenson's gear, although the method of driving it differed and there were other refinements in the control of the valve travel.

One other important development which occurred after 1850 is more appropriately mentioned here. In 1873–5 F. W. Webb, who had assumed charge of LNWR locomotives generally in 1871, started to abandon iron for steel in locomotive boiler construction. Tests had convinced him that a steel boiler pressed to 140 lb lasted longer than an iron boiler pressed to 120 lb. This pointed the way to general adoption of higher boiler pressures and to locomotives of greater power and speed.

Below: Fenton was a 2-4-0 of the GWR 'Hawthorn' class, built 1865-6, one of three types contributed to broad-gauge stock by Joseph Armstrong. He succeeded Gooch at Swindon when the latter retired as the GWR's locomotive Superintendent.

Chapter 9

Train travel in the early years

THE LOCOMOTIVE WAS new technology throughout, but the early railway carriage began as a recognizable offspring of the road coach. Prints of Liverpool and Manchester trains show first-class coaches looking like three conventional stagecoach bodies merged into one under a common roof, and mounted on a four-wheeled underframe with a wheelbase of about 7 ft.

At first coaches were painted black and yellow, and were named – two ideas brought over from the stagecoach. Passengers were seated three a side facing each other, foreshadowing the typical compartment railway coach of the years ahead. Some of the coaches had a box seat for the guard and rails round the roof so that passengers' luggage could be stowed. Continuous brakes were unknown at that time. The guards worked the brakes on their own coaches to supplement those on the engine and tender worked by the engine crew. Contemporary pictures often show three guards to a train.

Up to at least 1840 passengers could ride outside, as in coaching days, on the box seat. A travellers' guidebook of the day assured them that if they provided themselves with an extra greatcoat and a pair of gauze spectacles as a precaution against smoke and dust they would enjoy themselves ten times more than their fellow passengers. Before the train started, this vademecum went on, they would see from their vantage point,

several engines with red hot fires in their bodies, and volumes of steam issuing from their tall chimneys. One of them moves slowly towards you. The huge creature bellows at first like an elephant. Deep, slow and terrific are the hoarse heavings it makes . . . there it is, roaring, groaning and grunting like a sea-horse, and spouting up steam like a whale.

Mails were carried in trains from 1837 and in the following year the London and Birmingham Railway introduced a special first-class coach for this traffic with passenger accommodation inside and the mails in boxes on the roof. There was a projecting 'boot' at one end of the body, with the guard's seat on top. The boot could be opened from the adjacent compartment to provide leg room for a recumbent passenger lying on a padded board across the seats. Rudimentary sleeping accommodation was thus provided, but it seems likely that the facility was mostly used by invalids and the elderly, and that the London and Birmingham vehicle was

Left: First-class coaches were still crude in mid-century, as this Midland four-wheeler of about 1854 demonstrates. Note the roof rails to contain luggage.

therefore the ancestor of the later specialized invalid coach rather than of the sleeping car.

The Parliamentary trains

Second-class vehicles ranged from the austere to the downright uncomfortable. They were roofed, but sometimes open-sided. Even if passengers enjoyed the protection of side walls they might still have to put up with draughts from un-glazed windows. The third-class passenger had to make do at first with an open wagon, some-times with bench seating but often with none at all. The nickname 'Stanhopes' glorified these undeserving stand-up vehicles. A minor con-cession to comfort was made by drilling holes in the floor for drainage, so that on wet days the passengers were not actually ankle-deep in rainwater, even if they were otherwise soaked to the skin.

In time legislation improved the lot of the third-class passenger and brought order into the business of rail transport as a whole. After a Select Committee in 1839 had enquired into 'the state of communication by railway' the Regu-lation of Railways Acts of 1840 and 1842 laid down rules for the inspection of new lines, for safety in general, and for the fixing of fares. A Railway Department of the Board of Trade was set up, headed by an Inspector-General of Railways. Lieutenant-Colonel Sir Frederic Smith, the first holder of this office, inspected the Great Western Railway when its main line was opened throughout from London to Bristol in 1841.

A further Regulation of Railways Act in 1844 contained sections stipulating that at least one train in each direction should offer third-class passengers accommodation in carriages pro-tected from the weather and fitted with seats. The average speed of such trains was not to be less than 12 mph and they were to pick up and set down at every station. The fare was not to exceed one penny per mile. This so-called 'Cheap Trains Act' was not popular with the railways and some of them took care to run their 'Parliamentary trains' at inconvenient hours. Gradually in a changing society the third-class traveller was found to be good business, yet as late as 1872 the other railway companies were shocked when the Midland Railway began to carry third-class passengers on all its trains, including the crack expresses.

Various types of 'Parliamentary' carriage were built for operation in the Parliamentary trains. These were four-wheelers, but six-wheelers were beginning to appear by the middle 1840s.

In 1844 Joseph Wright took out a patent for 'multiple-axle' railway carriages and soon the first eight-wheelers were seen, although not necessarily carried on bogies. In some early examples the body was in two halves, with a hinged joint between them; the wheelbase of each half was fixed, although the axles were allowed liberal sideplay.

The first eight-wheel coaches to run regularly in express service were introduced by the broad gauge Great Western Railway in 1852. They were not bogie vehicles, but the axles of the pair at each end of the body were close together, with their 4 ft diameter wheels set at 5 ft centres. Equalizing beams between each pair of axles could pivot in the horizontal plane to allow some sideplay. A carriage with four-wheel bogies is said to have been tested on the London and Greenwich Railway in the 1840s but the details

re uncertain. For the most part the railway
traveller in the 1850s rattled along on four or
six wheels.

Communications

It was a lucky chance that railway traffic and
electrical science developed side by side. The
electric telegraph was demonstrated between
Euston Station and Camden in 1838 and its
principles were used later to provide signalmen
with the intercommunication essential for regu-
lating the movements of trains. At first, however,
signalling methods were rudimentary. A traveller
in the *Experiment*, the horse-drawn passenger
coach operated by the Stockton and Darlington
Railway in the intervals of its more important
freight traffic, noted that 'at any bends in the
road or other place where the view is obstructed

the coachman blows his horn to give warning of
his approach to any wagons or vehicles that may
be coming or going on the way'. By the 1830s
railways were employing men described as
'policemen to control train movements, giving
hand signals to engine drivers to tell them
whether they must stop, slacken speed, or
proceed at full speed'.

Hand signals and flags soon gave way to
mechanical signals of various kinds, still worked
by 'policemen' on the spot. The one most
recognizable as an ancestor of the type of signal
used on railways universally until the advent of
the colour-light was introduced on the Liverpool
and Manchester Railway in 1834. It consisted of
a red-painted board mounted on a vertical
spindle which could be turned to face the driver
of an oncoming train when he had to stop. When
the line was clear the board was turned through
90 degrees so as to be parallel with the track. It
was then hardly visible from a distance, and this
absence of a signal fulfilled the principle generally followed at the time that the line was
normally clear.

In 1838 the Great Western Railway introduced a disc and crossbar signal which worked
in a similar way, except that the disc and crossbar were mounted on the spindle at right angles
to each other so that one or other was always
displayed to the driver, the disc meaning 'all
clear'. A positive indication of 'all clear' was
soon generally recognized as necessary, so that
drivers could travel fast with confidence.

At first a train was allowed to proceed when
the 'policeman' judged that the preceding
train was far enough ahead. As late as 1850 an
instruction was issued on the London and
North Western Railway that the man in
charge of the down signal at Wolverton was to
'stop the 9 am express every day, and tell
the driver and guard how long the 3rd class has
left'. This seems to have left the onus on the

*Left: Second-class com-
partment of an Eastern
Counties Railway coach in
1847. At this time
Gladstone's 1844 Act had
not made enough impact in
improving third class to
persuade railways that
second-class passengers
deserved more than a roof
and windows.*

*Left: Experiment was the
name given the Stockton
and Darlington's first two
passenger coaches. The
first was just a shed on
wheels. This, the second,
was a horse-hauled vehicle
incorporating a stage-coach
body on flanged iron wheels.*

Right: Flag signalling on the London and Birmingham in 1844. From left to right: all clear; slow down; caution, bad track.

Below: An early GWR disc signal.

driver to regulate his speed so as not to catch up the train ahead.

The electric telegraph enabled the somewhat hazardous time interval system of signalling to be dispensed with. A signalman could communicate with his colleague down the line and find out if a train he had sent ahead had actually reached and passed the next signalling point. If so, he could let the next train proceed. Effectively, therefore, the line was divided into sections with a signalman at each end, and only one train was allowed into a section at a time. This was the block system of signalling, each bit of line being called a 'block section', and it came gradually into use from the early 1840s.

It was a natural step from the signalman walking round to his various signals and operating them individually to bringing control of all of them into his shelter. Traditionally this was first done on a do-it-yourself basis by a signalman at Watford in 1846. The shelter developed into the familiar signalbox. At first signals were mounted on posts at the box itself and when a driver sighted a signal applying to him as 'danger' he had to use his judgment about where to stop. The next step was to work signals at a distance from the box by wires;

Right: A junction signal of 1844. Note the notches on the post provided so that the attendant signalman could climb up to inspect the apparatus.

ment of mechanical methods to guard against conflicting signals being displayed. For example, if the signals were cleared and the points set for one route, the levers controlling signals on a converging route would be locked in the danger position; it would not be possible to set the points for the main route and then clear the signals for the converging route. This procedure is known as 'interlocking'. With the development of the electric telegraph it was soon supplemented by other locking arrangements to prevent a signalman from accepting a second train with his block instrument until the one already in the section had cleared it. This system could be extended from the instruments to the signal levers themselves, which would be locked until the section they protected was free. This is known as 'lock and block' working.

With many different railway companies following their own ideas, it is often difficult to establish where particular practices first began. The best claim to be the first interlocking, however, is that of Bricklayers Arms Junction on the London and Croydon Railway, where the branch to Bricklayers Arms Station diverged from the main line to London Bridge. Here in 1843 a four-lever frame was installed to control

he signal posts were located just where a train ad to draw up in order to be clear of other movements. The first authenticated use of this ystem was at Hawick on the North British Railway in 1846.

The concentration of levers working signals nd points in a signalbox led to the develop-

Left: In 1842 the LSWR *refused Wheatstone and Cook's offer of their electric telegraph, but because the Government wanted communication with Portsmouth, the* LSWR *installed it between Nine Elms and Gosport in 1845. At the time this was the longest telegraph line in Britain.*

Below: An impression of London Bridge A and B signalboxes and signals in 1866. Note the lettered route indication on each signal arm.

The inset photograph shows the inside of the South Eastern Railway's London Bridge signalbox in 1866.

Above: An early morning view of the South Eastern Railway's Redhill station in 1865. The iron pillars were later removed because enginemen leaning from their cabs were regularly injured by them.

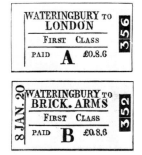

WATERINGBURY TO
LONDON
FIRST CLASS
PAID **A** £0.8.6
356

8 JAN. 20
WATERINGBURY TO
BRICK. ARMS
FIRST CLASS
PAID **B** £0.8.6
352

Above and right: Tickets and an Edmondson ticket-issuing machine of 1845. The first tickets issued were paper, but these were superseded by metal tags. The card ticket, subsequently adopted around the world, was the invention of a Lancashire Quaker named Thomas Edmondson, who after a varied career, became a Newcastle and Carlisle Railway stationmaster.

the junction signals. The signal wires were coupled to 'stirrups' in the frame, and to clear a signal for a train to pass the signalman had to press down the stirrup with his foot. That stirrup then fouled the stirrup connected with the lever for signalling a conflicting move, which thus could not be pulled. There was, however, no interlocking between signals and points.

The basic principle of the block system is still observed in modern colour-light signalling, although the signals are now controlled automatically by the passage of trains over long distances. There has, however, been a return to the original concept that the line is normally 'open' for trains, the signals showing green unless there is a train in the section they control. For most of the history of manual signalling in Britain the line was regarded as normally 'closed', even if no train was present; it had to be 'opened' by the signalman when a train was offered to him after all the conditions for safety had been fulfilled.

Signalling and safety were too important for individual railways to be left free to decide for themselves what standards they would adopt, and their arrangements were made subject to the approval of the Railway Department of the Board of Trade, as already mentioned. The first enquiries into railway accidents were held in 1840, and in the following year the comments of the Chief Inspecting Officer (or Inspector-General, as he then was) on a derailment in Sonning Cutting, GWR, in which third-class passengers had been flung out of their rude conveyances, hastened the legislation which improved their lot. Nonetheless, statutory authority to hold accident enquiries was not given until 1871. Even today an Inspecting Officer's recommendations cannot be enforced by law, although they are usually accepted.

The Railway Clearing Act

On the commercial side the railways got together among themselves to facilitate the handling of traffic which passed over different companies' lines. Nine companies participated in the Railway Clearing House scheme of 1842, which regularized accounting procedures when goods or passengers travelled over more than one railway, so that a single payment for a transit was fairly apportioned between the companies concerned. By 1845 sixteen companies were participating in the scheme, but then difficulties arose because the organization had no legal authority to enforce the payment of debts. The position was regularized by the Railway Clearing Act of 1850. The Railway Clearing House was then incorporated and issued its first classification of some 300 articles with their rates for carriage by rail. It was a highly variegated and rapidly swelling list soon embracing such diverse items as bands of musicians, fire engines, dogs and tramcars. By 1865 every railway of major importance belonged to the organization.

Early station design

At first passengers and goods traffic were handled on the same premises, but dual-purpose buildings were soon abandoned. One or two examples were long-lived. Outstanding was the flamboyant building put up at Newmarket in 1848 by the little Newmarket and Great Chesterford Railway, one of the Great Eastern's forerunners.

Most through stations were built from the start with platforms on each side of a double track, although the bulk of the station offices and passenger rooms would be concentrated in a building on one of the platforms – or not infrequently built into an over-bridge structure where the railway, in a cutting, had to be reached from a road at a higher level.

But in the earliest days some railway builders and station designers favoured a one-sided layout. The Great Western's Brunel was the best known practitioner of this style. At towns like Reading he erected a single, long platform well clear of the two through lines. The platform was served by a loop line divided in two, each half of which ran into and out of one of the running lines (the connections intersected in a scissors crossing at the platform centre), so that one end of the platform catered for down trains, the other for up. Each half of the platform had an identical set of passenger amenity buildings. The idea worked well when the train service was sparse, but became an operational handicap as trains grew longer and more frequent. The last station to be laid out in this way was the original Newcastle, in 1855, and the only surviving major example is Cambridge.

By 1850 the railway builders were already concerned not only to develop an individual architectural style for their stations, but also to refine their layouts for greater passenger comfort and functional efficiency. That is evident from a paper on stations read to the Institution of Civil Engineers in 1857 by a well-known engineer of the day, Robert Hood. For instance, he remarks that attempts to segregate the different classes of passenger were proving a failure. Passengers, he complained, were clogging platforms with luggage: the railway should make arrangements for luggage space on trains to be booked in advance. He urged the railways to get rid of the hand-operated turntables commonly used for shunting engines and vehicles from one station track to another, rather than point-work; they were both noisy and inefficient. And he particularly stressed the importance of providing ample paved and covered parking space in station forecourts!

Above: An LNWR *2-2-2 and train on the Bletchley-Cambridge line at Bedford in the 1860s.*

Left: Masham, country terminus of a branch built in 1875 by the North Eastern Railway from its Harrogate-Northallerton or Leeds Northern line at Melmerby. In this 1880 view the engine is NER *2-4-0T No. 84.*

Chapter 10

Early civil engineering masterpieces

PROBABLY MANY TRAVELLERS first became aware of railway civil engineering with the coming of the diesel railcar. The forward view from the front seats showed them for the first time the curves and gradients with which the civil engineer negotiated physical features of the country, the tunnel portal that loomed larger and nearer with the approach to a ridge of hills, and the narrow track ahead supported on unseen arches where the line crossed a valley.

The Menai Bridge

Some of these feats of engineering were greeted with as much enthusiasm as that which attended the opening of the first railway lines. The spirit of wonder was still alive in 1850, when on 5 March Robert Stephenson's tubular bridge across the Menai Strait carried the railway to Anglesey, Holyhead, and the dawning romance of the Irish Mail. A writer of the time recounted that when a test train ran through the tube 'a breathless silence prevailed; but when it emerged at the opposite end, loud acclamations arose, and the report of pieces of ordnance smote upon the ear'.

The crossing of the Strait had to be made with only two main spans, for to maintain un-

obstructed navigation the Admiralty would not allow a pier to be erected except on the Britannia Rock in midstream. Suspension bridges had not proved satisfactory for railway traffic loads and Stephenson was faced with the problem of building two spans over 400 ft in length. His answer was a rectangular tube of rolled steel plates for each tract, but this was only arrived at after lengthy calculation and experiment with a one-sixth scale model. A practical text followed when a tubular bridge of 425-ft span was built to cross the river estuary at Conway.

At Menai the two main spans were 460 ft long and allowed a clear height of 130 ft above the water. The great engineering works of the nineteenth century were objects of wonder because of their size and the boldness of their conception. Today these qualities are less astonishing than the fact that they were achieved in a period when earth-moving machinery and mechanical handling were unknown as engineering disciplines in their own right. We are told that the punching machine which perforated the iron plates 'with apparently as much facility as a child would push his thumb through a piece of blotting paper' was operated by a form of punched card control. There was much less automation in the process of fixing the plates together to form the tube:

Below: Robert Stephenson was forced into an unprecedented feat of prefabrication when the Admiralty refused to let him erect scaffolding in the waterway to build his Britannia Tubular Bridge over the Menai Strait in 1850. Each 460 ft-long wrought-iron tube had to be assembled on shore and lifted intact into place.

Left: Formidable engineering was involved in construction of the trans-Pennine route of the South Durham and Lancashire Joint line from the Stockton and Darlington extremity to Kirkby Stephen and Tebay. Its biggest viaduct was Belah, between Barras and Kirkby Stephen, a 196 ft-high, 1040 ft-long structure of sixteen 60 ft lattice spans. This is a view in BR days, the viaduct now having been dismantled.

As the bolts were heated, a lad snatched one up with a pair of pincers and flung it to another boy inside the tube, who picked it up and ran with it to the 'holder-up'. By an enormous hammer he forced it into the rivet hole till its end protruded the other side, where a couple of stalwart workmen soon moulded it into a head, and the bolt became a rivet. This, gradually cooling, bound the plates of iron together.

Completed tubes were floated on pontoons from the beach, where they were assembled on temporary supports at the foot of the piers. The first time this operation was performed it was watched by 'an immense concourse of visitors from all parts of Europe and even from the United States'. A steam press was mounted on top of the Britannia Tower to lift the tube into its final position, raising it 6 ft with each stroke of its piston. When all was done it was proposed to crown the Britannia Tower with a statue representing Science – for in those optimistic days on the eve of the Great Exhibition the effects of science were seen as wholly beneficent – but 'the depreciation of railway property induced the directors to abandon the design'. They made do with lions couchant at each end instead.

A feature of the bridge not mentioned in the above accounts was that the tubes were lined with timber. This fact was brought forcibly to public attention in 1970 when the timber was set alight by a fire started by vandals. One tube was so damaged that it was dismantled, but the other was repaired. The symmetry is spoiled, but in viewing what remains in its beautiful setting of sea, hills and distant mountains one can still feel the emotions that led an early commentator to write: 'Thus Science and Nature are mingled in harmonious contrast, and receive the grateful homage of every thoughtful observer.'

The Newcastle High Level Bridge

Robert Stephenson's High Level Bridge at Newcastle-upon-Tyne was in a less romantic setting than his Menai masterpiece. A few minutes' walk from the Central Station brings the visitor to its strange 'lower-level' roadway, with the trains rumbling overhead on the top-deck as they have done since 1849 when it first connected Newcastle with Gateshead and the south. At that time Newcastle Central was a terminus and trains continuing to Scotland had to reverse there. It did not become a through station until the present route crossing the Tyne on the King Edward Bridge and entering the station from the south-west was opened in 1906.

Stephenson shared the design of the High Level Bridge with T. E. Harrison. It crosses the deep ravine in which the Tyne flows between

Right: In 1859 Brunel had to prefabricate on shore the two 1000-ton, 455 ft-long spans of his Royal Albert Bridge at Saltash, then hoist them into position. Brunel, in the last days of his life, saw the bridge erected from a bed carried on an open carriage. The photograph shows diesel-hydraulic A1A-A1A 'Warship' No. D600 Active crossing the Tamar with the 'Cornish Riviera Express' in April 1958, before erection of the neighbouring Tamar road bridge.

Newcastle and Gateshead with six spans of 125 ft. The masonry piers support longitudinal 'bowstring' arches which carry the upper deck with its railway tracks. The roadway is level with the springing of the arches and is suspended from the railway deck by pillars. Height from water level to the roadway is 80 ft and to the railway deck 112 ft; the whole structure is 1372 ft long. When it was first built it was the first bridge of its size to carry both a road and railway. In later years structures of this kind became more common, but abroad rather than in Britain. Today the bridge of the Tyne and Wear Metro forms a new foreground for the panorama of bridges seen by rail travellers arriving at Newcastle from the south. This new bridge visually links the railway in its latest role as part of integrated urban transport with the era of main line construction represented by Stephenson's High Level Bridge in the background.

The Tamar Bridge

Brunel, like Stephenson at the Menai Strait, had to work under the constraint of Admiralty

Below: Another of Brunel's bridges, over the Wye at Chepstow, which was completed in 1852. His experience here was invaluable in design and erection of the Saltash bridge.

Above: The first Tay Bridge collapsed in a December gale of 1879, pitching a mail train and its 79 occupants into the estuary. This is the second bridge, the longest on British Rail, which was finished in 1887. Ex-NBR 4-4-2 No. 9872 Auld Reekie heads for Edinburgh with a 1930s express from Dundee.

requirements in bridging the River Tamar estuary to take the railway from Plymouth into Cornwall. The river here is 1100 ft wide and 70 ft deep at high water in the middle. Brunel was allowed a minimum span width of 300 ft and a minimum of 180 ft above high water. He solved the problem with a large-scale version of a bridge he had built earlier across the River Wye at Chepstow, in which the tubular and suspension principles were combined. When the Chepstow bridge was opened in 1852 it became a local tourist attraction, and a contemporary pamphlet noted that 'to the many objects of attraction this neighbourhood affords, the Railway Bridge may be considered an important addition; and strangers who come to the town appear to consider it as part of their business to pay the bridge a visit'.

Saltash has outlived the original Chepstow structure and was on a grander scale, with two river spans of 465 ft as against the single span of 300 ft across the Wye. Between the central pier in midstream and each shore pier are two slightly arched girders. The suspension chains are anchored to their ends and in their turn carry the deck with the single-track railway line, with the further support of vertical members and cross trusses. This variant of the pure suspension principle overcame some objections of the day to the idea of a railway suspension bridge. Today, however, Brunel's masterpiece survives in the shadow of the classic single-span suspension bridge across the Tamar. The bowed tubes of Brunel's Royal Albert Bridge where it crosses the water make it easy to overlook the magnitude of the work in other respects. The approach viaducts comprise 17 spans of 70–90 ft and the total length of the bridge is 2190 ft.

The Tay Bridge

One of the great bridges of the age of main line railway construction came to a tragic end. The Edinburgh, Perth and Dundee Railway was opened in 1849, but for many years travellers from Edinburgh to Dundee had to endure ferry crossings of the Firths of Forth and Tay. Thomas Bouch, as engineer of that railway, had

Above: A London Midland 'Crab' 2-6-0 heads a freight over Ribblehead viaduct, on the Settle-Carlisle line. The background is filled by Whernside.

Opposite: One of the two principal spans, each 1710 ft long, of the Forth Bridge. The rock of Inch-garvie Island, on which the centre cantilever stands, supports a total weight of 18,700 tons of metal. The whole bridge used over 54,000 tons of steel, held together by 6½ million rivets.

put forward plans for bridges at both places, but money was short and it was not until after the North British Railway had taken over that it was decided in 1869 to bridge the Tay between Wormit and Dundee Esplanade. Bouch was in charge of the work and decided on a viaduct of 89 spans. As the middle of the crossing approached the quality of the river bed deteriorated and the design of the piers and the middle section had to be changed. Here, in order to provide the necessary headway, the track was laid inside the girders instead of on top. These, in fact, were the 'high girders' inside which a train was later to plunge to destruction. But no misgivings were voiced at the opening ceremony of the bridge on 31 May 1878, when Bouch was knighted after Queen Victoria had travelled safely across the new structure with its total length of 11,563 ft.

Disaster struck little more than a year later in the furious gale of 28 December 1879. The high girders collapsed while a train was actually inside them, crashing into the Tay and killing all 73 people on board and the engine crew. The force of the gale had been unprecedented, and the whole structure was seen to shudder. A train inside the high girders presented a solid wall against which the wind could exert its furious pressure, sweeping the obstacle out of its path.

The enquiry found not only that lateral pressures had been inadequately calculated, but that there had been deficiencies in the quality and supervision of the work on the piers. Bouch suffered a nervous collapse and died soon after the enquiry. A new bridge across the Tay, designed by W. H. Barlow and his son, was opened in 1887 and remains in use today, the longest railway bridge in Great Britain.

The Forth Bridge

The second Tay Bridge was one of the last great structures based on wrought iron. When the next gap in the rail route to the north was bridged it was by a mild steel structure with two main spans of 1710 ft carried across the Forth by cantilever towers rising to 361 ft above high water. The overall length of the Forth Bridge with its masonry and lattice girder approach viaducts and girder spans between the cantilevers is 8296 ft. Opened in 1890, it stood for years in solitary majesty, enhanced by the fact that it could only be viewed from below except by railwayman or by those charged with the continuous task of keeping it painted. Viewed today from the road suspension bridge alongside it seems singularly diminished.

The great viaducts

The British railway system is rich in impressive masonry viaducts. The East Coast main line contains the Tay and Forth Bridges, Durham viaduct and the Royal Border Bridge at Berwick – a foursome which has earned it the name of 'The Great Bridges Route'. Some of the longest viaducts are in remote settings, like Ribblehead and Dent Head on the former Midland Railway route from Settle to Carlisle. The Settle-Carlisle line gave the Midland its own route to Scotland, but its East and West Coast competitors were already well established and the railway had to traverse desolate mountain country as the only choice left to it. At the same time the line had to be suitable for speed, since a 50 mph average at least was necessary to be competitive with the shorter Anglo-Scottish routes. As a result the line spanned valleys with great viaducts and pierced the ridges of hills with tunnels.

Ribblehead viaduct, in the shadow of Whernside, has 24 arches, the tallest 165 ft from the foundations to rail level. At Dent Head the viaduct across the Dent Valley is 600 ft long and the ten arches carry the railway 100 ft above ground level. The *Daily News* of 29 October 1872 had an account of the building of the line and of the navvies, who lived in small communities to which cartloads of food were sent from the moorland villages.

These men heap fuel lustily into the furnace of their vital energy. Many of them eat eighteen pounds of beef in the week. Beef is their fare. Mutton they reckon of little account, and bacon is only used to fill up the interstices . . . Within a couple of chains of the mouth of the tunnel we come upon a shaft, down in the depths of which twenty-five Cornish and

Devonshire miners are excavating to right and left of them along the level intended for the permanent way. They are working in blue-stone rock, hard as the nether millstone . . . we hear the clink of their drills, and every now and then the dulled report of a blast. Tub after tub comes to the surface laden with jagged fragments of stone.

This was Blea Moor tunnel, 7887 ft long, where there is a temporary easing in the 'Long Drag' from Settle Junction to the summit of the line at Ais Gill, 1169 ft above sea level.

Tunnels

The longest main-line railway tunnel in Great Britain is the Severn Tunnel on the Western Region from Paddington to South Wales. A bridge had been built across the river from Sharpness in Gloucestershire in 1879, but passenger trains from London to South Wales still made the long detour through Gloucester. Work on the Severn Tunnel began in 1877 and here manually worked shields were used with some success, but when the headings were little more than 300 ft apart water broke in.

The flooded workings needed considerable tidying up before tunnelling could be resumed, and the tunnel was not opened for regular passenger traffic until 1886. It is nearly four and a half miles long, but only two miles are under water. Steam excavators were used to make the approach cuttings – an unusual operation for its day.

Victorian station architecture

Before the railways came, journeys by public transport were most likely to start and finish in inn yards. Railway managements often decided in the early days that something should be done to impress on their patrons that they were entering a new age of travel far removed from the stagecoach and the carrier's cart. The triumphal arch proposed by the Directors of the London and Greenwich Railway for the first steam railway terminus in London at London Bridge never materialized. Passengers climbed stairs from a plain office building to exposed platforms on the railway viaduct, where an old sail was rigged as protection from

Below: A contractor's locomotive stands in the English entrance of the Severn Tunnel, begun in 1875 and completed in 1886. Apart from London's Tubes it is Britain's longest rail tunnel, measuring 4 miles 628 yards from portal to portal.

the weather if necessary.

The London and Birmingham Railway also proposed a triumphal arch, and achieved it. Philip Hardwick designed his famous arch as the approach to the first Euston Station. Four Doric columns supported the portico itself, which rose to a height of 72 ft, and lodges stood on each side. Critics of the period thought this splendour ought to lead to something more impressive than the plain two-storey station building beyond, but soon more buildings went up round the courtyard and in 1849 the Great Hall of Euston was opened, a combined concource and waiting room 125 ft 6 ins long by 61 ft 4 ins wide and 62 ft high. At the far end a wide double staircase swept up to a vestibule and gallery, with the doors to the shareholders' meeting room at the back of the vestibule. In 1852 a statue of George Stephenson was erected at the foot of the staircase. The panelled ceiling of the Great Hall, with its bas reliefs representing towns and cities on the London and North Western Railway, was said to be unparalleled outside Buckingham Palace. The Euston Arch was pulled down in 1963 despite the contractor offering to build it elsewhere. It transpired that BR had no intention of putting anything else there so that there was no reason why it should not have been left.

Early ventures in railway splendour were often classical in inspiration like the Euston Arch.

Above: The 1387 yd-long Severn Bridge under construction. Opened in 1879, it was built by the Severn Bridge Railway to connect the Severn and Wye and the Great Western at Lydney with the Midland's Gloucester and Berkeley New Docks branch at Sharpness.

enriched in a novel and effective manner by a course of Red Venetian tiles'; and it went on to note that in the centre there was a picturesque clock and bell tower, leading the contributor to suggest that although the style had been called Italian it might be designated more properly an English railway style, 'being designed to meet the peculiar circumstances of the case, and merely decorated with Italian forms'.

Years later, in 1852, Kings Cross was opened. Lewis Cubitt was again the architect and in the centre of his facade, with its two arches giving a glimpse of the arched roofs of the train shed behind, he placed a square clock tower with a clock in an Italianate turret. Some have thought that this feature spoiled the elegant simplicity of the design. For many years, however, the design could not be appreciated because of the medley of buildings in front of it, now happily cleared away. The design of the roof spans was based on the roofs of the Imperial Riding School in Moscow.

The Gothic style appealed strongly to the Victorians and was seen in railway station architecture as well as in church buildings. Examples could be found in many parts of the country, but the most famous was St Pancras Station in London. The platforms lay under a vast arched roof with a single span of 240 ft designed by W. H. Barlow, and the frontage seen by travellers entering from the roadway was the Midland Grand Hotel designed by Sir George Gilbert Scott. St Pancras has rightly been acclaimed as the finest example of Victorian secular Gothic and is probably the ultimate monument of the railway age. The theme is continued in the passenger concourse, which boasts a clerestory fit for a processional with lighted tapers and solemn chant.

That railway stations were the cathedrals of the nineteenth century can also be seen in the arches and ribs of Brunel's roof at Paddington (1852-4) which covers the station in three spans of 70 ft, 102 ft 6 ins and 68 ft, rising to a height of 55 ft above the platforms. The roof is intercepted by two transepts which enrich the pattern of the vaulting.

John Dobson, a leading architect of his day, provided another famous roof vista at Newcastle Central (1846-55) and gave the station a long classical frontage to which a portico was added later. At Derby (1839-41) Francis Thompson's light iron roof covered 140 ft in three spans. Originally there was only one very long platform behind a facade still notable for its length. These places were unmistakably stations, but at Huddersfield J. P. Pritchett's classical building

Below: Euston's Great Hall, the largest waiting room in Britain, was created when the LNWR built the station's central block of buildings in 1846-7. Hardwick was again the architect. Stephenson's statue at the foot of the staircase was put up in 1852.

Where the architect's aims were less pretentious an Italianate style was often favoured and in due course was adapted to form what became known as 'the English railway style'. When Lewis Cubitt designed a station at Bricklayers' Arms (1844) for the South Eastern and the London and Croydon Railways, the *Illustrated London News* commented on the 'noble frontage . . . crowned with a bold cornice and entablature

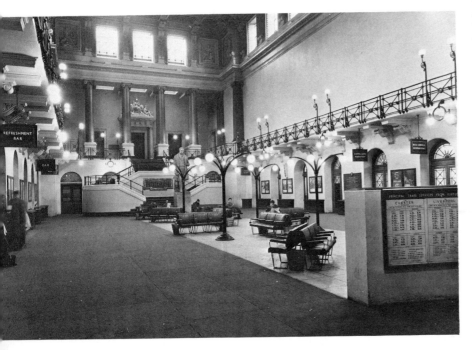

(1850) has been mistaken on numerous occasions for the town hall. A huge Corinthian portico, long colonnades and terminal pavilions fill one side of a public square from which the architecture can be appreciated more fully than in those places where urban development has encroached on the clear space in front of a station which the architect usually had in mind when he designed it.

The versatile Brunel was his own architect at Bath and Bristol Temple Meads, but he was more successful with the engineering proportions of his train sheds than in his exteriors, for both facades present a mixture of styles which are interesting rather than beautiful.

Railway station architecture is a worthwhile study, and photography can preserve pictorially much that will inevitably disappear. The modern terminus is often the ground floor of an office block but there are still country stations with individuality. Indeed, in many towns the station remains the most distinctive building. For many years, as an example, the station at Stoke-on-Trent was the only building with a preservation order in the whole city.

Opposite, above: The London and Birmingham Railway wanted the public to regard Euston station as London's gateway to the rest of the country. To strengthen that impression the architect, Philip Hardwick, conceived the famous Doric arch.

Left: Architects of the Midland Railway's 1867 London terminus at St Pancras were W. H. Barlow and Sir George Gilbert Scott.

Below: An 1860 view of Derby station in its original form, with only the one main platform face. In the foreground is the roof of the still surviving North Midland Railway locomotive roundhouse – the world's first building of this type (1840).

Chapter 11

The empire-building wars

Above: The London North Western Railway's coat of arms.

Below: A Liverpool-London Belfast boat express on Bushey water troughs in 1899. Taking water is Webb 'Dreadnought' class three-cylinder compound 2-2-2-0 No. 2063 Huskisson.

THE MID-NINETEENTH-CENTURY spread of Britain's railways was characterized by some of the most vicious in-fighting in the country's industrial history. We have already seen how parliament's failure to enforce stricter controls on both the financial practices and the route plans of the new companies gave a picaresque adventurer like George Hudson *carte blanche* for unscrupulous empire building. It also left the big companies, once they were established and had laid their principal routes, to work out their own frontiers.

Even if the Great Western had not built to an idiosyncratic gauge and Brunel had not publicly dreamed of extending 'the blessings of broad gauge to the North of England', the situation invited ruthless pursuit of self-interest. But the struggle to hem in Brunel's broad gauge was only one of the earliest and the more bitterly fought of a whole series of affrays as the big companies manoeuvred for the allegiance of smaller railways in the no man's land between their trunk routes, or for running rights over other railways which would gain them lucrative through traffic and a foothold on another empire's doorstep. The battle was to the strong: and the strongest alliances were forged by men just as masterful as Hudson, often just as machiavellian and generally more successful – men like Captain Mark Huish of the LNWR, his ally James Allport of the Manchester, Sheffield and Lincolnshire and later of the Midland, and Edward Watkin and James Staat Forbes.

Huish and the LNWR
Huish was arguably the most powerful character on the mid-nineteenth-century railway stage, and

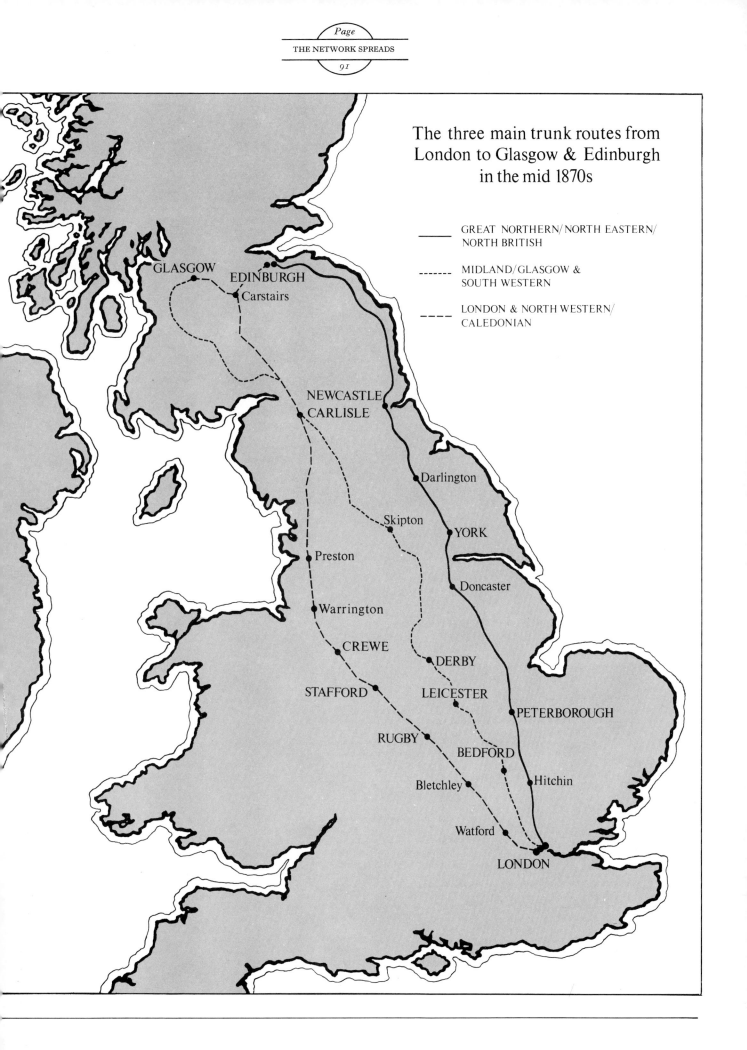

The three main trunk routes from London to Glasgow & Edinburgh in the mid 1870s

GREAT NORTHERN/NORTH EASTERN/ NORTH BRITISH

MIDLAND/GLASGOW & SOUTH WESTERN

LONDON & NORTH WESTERN/ CALEDONIAN

GLASGOW

EDINBURGH

Carstairs

NEWCASTLE

CARLISLE

Darlington

Skipton

YORK

Preston

Doncaster

Warrington

CREWE

DERBY

STAFFORD

LEICESTER

PETERBOROUGH

RUGBY

BEDFORD

Bletchley

Hitchin

Watford

LONDON

Right: A Paddington-Plymouth express of the GWR in Sonning Cutting, near Reading, shortly before the abolition of the broad gauge in 1892. In charge is one of the 'Convertible' 2-2-2s built at Swindon in 1891; they were modified to standard gauge in 1892, then rebuilt as 4-2-2s in 1894. Note quadrupling of the track is in progress.

at the same time one of the most devious. The London North Western Railway, of which he was General Manager, had come about through his machinations. Huish was then cutting his railway administrative teeth as secretary of the Grand Junction Railway, which ran from a junction with the Liverpool and Manchester at Warrington to Birmingham.

A quarrel with the London and Birmingham over its dalliance with the Manchester and Birmingham Railway, a combination which threatened to deprive the GJR of some of its business with the north–west, had alerted the GJR to a threat of isolation and its suspicions were intensified by L&BR interest in the independent Trent Valley Railway, via which a short route to the north–west avoiding Birmingham altogether would be created. Huish's astute counter was a proposal to transfer his GJR to the broad gauge camp, which was simultaneously

canvassing an extension from Oxford to Rugb and Birmingham. That would, he urged sancti moniously, avoid all the curses of monopoly – concern he never remotely revealed in his auto cratic LNWR years. The ploy paid off immediately An alarmed L&BR called for parleys and in 184 L&BR, GJR, M&BR and TVR amalgamated unde the composite name of the London Nort Western Railway, the LNWR.

No sooner had the LNWR come into bein than Huish's attitude to the GWR advance on th West Midlands switched to fierce opposition Now the LNWR's monopoly of the routes from London to the north had to be protected at an cost, not excluding the first of his nefariou share deals with the object of packing othe companies' meetings with his own nominee His aim in this episode was to oust the director of the company which would be the GWR's lin with the West Midlands, the Birmingham an

Below: Hitchin station, Great Northern Railway, in about 1870, looking south.

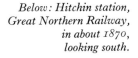

Oxford Junction. That failed, and since the LNWR's claim to hegemony was not a cause to touch the heart of Parliament, Huish had to try a new tack: righteous protestations about the inconvenience and expense to the public of extending break-of-gauge points. The outcome, as we have already seen, was the appointment of a Parliamentary Commission and the Gauge Act of 1846 which conceded the broad-gauge extension to Birmingham and subsequently Wolverhampton. The GWR was also permitted to lay down broad gauge to Rugby, but it lost interest in that part of the original plan. The broad gauge reached Banbury in September 1850 and its route to Birmingham Snow Hill was completed in October 1852.

Rivalry on the northern routes

Meanwhile Huish had become hotly engaged on another front, where hostilities had opened before the LNWR's formation. George Hudson was the first to take up arms at the threat of a new trunk route from the north to London when, in 1845, the West Riding MP Edmund Denison espoused a proposal to build a direct railway from London to York, with a loop between Peterborough and Lincoln to serve Boston and Lincoln. All Hudson's chicaneries failed to frustrate Denison, who got his Act in 1846 and had his Great Northern trains running out of London to York and the West Riding by 1850 though via the Boston loop: the direct Peterborough–Grantham line was not finished until 1852).

By 1850 Hudson had been kicked into oblivion, but Huish was in the saddle at Euston ready to deploy every artifice in the business manipulator's book to starve Denison's new London route of traffic. One after another, northern companies touched by the Great Northern were persuaded or coerced into a 'Euston Confederacy' whose sole objective was to 'black' Denison's railway. The Midland and the Lancashire and Yorkshire, which at the start were allowing GN trains into Leeds over their tracks, were compliant, but the Manchester, Sheffield and Lincolnshire, which had some working agreements with the GNR, was a slightly harder nut. However, the MS&L's General Manager James Allport eventually persuaded his chairman to sign up and then paid his dues to Huish by blocking the GN trains out of his territory at Grimsby, where they had been granted rights over MS&L tracks, and refusing to water GN engines at Retford. Huish failed to recruit the North British, but he did get a grip on the

Edinburgh and Glasgow, which denied GN trains any Scottish traffic beyond Edinburgh.

To avoid vicious and ruinous competition in the year of London's Great Exhibition, 1851, Denison allowed himself to be drawn into a highly partial receipts pooling agreement with Huish's Confederates. Within a fortnight of the Exhibition's opening the agreement's cheap fare clauses had been torn up in a furious bout of undercutting, and soon the two sides were squabbling over the division of receipts as well. Eventually Gladstone, no less, had to arbitrate and adjudged the GNR's share of the pool to be as much as 63 per cent. The apoplectic Confederates promptly devised ways to evade Gladstone's ruling, but their hand was nearly played out. The public was irritated by the inconvenience caused by their tactics and was beginning to like the GNR's civility to its passengers – in marked contrast to the way customers were sometimes treated on the LNWR and Midland. Queen Victoria's 1851 abandonment of Huish's railway for the East Coast route to Scotland on her journeys to Balmoral was the *coup de grâce*.

No episode dramatizes the immorality of Huish's wheeler-dealing more than his attempt to terrorize two stout little companies based on Shrewsbury. Huish had a satellite in the territory, the Birkenhead, Lancashire and Cheshire Junction, which he thought ensured him a monopoly, but his complacency was shattered when the Shrewsbury and Birmingham and Shrewsbury and Chester came to a working agreement to deal in through traffic between Birmingham and the north–west.

Written menaces unavailing, Huish soon resorted to force. He mustered a majority on the management of the jointly owned Chester

Above: The London South Western Railway's coat of arms.

Below: Perseus, one of Daniel Gooch's celebrated 'Iron Duke' class 4-2-2s of 1847-55 with 8 ft driving wheels, photographed in the late 1870s, in the declining years of the GWR broad gauge.

Station to bar the issue there of through tickets to Birmingham via Shrewsbury (the recalcitrant s&c booking clerk was bodily ejected from his office and his tickets flung after him), and forced his Birkenhead stooges to get as close to a total boycott of s&c traffic as they legally dared. Bloody but far from bowed, the Shrewsbury companies made a pact with the Great Western, by then only at Banbury. The enraged Huish riposted with one of his old ploys, buying up shares in the Shrewsbury and Birmingham and allotting them to LNWR staff so that the latter could disrupt the upstart's meetings – which they did: one s&b meeting in the spring of 1851 lasted a tumultuous four days. The outcome was illegal election of a new s&b Board which, using a forged seal, made an agreement with Huish (though even he lacked the gall to make much subsequent use of it), while the legal Board cemented an agreement with the GWR. A similar machination failed to

overturn the Shrewsbury and Chester Board however. In a last desperate move Huish tried physical force in the West Midlands to stop through trains between Birmingham and the north–west, but by 1854 he was beaten.

The GWR had one more tangle with the LNWR. The Oxford Worcester and Wolverhampton had been incorporated in 1845 to run, under Paddington's patronage, as a broad-gauge line from Oxford to a junction with the Grand Junction Railway at Wolverhampton, but with a stretch of mixed gauge to link the GJR with the Birmingham and Gloucester. However, Brunel badly underestimated the costs, the OW&W ran out of money and its directors fell out with the GWR, alleging breach both of financial guarantees and of faith, in that Paddington had become far more interested in the Banbury route from Oxford to Birmingham. Scenting a situation ripe for exploitation John Parson, a solicitor in the machiavellian Huish mould, gained control

Below: A London-Brighton South Coast excursion train at the turn of the century. Heading for Lewes and Seaford is one of Stroudley's Class B1 or 'Gladstone' 0-4-2s, built between 1882 and 1891.

of the OW&W and promptly made agreement with the LNWR and the Midland for completion of the line on the standard gauge. The GWR won an injunction declaring Parson's deal illegal and void, but Parson persisted with efforts to play off the GWR and LNWR against each other in the hope of benefit from escalating bids for his railway. Obliged to make it mixed gauge, Parson deliberately cobbled the job and talked his way out of every GWR protest. He did in fact persuade Huish to connect the OW&W with LNWR's Oxford–Bletchley branch at Yarnton and the first Worcester–London trains went that way, but the LNWR got little from the arrangement and soon lost interest in the OW&W.

By the end of 1853 the halting construction of the 'Old Worse and Worse', as it was soon tagged, was complete from a junction with the Birmingham and Gloucester outside Worcester to Wolverhampton Low Level, but with no money to buy its own locomotives and rolling stock the company had to engage a contractor to assemble a ramshackle collection for its inaugural trains. To the end when, as the West Midland Railway, it was absorbed by the GWR in 1863, it had evaded its broad-gauge duty and it was never traversed by a broad-gauge train.

South of the Thames the frontiers of the big companies were certainly not settled without incident, but the clashes were much more localized than the confrontations of empires on the other side of London.

Following pages: Afternoon calm at Birmingham New Street Station in September 1885, with a train of LNWR six-wheelers at the main-line platform on the left and a Midland train in the bay to the right. New Street Station was opened on 1 June 1854, whereupon the previous Birmingham stations, Curzon Street and Lawley Street, became goods depots.

The way west

The GWR's original routing to Exeter via Bristol and the LSWR's initial advance out of London to Southampton and Gosport (the nearest it got to Portsmouth at first) left a tempting tract of unexplored country between them. In 1844 both companies proposed what were eventually to be their main lines from London to Devon, the GWR its Berks and Hants from Reading as far as Hungerford, with an eye to eventual attainment of Taunton; and the LSWR a route from Basingstoke to Salisbury and Yeovil, plus a line from Southampton to Dorchester. The GWR won the day, though the Berks and Hants was not completed throughout from Reading to Taunton via Newbury and Westbury until 1906, and the LSWR therefore had to make do with serving Salisbury by a branch from Eastleigh and aiming for Exeter via Dorchester. The Salisbury branch and the Southampton and Dorchester Railway were both completed in 1847.

Although it was not inclined to pursue the Berks and Hants line beyond Hungerford at that time, the GWR was keeping other irons in the Wessex fire. Despite meagre traffic prospects and a costly construction (the GWR had to bale out the original sponsoring company, which ran out of cash), a railway was finished from the London–Bristol main line at Bathampton to Westbury and from there to Yeovil, to Salisbury and to Weymouth, by early 1857. But Parliament dashed any hopes of making this invasion of Wessex the springboard for a broad-gauge take-over in the south–west. Above all, the military establishment was not prepared to have the defence of the country's south coast handicapped logistically by break-of-gauge transhipment points in the immediate rear areas. The LSWR could therefore resurrect its original scheme for a main line from Basingstoke, Andover, Salisbury and Yeovil to Exeter, which carried its first trains throughout on 19 July 1860. After a good deal of skirmishing, it pressed on across the GWR to Exeter St Davids and via Okehampton and the northern flank of Dartmoor to Plymouth, to which through service from Waterloo was inaugurated on 17 May 1876.

The GWR tolerated the misuse of its initials as a mnemonic for the 'Great Way Round' to the far west until the end of the broad-gauge era, when it at last created, first a shorter route to Weymouth by the 1900 Patney–Westbury cut-off which bypassed Devizes, then – and much more significantly – the Castle Cary–Langport cut-off, which was the link that completed a route fully competitive in distance with the LSWR's to Exeter. One tends to forget that even so modern a train as the 'Cornish Riviera Express', when it was launched in 1904, had to start its career with two years' circuitous routing via Bristol.

Nevertheless the LSWR still contended keenly for Plymouth–London traffic, especially that off the transatlantic liners which docked at Plymouth. That rivalry was the stimulus for the GWR's epic Ocean Mails run from Plymouth to Paddington on 9 May 1904, when 102.3 mph was claimed for the 4-4-0 *City of Truro* on the descent of Wellington bank into Taunton. It led finally to the tragedy at Salisbury on 1 July 1906, when an LSW express inexplicably took the station's notorious curve at full speed and was wrecked, after which the chastened gladiators shouldered arms.

Rivalry in the south

The LSWR's early concern to make Southampton, not Portsmouth, the prime target of its first

main line from London, was odd. Southampton's maritime trade promise was certainly apparent by the mid-nineteenth century, but as the long-established base of the world's most potent navy and thus of of the country's most cherished assets Portsmouth had infinitely more national significance. The LSWR's neglect clearly invited someone else to step in, which the London Brighton and South Coast did. Its London–Brighton main line had been completed in September 1841 and the LB&SCR busily extended its domain along the coastal towns both east and west of Brighton, reaching Portsmouth in June 1847. But its London trains could only reach the naval town by reversing at Brighton. The LSWR slightly improved its approach to Portsmouth by building on from its first terminus at Gosport round the top of Portsmouth Harbour to join the LB&SCR line at Cosham (from 1 October 1848 the two companies agreed to joint ownership of the Cosham–Portsmouth section), but even then its route from London was as circuitous as the LB&SCR's. Portsmouth therefore remained a tempting bait.

It was grasped by the enterprising Thomas Brassey. By the 1850s it had become fairly common practice for one of the early contractors, by now well-heeled from the earlier construction mania, to promote and build a railway with his own capital in territory where it was a safe gamble that one or more of the existing railway companies would soon bid to buy it, lease it or at worst be happy to assume its operation. Brassey stepped into the gap between the Godalming terminus of an LSWR branch from Woking, and Havant, on the LB&SCR's Brighton–Portsmouth line. By 1857–58 he had virtually completed a railway between these two points which trimmed the London–Portsmouth distance of 30 miles compared with the LBSC route and 20 miles against the LSWR's.

For some months neither LSWR nor LB&SCR came knocking on Brassey's door. Brassey had expected an overture from the LSWR, but that company hesitated, apprehensive – justifiably so, as it turned out – that the LB&SCR would not take kindly to the idea of helping the new line to exploit its advantage of reduced distance by giving its trains hospitality over LB&SCR tracks from Havant into Portsmouth. Wise to the ways of a Huish in such an impasse, Brassey tried to tempt the South Eastern Railway with an offer to connect its Reigate–Guildford line to his new railway. Surprisingly, since it was frequently sparring with the LB&SCR, the SER refused. But knowledge of Brassey's move was enough to induce the LSWR to buy the new Portsmouth

Above: Sir Edward Watkin, who rose from the General Manager's chair of the Manchester Sheffield and Lincolnshire to Chairmanship of the South Eastern, the Metropolitan and the Great Central; it was he who extended the GCR to London in 1899.

Direct line, as it was and still is known, and to announce that it would run its first train that way on 1 January 1859.

The LB&SCR warned the LSWR of trouble, so the latter prudently made its inaugural working a goods train to spare passengers any insults or fisticuffs. When the goods arrived at Havant it found that the LB&SCR had blocked the junction with a locomotive and had removed a rail. Both companies had mobilized small forces of railwaymen and some scuffles broke out. Passengers travelling between Portsmouth and Brighton in LB&SCR trains were politely escorted past the scene of conflict to entrain again behind the lines.

The LB&SCR won that day and the LSWR train was forced to retreat to Godalming, but the right of the LSWR to send its trains to Portsmouth was upheld by an enquiry and the two railways then proceeded to outbid each other with cheap fares for Portsmouth traffic. Considering its much shorter route, the LSWR performance was not impressive. Foxwell and Farrer in *Express Trains English and Foreign* commented that, 'until 1888 neither Portsmouth

nor Southampton had ever had an "express" i.e. a train running at 40 miles an hour inclusive . . . Portsmouth is still out in the cold, and the Isle of Wight follows.' On the other hand the same authorities thought the Brighton company's London–Portsmouth express with an average of 43 mph 'the most praiseworthy' of the LB&SCR trains in that category' because of the steep gradients (1 in 80) it has to encounter'. By the time those words were written the LB&SCR had brought its London–Portsmouth journey down to 86 miles by means of a cut-off via Horsham and the mid-Sussex line to Ford opened in 1863.

The LB&SCR in its turn was nervous about invasion of the eastern end of its territory by the South Eastern Railway and built one or two lines of doubtful economic viability in east Sussex in order to keep the intruder out. It was unhappy, too, at the South Eastern's arrival in Hastings in 1851, although agreement had been reached for it to use the new Hastings station. But these were minor bickerings compared with the tough wars of the Euston Confederacy. In later years the two companies concluded an

*Left: The South Wales
Railway main line was
extended to Neyland in
1856. First called
Milford Haven, then
briefly Neyland in 1859,
the port was next known
as New Milford until it
became Neyland for good
in 1906. Brunel's hope of
attracting transatlantic
business to the port was
never realized.*

arrangement for sharing traffic receipts on the
Eastbourne route and the South Eastern put on
a through service from Charing Cross to Eastbourne via Tunbridge Wells and Hailsham in
1880, after extension of the Hailsham branch to
Eridge, but it lasted little more than a year.

Edward Watkin's influence

The Chairman of the South Eastern Railway
at this time was Sir Edward Watkin, who many
years earlier as plain Mr Watkin had distinguished himself in the negotiations leading to the
sale of the Trent Valley Railway, of which he
was Secretary, to the London and North
Western. Acquisition of the Trent Valley line
gave the LNWR a direct route from Rugby to
Stafford, avoiding the detour through Birmingham and Wolverhampton. Watkin joined the
LNWR and his expertise in negotiation fitted in
well with its aggressive philosophy.

In 1853 Watkin became General Manager of
the Manchester, Sheffield and Lincolnshire
Railway, which had once been a protégé of
Euston, but under Watkin struck out on its own
and challenged that august institution. There was
to be no more obedient harassment of the Great
Northern; instead, Watkin sought a closer
relationship with that company. By the time the
first fruits of his policy were seen in the shape of
a joint MS&LR/GNR service between Manchester

and Kings Cross in 1857, however, he had
resigned in annoyance over dealings with the
Midland while he had been absent in Canada.
He returned to Canada to become President of
the Grand Trunk Railway, but in 1863 he was
back in England and once more General
Manager of the MS&LR, which elected him to
its Board as Chairman in 1864.

Watkin seems to have long nourished an
ambition to bring the Sheffield company to
London. At first he had looked round for partners, but it takes two to make an alliance and
Watkin's reliability was suspect among the other
northern companies. Unabashed, Watkin took
his talents further, becoming Chairman of the
South Eastern Railway in 1866 and of the
Metropolitan Railway in 1872. Also in 1872 he
interested himself in the activities of the newly
formed Channel Tunnel company. Considered
together, these activities reveal a grand design.
If the Sheffield line were to be brought south
from its terminus near Nottingham to connect
with a northward extension of the Metropolitan,
its trains could travel through London and
emerge on the South Eastern by means of the
short East London Railway, also run by himself. Then the way would be clear to the Channel
coast and so, given a Channel Tunnel, even to
the Continent.

Watkin's Manchester–Paris express remained
a dream, but he saw the bill for the London

*Opposite, below: The scene
at Brackley, on the GCR's
new London extension,
on the formal opening
day, 9 March 1899.
Three specials conveyed
guests from the provinces
to Marylebone of which
this one, from Sheffield,
called only at Brackley.
One extremely distinctive
feature of the Great
Central extension was
that all of the stations,
with the sole exception
of Arkwright Street,
were built as islands.*

*Following pages: A
Midland express in the
summer of 1901, formed of
Clayton clerestory-roofed
coaches. No. 451, one of
Johnson's 4-4-0s of 1894
as rebuilt by Deeley, is
halted by signals on the
Ambergate avoiding line.
To the left is the former
Ambergate station, which
was superseded when the
town's celebrated
triangular station was
opened in 1876 (see
picture on page 61).*

Above: The crest of the Cambrian Railways.

Above: The crest of the Great Western Railway, combining the emblems of London and Bristol.

extension of the MS&LR receive the royal assent in 1893 after a long parliamentary struggle. A year later ill-health obliged him to relinquish all his chairmanships.

The Great Central, as the MS&LR was renamed after the line to London was sanctioned, was Watkin's most spectacular achievement, but by no means the limit of his interests. His chairmanship of the South Eastern and the Metropolitan Railways was marked by continual skirmishing with his opposite number on the Boards of the London Chatham and Dover and the Metropolitan District – James Staats Forbes. Both main-line companies competed vigorously for the Continental traffic via Dover and, although agreements were made between them from time to time, such as the pooling of receipts from traffic via Dover and Folkestone, both worked assiduously to create situations to which, hopefully, such arrangements would not apply.

In 1875 the Chatham company started a service from Queensborough to Flushing, which it contended was outside the pooling agreement. Watkin countered this by detraining passengers for the Continent at Shorncliffe and taking them by cab to the steamer in Folkestone Harbour. He maintained that this procedure was outside the pooling arrangement as it affected Folkestone traffic. He was taken to court by the Chatham company, responded with a counter-action over the Queensborough service, and lost both cases. Such oddities of behaviour explain the nervousness of the LB&SCR over the intentions of its South Eastern neighbour.

Through their chairmanships of the Metropolitan and the Metropolitan District, Watkin and Forbes were involved in the completion of an Inner Circle service for London. The Metropolitan District was in difficulties and the Metropolitan unhelpful. Progress was slow, but when exasperated city interests formed a new company to close the gap in the Circle route, Watkin pulled strings to hinder the raising of capital. In the end the line was completed by the railways themselves, but not until 1884. It would no doubt have been finished earlier had the two principal personalities been of more compatible temperament.

Expansion elsewhere in Britain and Ireland

While these struggles were going on in England, the railway map of Wales and Scotland was being filled in. Wales had its native system in the Cambrian Railways with a main line crossing the country from Welshpool to Barmouth and

Aberystwyth, and a branch southward from Moat Lane Junction to join the Brecon and Merthyr near Brecon. The LNWR served the North Wales coast, and the GWR penetrated South and West Wales, supplemented by various small companies thriving on the coal industry in the valleys, the steelworks and the ports. This industrial complex attracted the great railways of England. The LNWR had isolated sections in South Wales, reached by lines jointly worked, and it obtained running powers to the major centres. By means of its central Wales line from Craven Arms the LNWR reached out to Swansea, serving the Welsh spas of Llandrindod Wells and Llanwrtyd Wells *en route*, and happily still open. A Euston–Swansea through carriage survived into LMS days. Unexpectedly in Wales too was the Midland, which by acquisition and running powers made its way from Malvern Wells to Merthyr and Swansea.

Ham-fisted management, shortage of capital and a dearth of traffic combined to make the early advance of railways into East Anglia a halting business. Moreover, the first concern to strike north-eastwards out of London from a Bishopsgate terminus, the Eastern Counties Railway, had been persuaded by its engineer to adopt an idiosyncratic 5-ft track gauge, which within a few years was realized to be such a long-term handicap that re-laying to 4 ft 8½ ins was ordered. The ECR wilted from its travails when it got to Colchester in 1843 and another company, the Eastern Union, stepped in to complete a railway to Norwich; this infuriated the ECR, which for the five years until it absorbed the EUR in 1854 made sure the two companies' trains failed to connect with each other at Colchester. Meanwhile the ECR had in 1845 also reached Norwich over an easier route via Cambridge and Ely, and a year later projected a branch from Ely to Peterborough with the aim of establishing a main London–York railway to thicken its thin gruel of revenue from the East Anglian system. But, as already described, Parliament accepted the concurrent Great Northern Railway scheme.

London's Liverpool Street terminus – constructed at massive cost in the late 1860s and opened by stages in 1874–5 – did eventually become another starting point for the north. This followed the 1862 creation by mergers of the Great Eastern Railway from the two East Anglian trunk routes just mentioned, and their subsequent offshoots inland and to coastal towns like Harwich (in 1854) and Yarmouth (in 1859). In 1879–82 the GER contracted with the GNR for joint operation of the cross-country route from March, near Ely, to Doncaster via Spalding, Sleaford, Lincoln and Gainsborough; in addition the NER granted the GER running powers north of Doncaster, so that the GER could achieve its ambition of a through Liverpool Street–York express passenger service.

A third Anglo-Scottish trunk route was added to the map in 1876, extending the operations of the ever-thrusting Midland Railway from South Wales to the Clyde Valley. After Hudson's eclipse the GNR was prepared to forget his bitter – and unscrupulous – battle to kill the whole GNR main line project, and had allowed the Midland access to Kings Cross; the Midland gained the GNR by opening a line from Leicester to Hitchin in 1857. But the GNR had no intention of finding Hitchin–Kings Cross track space for Midland trains at the expense of its own. The Midland gritted its teeth at the cavalier treatment of its trains over this stretch until 1863, when it sought and gained powers to build its own approach to the capital; a new line from Bedford via St Albans was finished in 1868, together with the monumental St Pancras terminus.

Next the Midland made for Manchester, to challenge the LNWR for London business. In 1867 it extended its Ambergate–Buxton branch through the Peak Forest Hills in an enterprise that included boring the 1¾-mile Dove Holes tunnel. At first the Midland found a Manchester berth at the city's London Road station by grace of the MS&L (the MS&L's benign attitude was odd in view of its own involvement, already mentioned, in a London service via Retford and the Great Northern to Kings Cross). By the end of the century, however, the Midland had its own tracks all the way via Cheadle Heath and another long tunnel, the 2¼-mile Disley bore, to its own Manchester Central terminus. Further construction in the last quarter of the century – the Swinton and Knottingley line jointly owned with the NER, and the Melton Mowbray route from Kettering to Nottingham – combined with its existing network to give the Midland in essence two routes from Kettering for most of the way to the West Riding and York.

The LNWR had not taken kindly to the Midland's invasion of London on its tracks. One of the areas where it could and did vent its feelings was in Cumbria, where Midland traffic for Carlisle coming off the so-called 'Little North-Western' Clapham–Ingleton

Below: Great Western branch scene at Marlow in about 1880. The engine is a Class 517 0-4-2 saddle-tank, a type which epitomized the GWR loco-motive policy of refining an existing design time and time again, instead of building something new for the same job every two decades or so. First intro-duced in 1868 as a branch and suburban passenger engine, fresh batches of 517s were built up to 1885, then subsequently modern-ized so that the majority survived into the 1930s.

Above: The crest of the Lancashire and Yorkshire Railway.

Below: Derby Midland Station, the core of the Midland Railway, after dark in the fitful light of gas lamps on an April evening in 1908. The overall roof has since been removed.

branch of the Settle–Lancaster and Morecambe line had to finish its journey on the LNWR main line over Shap. The Midland was reluctant to start building its own expensive route over the fells, but its efforts to make a reasonable pact for joint operation between Ingleton and Carlisle were frustrated by LNWR intransigence. So, in 1866, it took the plunge and embarked on the Settle and Carlisle route, unarguably the most imposing of all British trunk routes, with its long, severe gradients, its nineteen viaducts, its 3 miles and more of tunnels and its wild setting high up among the moors and mountains. After completion of the Settle and Carlisle route in the spring of 1876 the Midland could open its own through service from London to Scotland in conjunction with the Glasgow and South Western and the North British – the latter had doubled its line from Edinburgh, the now vanished and mourned Waverley route, to open up Edinburgh as well as Glasgow to the Anglo-Scottish newcomer.

Early in the twentieth century, one should add, the Midland's domain reached into Ireland. In 1903 it absorbed the Belfast and Northern Counties Railway and the following year it completed a fine new harbour at Heysham, served by a railway, to stimulate a major expansion of the steamer service previously operated from Morecambe. Furthermore, in 1906 it took up joint ownership of the County of Donegal lines with the Great Northern Railway of Ireland.

The Midland Railway

The Midland was a remarkable railway – arguably the only truly national system in the country before the creation of British Rail. It was the only one of the major systems radiating from London which kept its focal point in the provinces, at the crossroads of trunk routes, not at the stub of just one. The Midland hub was always Derby, on the doorstep of the great East Midlands coalfield which from the start generated such a high

Above: The crest of the North British Railway.

Following pages: The down platform at Rugby, LNWR in the 1890s. The clarity and uniformity of the signposting of the various station offices and amenities are commendable.

proportion of its revenue. Where its own writ did not run, moreover, the Midland had liaisons which enabled its through passenger trains or coaches to interlace towns and cities the length and breadth of the island. Consider the list of principal through services beyond its borders which it was advertising on the eve of World War I (partnering railways are bracketed in each case):

London St Pancras	Edinburgh, Dundee, Aberdeen, Perth (North British) Glasgow (Glasgow and South Western). Bradford, Halifax, Huddersfield (Lancashire and Yorkshire). Harrogate (North Eastern).
Bath	York (North Eastern).
Birmingham	Bournemouth (London South Western). Cromer, Norwich, Lowestoft, Yarmouth (Midland and Great Northern Joint). Edinburgh (North British). Glasgow (Glasgow and South Western). Exeter, Kingswear (Great Western). York, Newcastle-upon-Tyne (North Eastern). Southampton (Midland and South West Junction).
Bristol	Scotland, York, Newcastle (North Eastern). Bournemouth (London South Western).
Leeds	Barrow (Furness). Exeter, Torquay, Kingswear (Great Western).

Besides these the Midland offered through services to a number of the 'foreign' destinations mentioned from Sheffield, Bradford, Liverpool and Manchester, and in summer its carriages reached the Kent coast at Deal and Dover over the South Eastern and Chatham. It touched the Essex coast, too, for in the final pre-World War I years, in 1912, the Midland engineered a takeover of the London Tilbury and Southend Railway in pursuit of better access to London dockland. Besides its service to Southend from London's Fenchurch Street terminus via the LT&S route, the Midland also went into partnership with the Metropolitan District Railway in 1910 to run through trains between Ealing and the Essex resort; the carriages were electrically hauled by the Metropolitan District to Barking, and steam-powered by LT&S engines for the rest of the journey.

The Midland's 1876 establishment at Carlisle in its own right set off the final development of south-west Scotland's railway network. The

Glasgow and South Western route from Clydeside to Carlisle via Kilmarnock until then had been largely discounted as a through route because, although more easily graded than the Caledonian line over Beattock, it was some 20 miles longer. Buoyed up by the prospect of the Midland's Anglo-Scottish' traffic, the G&SWR cut 10 miles from its disadvantage by building a more direct, if savagely graded, new line from Kilmarnock via Barrhead to Glasgow in 1873, setting the Scottish stage for operation of a fully competitive new trans-border service via the Settle–Carlisle and G&SWR systems. The last quarter of the nineteenth century also saw the emergence of Stranraer as an Irish packet port, and the upgrading of the railways leading to it.

The spread of the Scottish network

Except in this extreme south-west corner of Scotland the Caledonian and G&SWR systems intertwined in the west of the country. The relations between the two companies were oddly schizophrenic. In some areas they worked benignly hand in hand; the Caledonian, for instance, peacefully operated the new Glasgow Barrhead and Kilmarnock line in a joint arrangement with the G&SWR, even though the route furthered a rival Anglo-Scottish service, and a similar partnership harmoniously controlled the exit from Glasgow to Paisley. Moreover, they shared a Glasgow terminus at Bridge Street until 1879, when the G&SWR set up its own premises at St Enoch and the Caledonian made its home at Glasgow Central. But for the Clyde coast traffic the two companies were at each other's throats almost to the end of their separate existences. Rival routes to Greenock and Gourock and to Ardrossan took shape as late as 1869 and 1890 respectively (railways apart, each company had its own pier and operated its own steamers from Ardrossan), and the battlefront would have extended to Ayr if the Caledonian had not run out of financial wind when its line reached Irvine.

On the other side of Scotland the 1890 completion of the Forth Bridge knitted the North British Railway into an effective trunk route system. A new triangular junction was laid into the Edinburgh–Glasgow main line south of the Firth to make both cities equally accessible to the bridge, while across the water a much more direct route from Edinburgh to Perth was now created by coalescing existing branches into a main line with the addition of a

new link through the Ochil Hills at Glenfarg. In 1883, too, the North British had reached Kinnaber Junction and Aberdeen by using running powers over Caledonian tracks for the last few miles to the Granite City.

From the mid-1840s Aberdeen had been visualized as the rail gateway to the Highlands. True, a scheme had been advanced for a line to clamber over the mountains from Perth, but even in the heady years of the Mania, given the state of railway-building in the 1840s, that was too preposterous to attract investors. So the Great North of Scotland had set out from Aberdeen to Inverness in 1846. Desperately short of capital, it made such laborious progress that another company begun to build towards Aberdeen from Inverness. In due course the two met, but they never got on with each other and the Great North of Scotland never realized its ambition to dominate the Inverness business.

Eventually the railway north of Perth was built, reaching Inverness via Forres in 1863, becoming the Highland Railway in 1865, completing its northward projection to Wick and Thurso in 1874 and adding the Dingwall and Skye line in 1870; this last was extended to Kyle of Lochalsh in 1897, and in the following year the Highland opened the direct route from Aviemore to Inverness. The Highland main line touches the highest point on the British Rail system, the 1,484-ft summit at Druimuachdar between Aviemore and Blair Atholl. In the closing years of the nineteenth century two more gems were added to the Scottish railway crown. In 1870 the Caledonian took over a company struggling north-westwards from Callander and eventually reached Oban, generating considerable tourist traffic when trains began running in July 1880; and in August 1894 the spectacular West Highland line was opened to Fort William, from where it was extended to Mallaig in 1901 (the Mallaig extension, incidentally, had the highly unusual assurance of government-guaranteed dividends for its investors).

Assessment and appraisal

By the start of the twentieth century the United Kingdom railway map had essentially stabilized. Watkin's Great Central extension was the last major new project and the last of the great empire-building adventures. Even that was a competitive extravagance which would never have been authorized had railway expansion in Britain been rationally controlled as it was, for instance, in France. On several

Above: A Caledonian Railway 'Dunalastair II' 4-4-0, No. 766, heads a Euston-Glasgow express, including a 12-wheeled LNWR *diner, near Etterby, in the early 1900s. The semaphore route indicator at the head of the smokebox was a characteristic of Caledonian working.*

trunk routes the country was already over-endowed with railways, and in the big cities the multiplication of separately owned yards, depots, stations and connecting lines would fifty years later prove one of British Railways' major economic embarrassments as it wrestled with the problems of adapting to a road transport age. It was long possible, for instance, to travel from Manchester to London and arrive at Euston, St Pancras, Kings Cross, Marylebone and, with a little ingenuity, even at Paddington. Even if there had been more significant gaps in the network to fill, railway management in the early 1900s had the deterrent of unmistakeable sword-sharpening in Europe, which in 1912 prompted the general managers of nine leading British railway companies to unite in a Railway Executive Committee and prepare for the national emergency which few by then doubted was imminent.

Railway enthusiasts argue tirelessly over the ranking of the great pre-1923 companies. Was the London North Western the 'premier line', as its propaganda claimed, or did others have better claims to pre-eminence? Emotion or selective use of statistics could make a persuasive case for at least half-a-dozen systems, but objective comparison of a few facts about the leading companies' assets and performance in 1913, the last full year of peace before World War I, shows no one concern to be outstanding on all counts.

The Great Western was by a wide margin the biggest railway in terms of network size, with a route mileage of 2,678 exclusive of jointly operated lines. Its nearest rival was the London North Western with 1,802 and third in line –

surprisingly – was the North Eastern, the close-packed system of which aggregated 1,690 miles, whereas the Midland could only muster 1,519 – though if one takes jointly operated lines into account the Midland narrowly edges into third place. The only other company to muster more than 1,000 route-miles was the Great Eastern with 1,107.

If freight tonnage is the yardstick of merit, then – again to the astonishment of some, perhaps – the North Eastern took the honours. In 1913 it moved 10.82 million tons of merchandise, 44.17 million tons of coal and 15.53 million tons of minerals. Comparative and respective figures under each of the three heads for the other three big railways, in millions of tons, were: the Great Western 11.5, 37.17 and 10.44; the London North Western 13.27, 32.78 and 11.6; and the Midland 11.32, 31.3 and 12.47. One must remember, however, that the North Eastern freight movement was short-haul compared with that of the other companies. Its 1913 freight tonnage generated only 12.31 million miles of engine work, whereas the Midland's created 26.6 million, the Great Western's 20.17 million and the London North Western's 19.8 million.

The Midland may also be considered to have got better productivity from its freight working, since it covered the greater distances with only marginally more wagons than the North Eastern – just over 119,000 against just under 118,000. No other railways, incidentally, had anywhere near that size of wagon fleet; the Great Western in 1913 had just under 79,000 vehicles, the LNWR just over 75,000. It was a close thing between GWR, Midland and LNWR for size of locomotive stud at that time; the GWR had 3,146 engines on its books, the Midland 3,071 and the LNWR 3,049.

The Great Western clearly led the field in numbers of passengers carried, registerering over 109 million passenger journeys in 1913 – some 7 million more than the Midland. Under this heading the LNWR was edged out of third place by the Great Eastern, whose phenomenally intensive Liverpool Street–north-east London commuter service was responsible for most of its total of over 97 million, some 4½ million in excess of the LNWR figure. Once more the statistic of annual engine mileage in passenger train haulage points a contrast between the GER passenger service and those of the other lines mentioned; against a GER figure of 14.77 million miles that of the LNWR, for instance, was 31.77 million. The biggest fleet of passenger coaches was the LNWR's, standing at 9,502 in 1913, whereas the GWR's totalled 8,652, the Midland's 6,279 and the GER's 5,817. The North Eastern came back into the reckoning where passenger speed was concerned, since it was then operating the country's fastest train with an average of 61.7 mph start-to-stop, scheduled for a lunchtime express from Darlington to York. The only other railway offering a train at better than a mile a minute was the Great Central, which had an early morning newspaper train timed from Leicester to Nottingham at an average of 61.3 mph. Considering the general rather than the particular, however, overall speed standards were probably highest on the LNWR, where the weekday timetables showed over 60 trains daily making station-to-station

runs of over 100 miles at averages of 50 mph or more, nearly half as many again as the Great Western could boast.

As to profitability, the operating ratio – that of expenditure to gross income – is one commonly used measurement of railway performance. On that basis the frugal Scottish railways came top of the 1913 table, with the North British leading at 58.4 per cent, ahead of the Caledonian at 60.2 per cent. Parsimony paid off south of the border, too, for the star English turn was the infamously penny-pinching South Eastern and Chatham, on 62.4 per cent. Of the bigger systems which have chiefly figured in this summary, the Midland came out best at 63.7 per cent, followed by the North Eastern at 64.7 per cent, the Great Western at 64.9 per cent, and the London North Western at 65.7 per cent.

For investors the happiest havens for money that year were the LNWR and NER, each of which paid a total of 7 per cent to their ordinary shareholders, while the GWR managed only 6¼ per cent and the Midland 4½ per cent. The Great Central's sanguine supporters, incidentally, got nothing – they never did. When the line was the MS&L (Manchester, Sheffield and Lincolnshire), it was generally referred to by investors as 'Money Spent and Lost'. When the name was changed to Great Central, the barb quickly became 'Gone Completely'. The position of the premier line, however, must remain forever unresolved – the LNW had it by name, the Midland by penetration but for some the Great Western had the best claim – by route length, passengers and ultimately by emotion.

Above: Elaborate numbering of a Glasgow and South Western Railway coach.

Below: Inverness on the eve of the grouse-shooting season just before World War I. An overnight East Coast route express from Kings Cross is disgorging its passengers on the left – to the right is a Highland Railway train waiting to take passengers even further north. The remotest parts of Britain were transformed by the arrival of the railway.

Following pages: A photograph believed to have been taken on 24 May 1900, the first day of operation of Nottingham Victoria. The lack of smoke on the glass windows in the background certainly suggests that the time is very soon after the first train – the 1.12 am from Manchester to Marylebone – called. The joint owners each originally demanded that the station bear their name (Central after Great Central or Northern after Great Northern) but the clock shows the initials NJS, standing for Nottingham Joint Station – the name they agreed to. Fortunately, opening day was also Queen Victoria's birthday and the town clerk persuaded the parties to accept finally a sensible compromise – and the three earlier names were dropped.

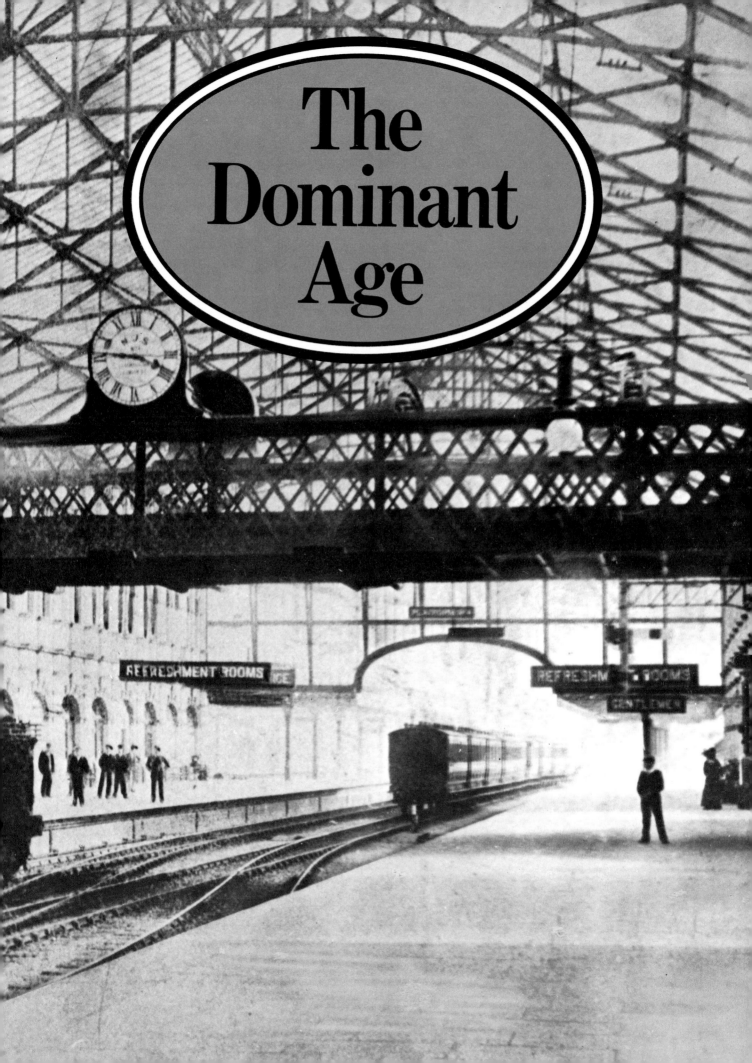

The Dominant Age

Chapter 12

The dawn of speed and comfort

Above: It was normal practice for Pullman cars to carry the Company's crest at each end of the vehicle.

Below: Following General Manager James Allport's visit to North America, Midland Railway shareholders were persuaded to allow the American George Pullman to export and operate on their system some of his parlour and sleeping cars, of which this is a 'drawing room car'.

OLD PHOTOGRAPHS AND early *Punch* cartoons often remind us that even well past the middle of the nineteenth century railway travel could be an austere business. Rugs and greatcoats were among the passenger's necessary impedimenta in winter, and usually he rattled along in a six-wheeled or even a four-wheeled carriage. There was no way he could leave his compartment between stations. Such conditions were accepted on the relatively short journeys in Britain, but by the 1870s a higher grade of accommodation had become available on long-distance trains in the United States through the enterprise of George Mortimer Pullman, whose Pullman Palace Car Company was formed in 1867. Pullman's first goal was to provide more comfortable conditions for night travel, but he soon added parlour cars for daytime use.

The introduction of the Pullman car to Great Britain is linked with the history of the Midland Railway. This company had developed as an important cross-country system based on Derby, but for many years it was dependent on other railways for access to London. Eventually powers to build a London main line were obtained, and on 1 October 1868 the Midland inaugurated passenger services to its own London terminus at St Pancras. Now it had the task of building up its image as a main-line railway on a par with that of its rivals at nearby Kings Cross and Euston. The company took its first and highly contentious step in this direction in 1872, when it admitted third-class passengers to all its trains. In the same year the company's General Manager, James (later Sir James) Allport, visited the United States and saw Pullman cars in service. He saw in them another way of putting the Midland on the map. A contract was signed for 18 cars, which were shipped to England in parts and assembled at the Derby Works. A Pullman sleeping car service was inaugurated between St Pancras and Bradford on 1 June 1874 and between St Pancras and Liverpool on 1 April 1875.

By 1875 another great Midland venture was nearing completion. This was the Settle–Carlisle line, which would give the railway its

Above: Interior of a Midland first-class dining car of 1906, designed by David Bain. Note the rare extravagance of the decor.

own route to the border and so onwards to Edinburgh and Glasgow by agreements with the Glasgow and South Western Railway and the North British Railways. This route to Scotland was longer than their rivals' so the Midland set out to establish new standards of passenger comfort. When the company introduced its first Anglo-Scottish expresses on 1 May 1876 Pullman 'drawing-room' cars were available for first-class passengers on the day trains, and Pullman sleepers on the night services.

By this time the Midland had abolished second-class travel, reclassifying its second-class carriages as thirds and from then onwards building third-class stock to the previous second-class standards. On the Anglo-Scottish trains ordinary first- and third-class passengers rode in comfortable compartment coaches carried on four-wheel or six-wheel bogies – when the six wheeler with rigid wheelbase was the norm on other companies' express trains.

In the long term, the comfortable Midland compartment coach proved more popular than the Pullman cars with their centre corridor layout, despite the latter's attractions of arm-chair seating, tables and a luxurious environment. There is little doubt, however, that their advent, combined with the Midland's own coach building policy, made other railways think earlier and more seriously about improving their own standards of passenger accommodation than they otherwise would have done. Curiously, the longest-lived Pullman services in Britain were those on railways in the south-east, where journeys are short.

Sleeping cars had appeared in Great Britain before the import of the Pullmans. A six-wheel vehicle with compartments convertible for night travel was built for the east coast route in 1873 by the Ashbury Railway Carriage and Iron Co. Ltd of Manchester, and on 1 October that year the LNWR introduced a sleeping car of its own design on the Euston–Glasgow service. For a time, however, the Pullman vehicles had the advantage over others of being equipped with an oil-fired heating system. Heating of rolling

stock by low-pressure steam from the loco-motive did not come until 1884.

Meals prepared in advance were served in the 'day' Pullmans on the Midland trains, but the first travelling kitchen was on a Midland special run from London to the north of Scotland in 1878; one of its vans was specially fitted out for the purpose. Two years later a kitchen was built into a Pullman car on the Great Northern Railway, and after a demonstration run between London and Peterborough the car began regular running on the Kings Cross–Leeds trains on 26 September 1879. Passengers taking meals had to pay the Pullman supplement. Although at this period some coaches had side corridors there was still no communication from end to end of a train, which obviously limited the number of passengers who could enjoy restaurant service. The first complete corridor train with vestibule connections between coaches was put on by the Great Western Railway in 1891, and in the same year the Great Eastern introduced a set of four six-wheel coaches gangwayed throughout on its 'North Country Continental' train from Har-wich. One vehicle was a dining saloon, and

although occupants of the third-class coach in the set were not admitted to it, one of the third-class compartments was fitted with a folding table on which meals could be served from the kitchen.

The true forerunner of the modern sleeping car was a vehicle built by the North Eastern Railway for the East Coast Joint Stock in 1894. It had four single-berth and two double-berth compartments, a pantry with a gas cooker, two lavatories and vestibules – in fact, the general arrangement of the modern sleeping car, for although currently two-berth compartments are confined in Great Britain to second-class sleepers, they have remained in use in first-class cars on the Continent.

Heating and Lighting

The late adoption of steam heating from the locomotive has been mentioned already. For many years travellers had to rely on the hot water footwarmer, at first hired but later pro-vided free (although the porter who brought it expected a tip). In 1880 Francis Webb of

compound locomotive fame introduced on the LNWR a chemical footwarmer which could be revived, after it had cooled, by vigorous shaking. A device of this kind came back into use as late as 1921 when the Great Western Railway introduced it to heat slip coaches.

Oil lamps predominated for carriage lighting until the 1880s and early 1890s, despite tentative experiments from time to time with gas – one of them as early as 1834 on the Liverpool and Manchester Railway. On some lines passengers could buy rubber sconces which adhered to the window pane and held a candle to supplement the light from the oil lamp. Gas lighting with oil on the Pintsch system was tested in an LNWR express in 1875 and first installed on a wider scale in Metropolitan Railway trains on the St Johns Wood branch on 22 January 1876. The London Brighton and South Coast Railway experimented with electric lighting from batteries in 1881, at first in a single Pullman car and then in a four-car Pullman train. At this stage the batteries were removed at night for recharging, but in 1883 William Stroudley of the LB&SCR equipped three suburban train sets with a dynamo, belt-driven from an axle in the guard's van.

Such was the ancestry of the system patented in 1894 by J. Stone and Co. Ltd of Deptford, which was long to remain the standard system of electric lighting for rolling stock. In this arrangement a belt-driven dynamo, suspended by a hinge so that the weight of the machine kept the belt under tension, was fitted under every coach to maintain the charge of a battery on the same vehicle. At high speeds, however, the mechanical power transmitted was greater than the weight of the dynamo could counterbalance, so that the belt slipped and the speed of the armature remained steady, holding the voltage output constant at high train speeds.

Slip carriages

Comfort and speed advanced together. The slip carriage was used on some lines to provide a fast service to intermediate stations without lengthening end-to-end journey times. The slip – one coach of a slip portion – could be detached from a train while it was travelling at speed and brought to rest in the station platform by the slip guard's control of the slip portion's air brake. The arrangement was most extensively used by the Great Western Railway, but the slip coach working off an express in Great Britain began in February 1858, when coaches for Lewes and Hastings were slipped at Hay-

wards Heath off an LB&SCR London–Brighton fast train which did not stop between East Croydon and Brighton. Only the GWR was still operating slip coaches by the time of railway nationalization in 1948, and they continued on Western Region until the end of the 1950s. Slipping was basically a simple idea, achieved by means of a hinged coupling hook operated through a lever by the slip guard, but a special adaptor was necessary in the connection between the vacuum brake systems of the main train and slip, so that when the hoses separated the brake on the main train was not automatically applied, as would have occured in an accidental breakaway. On the slip coach the brake pipe was sealed by operating the lever. In the last years on the GWR and Western Region, slip portions were supplied with steam heating through a new design of pipe coupling.

The railway races

The steam train was for many years the fastest method of surface transport, but there were constraints on the exploitation of locomotives' speed capacity. Braking distances, signal spacing, traffic density and curvature of the track all had to be considered in planning the timetables, and daily running was pitched at a level below the optimum. On two famous occasions, however, the railways of the west and east coast routes pushed their trains to the limit.

These were the so-called railway races of 1888 to Edinburgh and 1895 to Aberdeen. The

Above: Details of gas and early electric lighting in the clerestory roofs of Great Western saloons. Queen Victoria favoured oil lighting to the end of her days; when the GWR built her a new train for her Jubilee year travels in 1897, she insisted that her own saloon be oil lit even though the rest of the train was electrically illuminated.

Left: The business end of a Lancashire and Yorkshire slip coach. The hinged slip coupling is open. Note the headlamp denoting the coach as a 'stopping passenger train' once it was detached.

*Above: Number 2 plat-
form at Euston on a
summer evening in the
1920s as GPO vans arrive
with mail for the nightly
classic 'West Coast
Postal' to the north west
and Scotland.*

Edinburgh race was triggered by a Great Northern Railway announcement in November 1887 that it would admit third-class passengers to its 10 am expresses between London and Scotland, then taking nine hours to Edinburgh. The west coast expresses from Euston already had third-class accommodation, but their trains to Edinburgh took an hour longer. The west coast side did not retaliate until the following summer, when Euston proclaimed that from 2 June its 10 am train would equal the Kings Cross performance by reaching Edinburgh in nine hours. Move and counter-move by both routes followed during the summer months, reaching a climax on 13 August, when the east coast companies began running their train from Kings Cross to Edinburgh in $7\frac{3}{4}$ hours. On that day the train from Euston made the run in 7 hours 38 minutes but 'the East Coast got in late,

because of wind'. It made up for it on 14 August, however, with a time of 7 hours 32 minutes. After this the rivals conferred and agreed that the scheduled times should revert to 8 hours by the west coast route and $7\frac{3}{4}$ hours by the east coast until the end of the month.

In a final fling on 31 August the train from Kings Cross improved on its previous best. A passenger who rode on it reported that:

our train of seven carriages drew smartly up at the Waverley platform at 5.27. A crowd at once surrounded the engine, one of Mr Worsdell's new [North Eastern Railway] compounds, and the driver was besieged with many a query while the fireman stoked the engine here and there.

Timings like these were too tight to be scheduled for regular operation all the year round, and after the race they were lengthened to $8\frac{1}{4}$ hours

to Edinburgh by the east coast and 8½ hours to the west coast, whose route was 7¾ miles longer.

With the opening of the Forth Bridge in 1890 the distance from Kings Cross to Aberdeen became 16 miles less than from Euston. By 1895 tourist traffic to the Highlands was enjoying a boom and the east coast route was eager to exploit its advantage. In the summer months of that year both routes began cutting the time of their overnight tourist express to Aberdeen with scant regard to the published timetable. The sporting British public quickly scented another race in the air, this time with the added piquancy that both routes converged at Kinnaber Junction, 38 miles south of Aberdeen, from which point the east coast train had to run over the line of the Caledonian Railway, a west coast company.

In August the heavy traffic of 'the Twelfth' for the grouse-shooting caused the competitors to relax their speed efforts a little, but from 19 August the contest was at its fiercest. Sporting instincts prevailed, and on one occasion when the signalman at Kinnaber Junction was offered the east coast and west coast trains simultaneously he, as a Caledonian man, gave the road to his east coast rival, which reached Aberdeen in 8 hours 40 minutes from Kings Cross. The best east coast time was 8 hours 38 minutes, achieved on 22 August, and on the same date the west coast train achieved 8 hours 32 minutes for an average speed throughout of over 60 mph, despite stops *en route* at Crewe, Carlisle, Stirling and Perth. The load for this special effort was cut to 72½ tons and the highest start-to-stop average speed was achieved on the difficult section from Preston to Carlisle, over Shap Summit, where the 2-4-0 locomotive *Hardwicke* averaged 67.2 mph. In those days, and indeed long after, 'a mile a minute' was viewed with some reverence, like Concorde's Mach 2 today; the west coast train surpassed that standard on every section of its run. Even Carlisle to Stirling, including the ascent of Beattock Bank,

was achieved effortlessly by the Caledonian locomotive at an average speed of 61.8 mph.

With the motive power available, there was no possibility of perpetuating the schedules of the racing period. A general reduction of speed followed, and in 1896 the derailment of the night tourist train while taking the curve at Preston at excessive speed put an end to further speed ambitions. The companies had already agreed on 18 June that year to a minimum day schedule of 8½ hours between London, Edinburgh and Glasgow, reduced to 8¼ hours by a second agreement of 1 December 1900 to take account of the wider use of restaurant cars and the resulting reduction in meal stops. Anglo-Scottish services were not accelerated again until after Grouping, when the LNER and LMS together agreed in 1932 to relax this long-standing constraint.

The mail trains

Something of the romance of the racing trains also surrounds the night mails. The carriage of mails by trains began early – the first occasion was on the Liverpool and Manchester Railway on 11 November 1830. In the following years a contract was sealed with the Postmaster General, but the scheme could not demonstrate its full importance until the railway network had grown and there was continuous rail communication between London, Birmingham, Manchester and Liverpool. In the days of the stagecoach it had been suggested that time could be saved by sorting mail *en route*. The idea was first put into practice by the Grand Junction Railway, which fitted up a horsebox as a sorting carriage and ran it for the first time between Birmingham and Liverpool on 6 January 1838. Satisfied with the experiment, the GJR decided to build a special-purpose vehicle and to equip it with an apparatus for picking up and dropping mails at speed, which had been devised by John Ramsay of the Missing Letter Branch in the Post Office. By February 1839 the vehicle was reported to be 'perfectly efficient'. With minor improvements, Ramsay's apparatus was the basis of mail exchange with moving trains right up to 1971, when wide use of road transport for conveying mails to and from the stopping-places of the postal trains made it unnecessary.

A Travelling Post Office (TPO) service from London to the north was begun in March 1838, before completion of the London and Birmingham Railway. The mails were taken by train from Euston to Denbigh Hall, north of Bletchley, from where they travelled by coach along

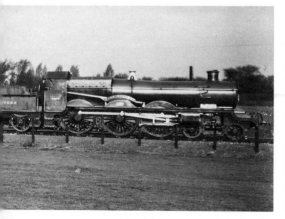

Left: GWR '*Star*' class 4-6-0 No. 4029 King Stephen *heads the* GWR Royal Train *in a photo of the early 1900s. When the train was built in 1897 it included a remarkable vehicle which fitted intact on to a new frame the body of an 1874 saloon to which Queen Victoria was greatly attached and which she had ordered must not be scrapped.*

Watling Street, to be put on board a GJR train in Birmingham. After the rail gap between Denbigh Hall and Birmingham was closed, a through TPO began running between London and Preston on 21 October 1838. This was the beginning of the TPO network which at its peak comprised some 70 mail-carrying trains and about 160 specially constructed vehicles.

At first the mail coaches were attached to ordinary passenger trains, but these were often subject to delays and complaints at the irregularity of the mail service led at length to a House of Commons enquiry. As a result the Postmaster General, Sir Rowland Hill, arranged for the running of certain 'special mails' for Post Office traffic only. The first of these was inauguarated between Paddington and Bristol on 1 February 1885 and was the first train of its kind in the world. In later years the Post Office agreed to one first-class passenger coach being attached, and the train was called a 'limited mail'.

One celebrated postal service developed in the opposite way. A 'limited mail' for Scottish traffic, inaugurated on 1 February 1859, became a 'special mail' running between London and Aberdeen from 1 July 1885. Officially the train was the Down Special TPO and the Up Special TPO, but the service has been known for many years as the 'West Coast Postal'. With its many connections it continues to provide the backbone of the postal service for large areas of the country.

Into the twentieth century

The standards of speed, comfort and service which developed in the last thirty years of the nineteenth century created the modern railway. Tastes and styles change, and although the centre corridors of Pullman's parlour or drawing-room cars did not find lasting favour in their day they were to be

Below: Departure of the inaugural Great Central train from Marylebone on 9 March 1899, headed by Pollitt Class 11A 4-4-0 No. 861. It was the last major line built in Great Britain. Behind the train is the temporary banqueting hall seating more than 700 which was erected over the platforms and their tracks for the inaugural lunch. (From Great Central recalled *by George Dow, published by Bradford Barton Limited.)*

accepted almost without question a hundred years later in Inter-City 125, by which time the layout had become associated in many travellers' minds with attentive air hostesses dispensing duty-free alcohol and cigarettes. The survival of the Pullman tradition south of the Thames has already been noted. A popular Sunday train from Victoria to Brighton in the 1890s consisted sometimes of seven Pullmans as well as six or seven ordinary first-class coaches. A 'Pullman Limited Express' to Brighton consisting of four cars was introduced in 1881 but was not an immediate success, though the introduction of the first non-stop Pullman Limited between Victoria and Brighton on 2 October 1898 began the 'Brighton-in-one hour' tradition and was the precursor of the Southern Belle, which first ran on 1 November 1908 and was once hailed as 'the most luxurious train in the world'.

At the close of the century the main-line railway map was completed with the arrival in London of the Great Central Railway and the opening of its Marylebone terminus on 15 March 1899. The staple Great Central main-line services were London to Leicester, Nottingham, Sheffield and to Manchester,

with certain through coaches or trains serving Bradford. The GCR had few friends among the other companies, having offended the major ones during the long manoeuvres preceding the granting of its Act. Some commercial interests in the Midlands, however, welcomed the competitive element brought by the new line into a somewhat complacent railway industry, and there was public interest in the venture - perhaps even admiration, particularly for the dramatic new station in Nottingham. The GCR set out to create a distinctive image and its publicity dwelt on the aspects of railway travel which were not of major commercial importance. 'Rapid travel in luxury' was one slogan, and the cover of the Great Central timetable read: 'Each express train is vestibuled and has a buffet car attached available for first- and third-class passengers.' If a certain complacency had settled upon the other lines they now had to discard it. But more than competition from the GCR lay in the future. In the coming century there would be less room for inter-company rivalries and more need for united action by all railways in making known and demonstrating their advantages in the face of challenge from the roads.

Above: Stirling 8 ft 4-2-2 No. 53 heads a Great Northern express out of Kings Cross past the one-time Holloway ticket platform in the 1880s. Note the characteristic GNR somersault semaphore signals.

Chapter 13

Late-Victorian locomotives

IN THE FIRST fifty years of British railways following the opening of the Stockton and Darlington Railway, average express passenger train speed had progressed to around 41½ mph, allowing for intermediate stops *en route*. This was enough to give Britain the world lead by a substantial margain. Trains in the USA were recording a similar figure, but on services covering only a fifth of the daily mileage of British expresses. Average speeds in the rest of Europe were 8–10 mph slower, but here again the number of trains ranking as expresses was far smaller than in Britain; France, for instance, showed only a sixth of Britain's daily express train mileage, at an average speed including intermediate stops of only 32.8 mph. By the early twentieth century, the Americans and French closed the gap.

Below: A GWR *stopping train of approximately World War* I *period, headed by 3001 class 4-2-2 No. 3056* Wilkinson. *The second and last vehicles are slip coaches, identifiable by the independent vacuum brake reservoirs flanking the clerestories of their roofs.*

Braking systems

An important factor in the rise of express train speed was the adoption of continuous, auto-matically acting train brakes. At first locomotive designers had been unwilling to fit the engines themselves with any brakes whatsoever, fearing mechanical damage. Even in the 1870s many passenger trains were still running with only tender brakes, applied by the fireman, and brake vans at the front and rear of the train, with hand control by guards obeying whistle codes from the engine driver.

In 1873 the American George Westinghouse, spurred by an appalling collision he had personally witnessed seven years earlier, patented his continuous compressed air brake; its vital feature was that, in the event of a train parting while on the move, both sections would be automatically halted. It was eventually adopted by several British railways – the Great Eastern, North Eastern, London Brighton and South Coast, and London Chatham and Dover, for instance – but the majority of British companies eventually opted for the continuous vacuum brake alternative. There was little to choose between the two at the

time in terms of efficiency, but it was a different matter after mid-twentieth-century development of air brake technology, when quick-acting air brakes became a prerequisite for higher-speed operation of all traffic; then their predecessors' near-standardization of the vacuum brake was to become one of the nationalized British Railways' major technical handicaps to thorough going modernization. In the 1870s and 1880s most railways adopted continuous braking reluctantly, because of the expense of fitting it to all vehicles. Parliament, however, made both this and the block-interval system of train working mandatory for passenger trains after a catastrophe at Armagh in 1889 when 78 people were killed in an accident that both precautions would have prevented.

The new locomotives
By the 1870s the standard gauge railways were producing locomotives which could match those of the GWR's broad gauge engines. This was attributable partly to improved design, partly to lack of advance on the broad gauge. Even on the GWR the end of the broad gauge was now accepted as inevitable, as witness the construction in 1872 of some goods tank engines capable of conversion to standard gauge when the word was given. In the 1870s the Gooch 4-2-2s built in 1847–55 were getting old, but they were replaced by new engines of

almost identical design; these worked the broad gauge expresses up to final conversion to narrow gauge in 1892. No modern engine taking design advantage of the more generous 7 ft o¼ in. gauge was ever built. In the last few months of the broad gauge the GWR fleet was reinforced by eight 2-2-2 'Convertible' engines, which were essentially standard gauge locomotives adapted to run on the broad gauge track; they were quickly converted to standard gauge after 22 May 1892.

The eight Convertible 2-2-2s were soon joined by other 2-2-2s of similar design built expressly for the standard gauge. They had 7 ft 8½ in. driving wheels but they carried an excessive weight on the leading carrying axle. After No. 3021 *Wigmore Castle* had been derailed in the Box Tunnel in September 1893 they were rebuilt as 4-2-2s and thenceforward all new single-drivers were built with bogies. These 4-2-2s, designed by William Dean, were among the best singles ever to run in Britain. The most significant high-speed performance by a nineteenth-century engine was made by one of them, No. 3063 *Duke of Connaught*, though it took place in the early years of the twentieth century. On 9 May 1904 *Duke of Connaught* ran a 120-ton Plymouth Mail Special from Bristol to Paddington, 118.7 miles, in 99 minutes 46 seconds start to stop; 70 miles were covered at an average speed of 80 mph. The sustained character of this run makes it more important

Above: Watford Junction in February 1898. An up express passes behind a 'Precedent' class 2-4-0. To the right of the station is the motive power depot.

than spectacular short downhill bursts of 90 mph or over.

Train speeds rose considerably during the last decade of the nineteenth century and classes of locomotive which had rarely if ever exceeded 75 mph in the 1880s were timed at around 85 mph in the 1890s. E.L.Ahrons attributed this mainly to the use of harder rails and tyres. By this time the majority of express passenger engines were either 2-2-2, 4-2-2, 2-4-0 or 4-4-0 types. The British track was strong and firm by contemporary standards and the six-wheeled engines were proving quite safe at high speeds. Some of the best British 2-4-0s were notable performers which yielded no points to the Gooch broad gauge 4-2-2; the Kirtley 800 class of the Midland Railway and the 901 class of the North Eastern, built by Fletcher, were outstanding.

However, the standard gauge engines which first captured public imagination to the same extent as the broad gauge flyers were the 4-2-2s with 8 ft driving wheels built by Patrick Stirling from 1870 onwards for the Great Northern. The first of these, the famous No. 1, is still preserved. The use of outside cylinders and a leading bogie conflicted with Stirling's usual practice of building six-wheeled engines with inside cylinders. He took this course to lower the centre line of the boiler and the result was one of the most graceful-looking engines in British railway history.

Stirling continued to build 'eight-footers' with only slight design variations until 1893. Between 1885 and 1894 he reinforced rather than replaced

them with some 2-2-2s with 7 ft 6 in. driving wheels and inside cylinders. The two classes were built side by side and were used for the same duties with no significant difference in performance.

By 1893 train loads were increasing after the introduction of corridor coaches and dining cars, and the Stirling singles could no longer be counted upon to keep time when pulling a heavy train on a wet day with strong side winds. Until then Stirling had refused to have his singles double-headed but from the beginning of the 1894 summer timetables he relaxed the rule, although double-heading never became as prevalent on the GNR as it was on the Midland or the LNWR.

In November 1894 Stirling made his final attempt to prolong the life of the single when he built a last batch of 'eight-footers', the 1003 class. These six enlarged 4-2-2s were relatively less successful than the earlier singles. At times they put up individual runs of great merit, but the everyday standard was little different from that of the earlier 4-2-2s and 2-2-2s. There was trouble over the weight in the driving axle, which some critics claimed was responsible for the broken rail which caused the St Neots derailment of 1895. Stirling's successor, H.A. Ivatt, therefore reduced the axle loading from 20 to 18 tons and the engines became less effective.

There is little doubt that, in favourable conditions, the single-driver wheeled engine gave a very good account of itself. It needed less power to move it than a coupled engine of the same size, and that made more horsepower

Below: For the 50th anniversary of the 'Flying Scotsman' on 30 June 1938 the GNR Stirling 8 ft driving wheel 4-2-2 No. 1 is steamed again. It is seen passing Wood Green with a typical six-wheeler express train of the 1880s.

Above: A Whitby locomotive
of 1864-65, designed by
Edward Fletcher to run on
the heavily graded, steeply
curving line from
Whitby to Pickering.

available at the drawbar. This, however, assumed that the driving wheels would grip the rails without slipping. A sudden rainstorm could and frequently did reduce the effective power of the engine. Consequently, many railways regarded the 2-4-0 or 4-4-0 as more suitable for everyday work in all weathers. The single was given a further lease of life from the middle 1880s by a Midland engineer's invention known as the Holt sand blast; sand was blown under the driving wheels – at first by compressed air but later by steam – and helped the wheels to get a better grip on the rails.

The Midland itself had not built singles for many years, but in 1884 its engineer, Samuel Johnson, turned out a very handsome 4-2-2 single with inside cylinders. This was the first of several batches of Midland singles with driving wheels varying between 7 ft 4 in and 7 ft 9½ in. However, side by side with these engines Johnson built 4-4-0s. The difference in performances was not significant; the singles occasionally rose to great heights, but the coupled engines were more consistent in bad weather. It was generally believed that the singles were lighter on coal but reliable test results were never published, and Rous Marten wrote that the difference was 'a moot point'. Rous Marten timed his first 90 mph maximum speed with a Midland single in 1897, and on occasion these engines handled loads of over 300 tons, as did the GNR and GWR singles.

On the LNWR Francis William Webb tried to combine the good qualities of both single and coupled engines in his double-single compounds. These engines had two outside high-pressure cylinders driving the rear pair of driving wheels, while a single and very large inside low-pressure cylinder drove the leading pair. The driving wheels were uncoupled. The best of these were the ten Teutonic class engines built in 1889 and 1890. No. 1304 *Jeanie Deans* of this class worked the mid-day Scottish dining car express from Euston to Crewe and back almost every day from January 1891 to August 1899, keeping very good time with loads which at times exceeded 300 tons. Webb's later 2-2-2-2 compounds of the Greater

Above: No. 2202 was one of the first batch of S. W. Johnson's enlarged 4-4-0 express passenger engines of 1892 for the Midland Railway. She was photographed at Bedford circa 1904.

Britain and John Hick classes were less successful, and after these he progressed to 4-4-0 four cylinder compounds. Throughout Webb's compound period the LNWR was still heavily reliant on the small, simple expansion 2-4-0s of the Precedent class. In 1897 Dugald Drummond of the LNWR built a 4-2-2-0 four-cylinder simple 'double single' but on the simple expansion principle, and added five more in 1901. As with the Webb engines, their performance was variable.

The potential speed capacity of the nineteenth-century express locomotive was demonstrated in the 1895 'Races to Aberdeen', when light trains were rushed north by the east and west coast companies in fierce competition.

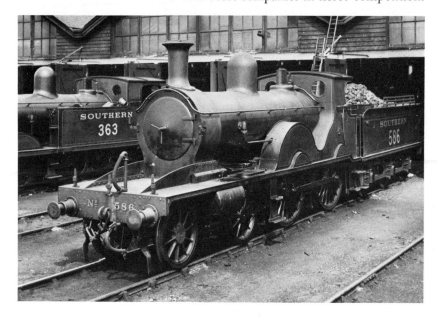

The most outstanding run was made by the smallest engine involved, the LNWR simple 2-4-0 *Hardwicke*, which is still preserved and steamable. On the night of 22 August 1895 this engine took the west coast race train from Crewe over Shap Summit to Carlisle, 141 miles, in 126 minutes start to stop. The GNR used their 4-2-2 singles, but the NER, the NLR and the Caledonian employed 4-4-0s on the race trains in their sectors.

Possibly the most significant design of the nineteenth century was built for the Caledonian Railway by J. F. McIntosh in 1896. McIntosh introduced no adventurous design features, but merely put a larger boiler on a 4-4-0 of similar basic design to those which his Caledonian predecessors had used in the 1895 races. As it happened, this was just what was wanted. The new locomotives were known as the Dunalastair class.

In the summer of 1896 the down Tourist express, hauled by one of the new Dunalastairs, was scheduled to cover the 117 miles from Carlisle over the 1000-ft-high Beattock Summit to Stirling in 125 minutes start to stop with a load of 150–200 tons.

The favourable publicity gained by these Scottish engines induced other designers to adopt large boilers for their own 4-4-0s. The North Eastern just managed to get their Class R 4-4-0s designed by Wilson Worsdell into the nineteenth century, but the Johnson Belpaires of the Midland and the Claud Hamiltons of the Great Eastern did not appear until the early months of 1900. In 1897 McIntosh

brought out an enlarged Dunalastair and a still larger example just squeezed into the nineteenth century in December 1899. The Belgian State Railway puchased five of the second Dunalastair class and later added 230 of a slightly enlarged version to the five built in Scotland. The big-boiler 4-4-0 was to play a key role hauling expresses in the early twentieth century.

The advent of the Atlantic

On the GNR H. A. Ivatt, while he was turning out the last batch of 4-2-2s to be built in Britain, was pondering something bigger still as the logical successor to the Stirling singles. The 4-4-2 or Atlantic type was gaining a high reputation from the high speed running in the USA of the Atlantic City Flyers of the Philadelphia and Reading Railway. So, in 1898, Ivatt built Britain's first Atlantic-type engine, No. 990 *Henry Oakley*, which still survives in the National Railway Museum. *Henry Oakley* was not a true Atlantic in the American sense of the word, as it had a narrow firebox, but Ivatt was to build some larger-boilered Atlantics of the American wide firebox type from 1902 onwards. Ivatt's lead was followed in 1899 by John Aspinall, who built some inside-cylinder 4-4-2s for the Lancashire and Yorkshire Railway. The Atlantic was the logical successor to the single and shared to some extent its tendency to slip in bad weather,

but several railways, notably the east coast companies, adopted the type in the 1900s.

The beginning of the 4-6-0

At the Paris Exhibition of 1900 two contrasting British locomotives stood side by side. One was *Princess of Wales*, a Midland 4-2-2 single typical of much that was best in the nineteenth century, but which had been built early in 1900; the other was North Eastern's 4-6-0 No. 2006, one of the first class of six-coupled express engines. There had been earlier 4-6-0s on the Highland Railway and the GWR, but the NER engines were the first intended specifically for heavy express passenger trains. Later the 4-6-0 was destined to outclass the 4-4-0 and the 4-4-2 Atlantic types and to press close on the heels of the larger 4-6-2 Pacific type. The single was symbolic of a type with an honourable record but it was already threatened with extinction by the increasing weight of trains. The 4-6-0 was far from an unqualified success, but it pointed to future development.

The steam locomotive had progressed far in the half century from 1850 to 1900. Despite the brilliance, for the period, of the broad gauge Gooch 4-2-2s on test in 1847, the standard gauge Dunalastair of 1896 could produce almost twice the horsepower from a boiler of much the same size and grate area, and so could haul trains of twice the weight at comparable speeds.

Above: The Highland Railway was the first to employ the classic 4-6-0. Pioneer of this wheel arrangement was the HR 'Jones Goods' and from that was developed the 'Castle' for passenger work. No. 140 Taymouth Castle was one of six built by Dübs in 1900.

Opposite, below: Following the opening of the LSWR's direct route from London to Bournemouth via Sway in 1888 and an acceleration of the passenger service, William Adams designed a new range of express passenger 4-4-0s for the railway. Class X2 was built in 1890-92 and of these No. 586 is seen in Southern Railway ownership at Eastleigh in 1942.

Chapter 14

The commuter is born

THE EARLIEST LONDON commuters travelled of necessity. Many small houses were demolished when the railway built their lines to the London termini and workers had to find new accommodation, usually further out. To minimize the expense of the journey to work, the Great Eastern Railway was obliged by an Act of 1854 to convey workmen from Edmonton and Walthamstow to its Bishopsgate terminus in London for twopence return. By the following year 2.14 million passengers passed through the station, and as the tide swelled Bishopsgate became inadequate for its traffic. An extension to Liverpool Street was opened to local services

on 2 February 1874. Less than thirty years late traffic at Liverpool Street had risen to 65.3 mil lion passengers a year and the Great Easterr terminal was the busiest in London.

At the beginning of the railway age in 183 London covered an area of some 18 square mile and had 1.65 million inhabitants. Its growth ha already caused concern to some observers 'Whither will this monstrous city extend? Daniel Defoe had asked at a much earlier date and in the 1820s William Cobbett complaine that the capital was draining the provinces o wealth, culture and talent.

The first railway in London was the Londor

Below: A London suburban branch scene at the turn of the century. LNWR 2-4-0T No. 999 waits to return from Stanmore to the main line at Harrow and Wealdstone.

and Greenwich, opened as far as Deptford in 1836 and throughout in 1840. An early print shows the line on its brick viaduct winding away among the roof-tops and factory chimneys of Bermondsey to open country in the middle distance. When the London and Croydon Railway was opened in 1839 day tickets allowing a break of journey at any station were issued 'in order to afford the public an opportunity of viewing the beautiful scenery upon this line more at leisure than the rapid transit of the trains will now permit'. It was also announced that 'marquees, etc., are erected in the wood close to the Anerley station, and parties using the railway will be permitted to angle in the adjacent canal, which abounds in fish'.

Such sylvan pleasures in the shadow of the metropolis were not to last long. Railways accelerated the expansion which had alarmed Defoe all those years before, and Arcadia moved further away.

North London and Great Eastern

Commerce brought growing numbers of clerks to the City. The North London Railway came to Broad Street station in 1865 and tapped a belt of suburbs extending as far west as Rich-mond, from which a swelling daily tide flowed and ebbed between home and the offices of the Square Mile of the City of London. Between them the North London and the Great Eastern were largely responsible for the spread of the

suburbs northwards. Their clientèles were some-what different, North London having a higher proportion of management and its growing swarms of acolytes; it was not obliged to carry third-class passengers until 1875. The Great Eastern was – in the words of an LCC report – 'especially the workman's London Railway – the one above all which appears to welcome him as a desirable customer'.

Up to its last days the Great Eastern continued to work its ever-growing commuter traffic with steam locomotives in spite of pressure for electrification. The first electrics were not seen at Liverpool Street until the main line was electrified as far as Shenfield in 1949. They would have been earlier but for World War II, as Liverpool Street–Shenfield was scheduled for electrification in 1935 under a government aid scheme, and work was in hand by 1939. The advocates of electrification at the beginning of the century had pointed to the high acceleration of the electric multiple-unit train, which could attain 30 mph in 30 seconds from rest. To show that steam could do as well the Great Eastern built an 0-10-0 tank locomotive, the Decapod, which with a train of about 250 tons actually improved on the electric performance. The demonstration appears to have rather easily silenced the electric lobby of the time, for the Great Eastern never put the design into general production.

To eliminate one operating disadvantage of any steam locomotive in intensive suburban service terminal conditions – that it had to run round its train at the end of every journey – some railways practised 'push-pull' working with steam 'auto-trains' or 'rail-motors'. But not more than two coaches could be propelled, so the system was confined to routes of low traffic density.

Commuter services at Liverpool Street reached their peak intensity with steam working in the timetable introduced on 12 July 1920, in preparation for which new engine spurs were laid at the terminus in which locomotives could wait to take over arriving trains and work them back to the suburbs. Platform occupation was cut to a minimum of four minutes, providing that unloading and loading proceeded smoothly. A train entered each platform every 10 minutes and 51 trains left the terminus between 5.00 and 6.00 pm, 27 for the Hackney Downs lines, eight for the Loughton line, and 12 for Ilford and beyond. It was described at the time as 'the last word in steam-operated suburban services'. To help passengers, yellow and blue stripes were painted under the carriage roofs to distinguish first- and second-class accommodation,

an adornment which earned the operation the nickname of the 'Jazz Service'. After World War II European railways began to identify first class similarly; in due course British Rail took up the idea and added a red stripe for catering vehicles.

Commuting from the south and north-west

South of London the London, Chatham and Dover Railway instituted workmen's cheap trains over its 'London Extension' line in 1865. Trains ran daily in each direction between Ludgate Hill and Victoria via the west curve at Loughborough Junction, serving Walworth, Camberwell, Brixton and Battersea. They left in the morning at 4.55 am and returned in the evening at 6.15 pm (2.30 pm on Saturdays). A contemporary report described them as being 'for the exclusive accommodation of artisans, mechanics and daily labourers, both male and female'.

According to the LC & DR Chairman, James Staats Forbes, the company had agreed to run workmen's trains as a 'graceful concession' to

Below: Bishopsgate, the original London terminus of the Eastern Counties Railway and then of the Great Eastern until they built the delightful Liverpool Street at enormous cost in the late 1860s.

meet criticisms that it had been a 'great destroyer of house property in London' when building its London extension. A clause regarding the running of the trains and the fares to be charged was inserted in the Act sanctioning the construction of the line, but remembering that similar responsibilities had been placed upon the Great Eastern Railway in 1854 it seems that Forbes was taking credit for magnanimity which he did not necessarily deserve.

The principle of helping workmen obliged to live at some distance from their jobs was applied more generally in the Artisans' and Labourers' Dwellings Act of 1868, which recommended an obligation on railways running out of London to provide transport at the rate of one penny for seven or eight miles. This ruling was enforced at the discretion of the Board of Trade and some companies were highly imaginative in finding reasons why it should not apply to them. Workmen in some areas walked long distances daily to join a train at a station on a line where cheap tickets were available. Even the companies which made the concessions were sometimes arbitrary in applying them. Sir Edward Watkin, Chairman of the South Eastern Railway, suspended workmen's trains in 1874 during agitation for a nine-hour day.

Among the well-to-do the idea of commuting between the south coast and the City dawned early. An annual season ticket rate of £40 between Brighton and London was quoted in 1862, and in 1865 a business express ran between Brighton and London Bridge in 65 minutes. This timing did not last long but the 8.45 am up service and the 5 pm down became well-established and were the forerunners of the LB & SCR's City Limited, a first-class-only train with a Pullman car. The name was first used in 1907 when new rolling stock was built for the service. Third-class passengers were not allowed to use the City Limited until 1921.

The commuting habit spread along the south coast, but Hove and Worthing passengers were at a disadvantage at first because their trains to town had to run into Brighton station and out again. In 1879 the Cliftonville spur was opened from Hove to the London main line at Preston Park, avoiding Brighton station.

Old timetables often contain reminders of how the status of suburban stations has changed with the years and with the expansion of London, which increased its area tenfold between 1867 and 1901. For example, Forest Hill, only $5\frac{1}{2}$ miles from London Bridge on the Brighton line, attracted some important services in the 1850s. For some years the 10 am first-class train from Brighton to London Bridge stopped only at Reigate (now Redhill) and Forest Hill, while three other up trains stopped at Forest Hill but omitted Croydon. Two down trains stopped by the signal if there were passengers to pick up.

Above: The North London Railway operated its passenger services with distinctive 4-4-0Ts. No. 51 was one of a class of eleven built in 1865-69 with inside cylinders.

There was also long-distance commuting in the north-west, and in 1895 it took a particular form when a group of Manchester businessmen who travelled daily from Blackpool proposed to the Lancashire and Yorkshire Railway that a carriage should be set aside for their use. A bogie saloon was fitted up with armchair seats and an attendant's compartment from which refreshments could beserved, and was soon followed by a second 'club car' of this kind. Both vehicles ran together in one service, which became known as the 'Blackpool Club Train'. Other club trains were run by the London and North-Western Railway on the Manchester–Llandudno and Manchester–Windermere routes, by the Midland between Bradford and Morecambe, and by the Lancashire and Yorkshire from Southport. The Manchester–Blackpool 'club' facilities were carried on by the LMS and a new club saloon was built as late as 1935. This commuting elitism did not survive World War II, in which there also vanished Pullman Cars between Aylesbury, Chesham and the City which had been introduced by the Metropolitan Railway on certain morning and evening trains and were continued by London Transport.

Electrification to improve commuter services around Manchester, Liverpool and Newcastle-upon-Tyne is dealt with in a later chapter. Merseyside had a special problem in that residents in Birkenhead and the Wirral peninsula who worked in Liverpool had to cross the river twice daily by ferry. It was not the most comfortable or convenient means of transport,

particularly in the British climate, and in 1868 Mersey Railway Company was formed to build an underground railway between Liverpool and Birkenhead that would pass under the Mersey in a tunnel. The line was formally opened on 20 January 1886 and public services between Green Lane, Birkenhead, and James Street, Liverpool, began on 1 February. The line was worked by steam, and the powerful locomotives necessary to cope with a ruling gradient of 1 in 27 created an atmosphere inside the tunnel which some travellers found more hostile than the breezy decks of the ferries. There was general relief when the line was electrified in 1903; it was the first steam railway in Britain to be converted.

The Mersey Railway did not reach its full potential until an extension took it to Birkenhead Park, where from 2 January 1888 its trains connected with those of the Wirral Railway, a line serving a developing suburban area extending across the Wirral peninsula from Hoylake to New Brighton. On 15 June 1891 another Mersey Railway extension connected at Rock Ferry with services to Chester and the south by the Birkenhead Joint Railway (jointly owned by the Great Western and the LNWR). On the other bank of the river the Mersey Railway was carried on in a tunnel from James Street to Liverpool Central, a service opened on 11 January 1892, connecting there with the services of the Cheshire Lines Committee.

The Wirral lines were electrified by the LMS in 1938, the trains running through, to and from Liverpool Central over the Mersey Railway.

Important changes in the railway geography of central Liverpool were made in 1977, and today trains arriving at James Street from the Wirral continue over the loop line through Moorfields, Lime Street and Central to re-enter James Street from the opposite direction, ready to continue on their next outward journey.

Underground lines

The Mersey Railway was concerned primarily with getting commuters into and out of the city, but underground lines had been built much earlier for internal city transport. The first underground railway in the world was the section of the Metropolitan Railway between Bishops Road (Paddington) and Farringdon Street in the City of London, opened on 10 January 1863. This was built on the 'cut-and-cover' principle, only a short distance below street level under what is now the Marylebone and Euston Roads. The same form of construction was used for the Metropolitan District Railway, opened between South Kensington and Westminster Bridge (now Westminster) on 24 December 1868. After many vicissitudes and much mutual recrimination the two railways extended their lines to form the present Inner Circle, which was completed on 6 October 1884. Both railways were

steam-worked until electrification began in 1905.

The District (to use its popular, short title) extended to suburbs east and west of London, and through a connection with the London Tilbury and Southend Railway shared in the working of a through train between Ealing and Southend. The Metropolitan pushed out north-westwards from Baker Street into Middlesex, Hertfordshire and Buckinghamshire. Its Chairman in the 1890s was Sir Edward Watkin, also Chairman of the Great Central and mastermind of the Great Central extension to London. To reach Marylebone, Great Central trains joined Metropolitan metals at Quainton Road in Buckinghamshire and followed them to Canfield Place, near West Hampstead, where they diverged on to their own tracks for the short distance, mainly in tunnels, to the terminus.

In addition to providing access for Great Central trains to Marylebone, Watkin's extension of the Metropolitan became the backbone of a new commuting area in which the Metropolitan Railway itself, through a subsidiary, actively encouraged building development. This was 'Metroland', beginning in the shadow of Harrow Hill and extending through the outer suburbs into 'beechy Bucks' and the Chilterns. 'Live in Metroland' said the posters aimed at potential season-ticket holders, and *Country*

Left: Horse-drawn public and private transport in the forecourt of Brighton Station in 1903.

Walks in Metroland swelled the sales of cheap day returns besides stimulating ambition to become a resident in this favoured area. Desirable residences and small parades of shops sprang up near the stations, but in this undulating landscape they were not obtrusive.

At first the Great Central trains using the Metropolitan line were not allowed to carry local traffic, but in due course the Metropolitan and Great Central Joint Committee was formed and both railways provided the service. The Metropolitan, which always looked upon itself as a main line, ran freight trains and road collection and delivery services, but after the formation of the London Passenger Transport Board these activities were considered unsuitable and goods working passed to the LNER.

As well as inheriting the first underground railway in the world, the London Passenger Transport Board inherited the first city underground electric railway and the first of London's deep-level 'tube' lines. This had started life on 18 December 1890 as the City and South London Railway, running from King William Street, near the Monument, to Stockwell. From 25 February 1900 the opening of a new line from near Borough Station to Moorgate via London Bridge meant that King William Street found itself on a disused spur, visited from time to time by the curious to see those relics of the old line that remained *in situ*, and the City and South London became more recognizably the ancestor of London Transport's Northern Line.

Originally the City and South London was to have been cable-worked, but the bold decision

was taken at that early date to use small electric locomotives instead. Glasgow, however, did solve its internal transport problem with the cable-worked Glasgow District Subway, first opened on 14 December 1896 but quickly closed after a breakdown and a collision. It reopened on 21 January 1897 and remained cable-worked until it was electrified in 1935. The route was circular – two independent lines, one for each direction of travel, in separate tube tunnels, covered 6½ route miles.

Overhead lines

The London and Greenwich Railway can claim to have been the first overhead line in the country, as it was carried on a viaduct throughout its length, but in the 1830s transport from London Bridge to Deptford or Greenwich was not regarded as urban. The first, and only, urban overhead railway in the country was the Liverpool Overhead. Its 6¼ miles of double track ran the length of the Liverpool docks and quays on a viaduct which followed the line of the roadways below and came to be called the 'dockers umbrella'. The Liverpool Overhead was electrified from the start, and when its first section was opened on 4 February 1893 it was the first elevated railway in the world. The LOR continued in operation until 30 December 1956, and it issued 'workmen's tickets' to the end. Similar facilities had been renamed 'early morning tickets' in the London area since 1 October 1950, and from 1 September 1952 this less divisive term was adopted by BR.

Below: An early steam train of the District Railway, which in its steam days made exclusive use of Beyer Peacock-built outside-cylinder 4-4-0Ts. No. 33 was one of a batch built in 1880; it was scrapped in 1925.

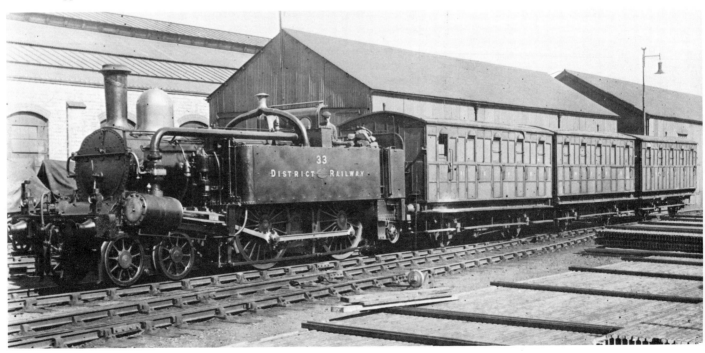

Electrification

The early years of the twentieth century were the years of the electric tram. Diligent attenders at Sunday School in those days were liable to be rewarded with a book of improving verses, one of which began:

It's a wonderful thing, an electric tram
As I said today to my sister Pam;
There's a little wire and a wheel and lo!
A handle is turned and off we go.

A tram moving off in effortless majesty was beginning to attract a fickle public which suddenly found suburban trains slow, uncomfortable and even dirty.

One of the lines particularly badly hit by the new competitor was the South London line of the LB&SCR from London Bridge to Victoria, passing through an area where the LCC tram at the street corner was stealing the customers who formerly had accepted that they must make their way to a station and perhaps wait some time for a train. In these circumstances the LB&SCR decided to electrify its South London line, and to adopt an alternating current system at relatively high voltage which would be suitable for a main-line electrification at a later date. Electric working on the South London line began on 1 December 1909. It was later extended to Crystal Palace, to Sutton and Cheam, and down the Brighton main line as far as Coulsdon.

When the Kennedy Committee on railway electrification sat in 1920 it had before it detailed LB&SCR proposals for extending the AC system to Brighton, but Grouping was in the air and the committee favoured a standard system for the Southern lines, where the London and South Western had adopted a 630v third rail and the South Eastern and Chatham was electrifying similarly. After Grouping all the LB&SCR AC lines were in due course converted to DC; the last AC electric services ran in 1929.

Electrification on the Brighton line came in 1933, but on the DC third-rail system. It was less a main-line electrification than an extension of a suburban system. In announcing the project the Chairman of the Southern Railway described it as 'outer suburban'. The phrase was a commentary on how far London had spread.

Above: Metropolitan Railway Class B 4-4-0T No. 55, built in 1880, approaches Aldgate junction with a Hammersmith train in 1885 in the days when the Metropolitan was still operated by steam engines.

Chapter 15

Light railways and narrow gauge

OVERSHADOWED BY THE momentous expansion of the main-line railways, another system, puny by comparison, had been born of the Industrial Revolution. Its cradle was on the opposite side of the country to Stephenson's railways, in the slate quarries of the North Wales mountains, where the expanding demand of the new towns and factories for building material was hopelessly overtaxing transport that was still virtually medieval. Up in the heights the roads – if one can call them that – were so poor that they were unfit even for horse-drawn wagons; panniers had to be slung over mules to get the slate well down the mountain-sides before it could be transferred to wheeled transport.

As early as 1801 a railway was constructed from the Penrhyn Quarry, one of the two largest in the world, to the Menai Strait at Port Penrhyn, six miles away near Bangor. Whether this was the first in the area is not verified, but it was certainly the first of substantial length. Worked entirely by horses until 1874, the Penrhyn Railway was built to a narrow gauge of 2 ft. In later years the planners of public passenger and freight railways were to realize the economy of a narrower gauge in projecting a railway through difficult terrain where train speed was a minor concern, because of its facility for sharper curvature to avoid expensive earthworks. Even on the flat it became a cheap way to establish rail transport in areas where traffic prospects were slender. The Penrhyn builders, however, are most likely to have picked on their 2-ft gauge as the widest they could conveniently fit into the tunnels and on to the terraced working faces of the quarry.

The narrow gauge in Wales

Throughout the first half of the nineteenth century no-one in Britain dreamed of scaling the steam locomotive down to narrow-gauge use. Nor were passengers carried on the narrow gauge until the Festiniog Railway wrote new history on both counts. It was early in the 1830s that a civil engineer named James Spooner proposed a construction of a narrow-gauge tramroad from the quarries at Blaenau Festiniog to the coast at Porthmadog (Portmadoc). He took a leading part in promoting a bill before Parliament which received the royal assent in 1832 and incorporated the Festiniog Railway Company. The railway still operates as a tourist line, and the English spelling of Ffestiniog with one 'F' remains in its official title, although the 'Portmadoc' of the original Act is now generally known as Porthmadog.

The Festiniog Railway was built to the 1 ft $11\frac{1}{2}$ in. gauge, winging through the mountains in a series of almost continuous curves of radius between 8 ch and as little as $1\frac{3}{4}$ ch, (40–175 yd) and climbing through 700 ft between the coast and the quarries. For many years the line was worked by gravity, the loaded wagons coasting down from the quarries and being hauled back empty by horses. One of the sights of the line was to see the horses, after being unharnessed on arrival, walk unled to take their place in the 'dandy car' in which they rode down to Porthmadog at the back of the next train in order to repeat the performance.

Slate traffic increased steadily and outgrew the capacity of horse haulage. In 1860 the railway made an enquiry about steam locomotives and in 1863 four 0-4-0 tank engines were delivered by George England and Company of New Cross. This was the year in which George Borrow published *Wild Wales*, a book which made thousands aware for the first time of the romantic scenery of Snowdonia. It may well have been that the upsurge of interest in Welsh travel which it stimulated encouraged the board of the Festiniog Railway to run an experimental service in 1864 on which passengers could travel at their own risk and without payment of a fare. The venture proved so popular that application was made to run regular passenger trains. After an inspection by the Board of Trade the application was approved and an official passenger service was inaugurated on 6 January 1865. It was a far-sighted move, for when slate traffic eventually declined, in particular in the years after World War I, passenger traffic continued buoyant for some time. The Festiniog Railway is best known, probably, for its Fairlie double-

ended locomotives.

In 1867 the Cambrian Railways line from Barmouth Junction to Pwllheli was opened. At Minffordd it passed under the Festiniog Railway and in 1871 the Festiniog opened sidings at this point so that traffic could be exchanged with the Cambrian. The passenger stations on the two lines were adjacent and tourist traffic from Barmouth was encouraged by the issue of cheap through tickets.

In later years such inducements failed to offset the decline of slate traffic which had followed World War I, and universal motoring aggravated the problems. By 1935 the losses on the Festiniog were serious. Passengers continued to be carried up to the outbreak of World War II but from 15 September 1939 no further passenger trains were run. A post-war application for a grant to resume tourist trains was unsuccessful and the line was closed on 1 August 1946.

Below: BR's only narrow-gauge line is the 1 ft $11\frac{1}{2}$ in. gauge Vale of Rheidol, opened in 1902 over an $11\frac{3}{4}$ mile route from Aberystwyth to Devil's Bridge, then taken over by the Cambrian Railways and hence the GWR at the start of 1923. No. 8 Llywelyn *is one of the two VoR 2-6-2Ts built at Swindon works.*

Above: Welshpool and Llanfair 2 ft 6 in. gauge 0-6-0T No. 822 The Earl in 1935.

Below: An early Festiniog train with 0-4-0T The Princess at Duffws.

Its subsequent history saw a turn of fortune. The line was rescued by the Festiniog Railway Society and reopened in stages, starting from Porthmadog. In the meantime, however, part of the old route to Blaenau Ffestiniog had disappeared under a reservoir, and a deviation with a new tunnel had to be built. The diverted line was opened to traffic as far as Llyn Ystradau on 7 July 1977.

Three years after the Festiniog received its first steam locomotives, the 2 ft 3 in. gauge Tal-y-Llyn Railway was opened from Tywyn (Towyn) to Abergynolwyn. Also a slate line, the Tal-y-Llyn served quarries at Bryn Eglwys. The railway's Act only authorized a line to Abergynolwyn, but from there it built on private land an extension three-quarters of a mile long to the foot of a gravity-worked incline by which slate was sent down from the quarries. Soon after the opening a passenger service for tourists began to be operated in the summer months, but it terminated at Abergynolwyn, as the so-called 'mineral extension' was not passed for passenger traffic. Nearby was the terminus of the 2 ft 3 in. gauge Corris Railway, originally a horse tramway running to Machynlleth, which stepped up to steam haulage in 1879 and inaugurated a passenger service on 4 July 1883. The two railways linked their railheads with a bus service which enabled summer visitors to travel over both lines and complete the circuit by taking the Cambrian Railways from Machynlleth back to Tywyn.

The Tal-y-Llyn lost an important source of revenue when the Bryn Eglwys quarries closed in 1948, but the company's Chairman, Sir Henry Hayden Jones, kept his pledge to maintain a railway service. He died in 1950, but in the meantime the Tal-y-Llyn Railway Preservation

Society had been formed and was able to keep the line open. It is still running and in 1976 extended its passenger services from Abergynolwyn over the 'mineral extension' to the foot of the incline at Nant Gwernol, having restored this long-derelict section of track, never before used by passenger trains, to satisfy the safety requirements of the Department of the Environment.

The Welshpool and Llanfair Light Railway was a 2 ft 6 in. gauge line opened in 1903 to connect Welshpool, on the Cambrian, with Llanfair Caereinion. It was taken over by the Cambrian, and so on Grouping came under the Great Western Railway. The GWR replaced its passenger trains with a bus service in 1931, but goods traffic continued until 1956. This line, too, is now worked over a part of its original length by a preservation society.

Contemporary with the Welshpool and Llanfair was the Vale of Rheidol Railway, a 1 ft 11½ in. gauge line from Aberystwyth to Devil's Bridge, a remarkable triple bridge up in the hills, opened in 1902. It, too, joined first the Cambrian and then the Great Western, but it survived to become the only steam-worked line of British Railways, continuing as a strong tourist attraction under BR management.

Narrow gauge railways in England

Narrow gauge lines in England were not numerous, and the years between the two world wars saw their numbers reduced. The best-known was the 1 ft 11½ in. gauge Lynton and Barnstaple in the West Country, opened on 11 May 1898 to provide Lynton with a connection to the main-line railway system. Its founder was Sir George Newnes, the publisher who had already provided Lynton with a cable railway to Lynmouth at the foot of the cliffs. The Lynton and Barnstaple enjoyed a reasonably rewarding seasonal traffic up to the time of the Grouping, for the scenery of its 19½ mile route was a popular attraction to holidaymakers. After absorption by the Southern Railway, train services continued until the end of the 1935 summer service. For the next 25 years Lynton was distinguished by being the town furthest from a railway station in Great Britain.

Older than the L&B but less widely known was the Southwold Railway, which also served to connect a somewhat isolated coastal region with the main railway network. The Southwold Railway was a 3 ft gauge line opened in 1879 between Southwold in Suffolk and the Great Eastern main line at Halesworth, 8¾ miles away.

Left: The 2 ft 3 in. gauge Tal-y-Llyn Railway was opened to goods traffic in 1865 and to passengers in late 1866. It was the first of the Welsh narrow-gauge railways to be saved by voluntary preservation effort, in 1951. Locomotive No. 1 Talyllyn was built in 1865.

It was an early victim of road competition and closed in 1929. Another narrow gauge coastal venture was the 3 ft gauge Rye and Camber, in Sussex. The changing coastline had left the ancient port of Rye high and dry centuries earlier, but the sea was only three miles away and the Rye and Camber bridged the gap in 1895. A golf course and Camber Sands encouraged travel for a time, but in the inter-war years the line succumbed to the inexorable advance of the private car.

The 2 ft 6 in. gauge Leek and Manifold Light Railway in Staffordshire was opened in 1904 between Waterhouses and Hulme End. At Waterhouses it connected with a branch of the North Staffordshire Railway from Leek and it was worked from the start by the North Staffordshire. Transporter trucks enabled standard gauge wagons to be worked through to Leek and Manifold stations. A proposal to extend the light railway to Buxton did not materialize and both ends of the line remained somewhat remote; so, despite its scenic attractions, it became yet another victim of the fatal 1930s, and closed on 12 March 1934.

Two 15 in. gauge lines still in operation are in a category of their own since their motive power was consciously modelled on that of main-line railways. The Romney, Hythe and Dymchurch Railway, opened in 1926, set out to be a main-

that the stringent requirements of earlier legislation were retarding railway development in some rural areas, the Regulation of Railways Act of 1868 authorized a railway to be licensed as a 'light railway'; as such it might dispense with certain amenities and safety devices at stations which had previously been mandatory, subject to speed restriction of 25 mph and a maximum axle load of 8 tons. Procedures were further simplified by the Light Railways Act of 1896, which was described as 'an Act to facilitate the construction of light railways in Great Britain'. Among other things it provided for financial asssistance from the Treasury and from local authorities.

The choice of standard gauge for a light railway had several advantages. Motive power and rolling stock could be bought second-hand from larger companies, freight traffic could be worked through, to and from a main line without transhipment problems, and there was always the possiblity that a light railway might eventually be taken over by the main line with which it was connected. Often one or more of the light railway directors were also members of the board of a main-line company. This was the situation of the Culm Valley Light Railway in Devon, one of the first lines built under the relaxed requirements of the 1868 legislation. Its Chairman was a Bristol and Exeter director and that company worked the line from the beginning. Hopes that the Bristol and Exeter would eventually buy it on favourable terms were, however, frustrated by the fact that the B&E itself was taken over by the Great Western, which bought the Culm Valley line, but on less generous terms than its promoters had anticipated.

One name stands out in the history of light railways in Great Britain: that of Lieutenant-Colonel H. F. Stephens (1868–1931), whose diverse activities in this field earned him the title of 'the father of light railways'. His first venture was the construction and equipment of the narrow gauge Rye and Camber Tramway. Next he was involved with the standard gauge Hundred of Manhood and Selsey Tramway, another example of a light railway serving a coastal area bypassed by other lines. The territory was the Selsey peninsula, and the line ran from a terminus adjacent to the LB&SCR station in Chichester to Selsey Town, a distance of 7½ miles. It was a classic light railway with minimal engineering works, since it followed the contours of the ground for most part. Opened in 1897, it changed its name to the West Sussex Railway in 1924 when steps were taken to

line railway in miniature, but as well as having a 'small is beautiful' appeal it served a useful purpose on a stretch of coast without other railways. The roots of the Ravenglass and Eskdale Railway in Cumbria go deeper. Originally it was a 3 ft gauge line opened in 1875 to carry iron ore from Boot to the coast at Ravenglass. Tourist passenger traffic began a year later, but it gradually declined and the line was closed in 1913. The Ravenglass and Eskdale's revival and restoration as a 15 in. gauge tourist line, beginning in 1915, were inspired and accomplished by two famous figures in the world of miniature railways – W. J. Bassett-Lowke and Henry Greenly.

Standard gauge light railways

The term 'light railway' does not necessarily imply a narrow gauge line. When it was found egularize its unusual status with an Act of Parliament (its whole route was on private ground). A visitor to the line shortly before it was closed on 19 January 1935 reported that by that time 'the greater portion of the track was so overgrown with grass and weeds, in some places two or three feet high, as to be almost invisible'.

Since the end of World War I the railway had been paralleled by a bus route which took passengers to and from the centre of Chichester in considerably greater comfort. Travellers in that period were insensible to the charm of riding in old London Chatham and Dover rolling stock bought second-hand from the Southern Railway, and they preferred a bus on rubber tyres to the petrol-engined railbuses converted from road vehicles which were a Stephens speciality.

The list of light railways with which Stephens was associated as engineer, manager or consultant, or in other capacities, is extensive and shows how widespread his activities were: Rother Valley (later Kent and East Sussex), Sheppey Light, Bere Alston and Calstock, Burry Port and Gwendraeth Valley, Shropshire and Montgomeryshire, East Kent, and Weston Clevedon and Portishead. His reputation brought him the appointment of Civil Engineer and Locomotive Superintendent of the Festiniog and Welsh Highland Railways in 1923, and he became Chairman and Managing Director in 1925. The Welsh Highland had begun life in 1872 as the North Wales Narrow Gauge Railway and its main line extended eventually from Dinas Junction, on the LNWR line between Caernarvon and Afon Wen, to Porthmadog. It sustained a precarious existence until the middle 1930s, with some seasonal passenger traffic stimulated by through bookings from LMS stations to Welsh Highland and Festiniog destinations.

Originally the Kent and East Sussex Railway was 21½ miles long, connecting Headcorn (on the main line to Dover) with Robertsbridge (on the line from Tonbridge to Hastings). Its territory included Bodiam Castle, which brought it tourist traffic, and it operated road collection and delivery service for parcels. Stephens combined the posts of General Manager and Engineer of the Kent and East Sussex for many years.

Less successful than the Kent and East Sussex were the East Kent Light Railways, another Stephens system, which were planned to extend for some 56 route miles and serve a large area of Thanet. World War I held up construction and in the end only 19 miles of main line between Shepherdswell and Wingham Colliery were built, plus a branch line to the port of Richborough. In 1921 the branch carried an experimental train of ferry wagons bringing fruit from the south of France to Southwark, but this venture was not continued. Passenger service over the branch was discontinued in 1928. Both the Kent and East Sussex and the East Kent survived long enough to be taken over by British Railways in 1948, but were closed shortly afterwards, except for a short section of the East Kent serving Tilmanstone Colliery. Today four miles of the Kent and East Sussex between Tenterden Town and Wittersham Road are operated as a preserved line by the Tenterden Railway Company.

Below: On the Weston, Clevedon and Portishead, one of Colonel Stephens' light railways. Ex-LBSCR 'Terrier' 0-6-0T No. 4 is attached to a coach bought in 1899 from the Lancaster Wagon Co., which is believed to have built it for a cancelled South American railway order.

The
Grouping
Years

Chapter 16

The era of the big engine

IN THE DAWN of the twentieth century the large-boilered 4-4-0 was firmly established as the type of express locomotive most likely to be built in large numbers in the immediate future. But rising traffic and increasing train weights were already emphasizing that something bigger would soon be needed. During the closing years of the nineteenth century the GNR and the L&YR had introduced 4-4-2 Atlantic locomotives, and the NER had built some passenger 4-6-os which pointed the way to future development.

The next significant event came in 1902, when Ivatt built for the GNR his No. 251, an Atlantic with a much larger boiler and a wide firebox, more like that of the American Atlantics. With this feature but relatively small cylinders, No. 251 contrasted sharply with the final batch of Stirling 'eight-footers', which displayed the exact opposite. Blessed with such ample steam-raising capacity, No. 251 should never have 'run out of breath' however hard it was driven, and in general this was true of the large-boilered GNR Atlantics, but in the early days their performance was often disappointing. They were fast downhill and on the level, but were slow in acceleration and in climbing banks. On special occasions, such as a test run, they could put up a vigorous climb, but their everyday uphill work was often inferior to that of smaller 4-4-os. The remedy was to be found in the subsequent development of steam superheating.

In 1901 Wilson Worsdell of the NER built a large-wheeled version of his 4-6-0 for high-speed express work. Some of its initial performances were very promising, but in 1903 Worsdell switched in his No. 532 to an Atlantic larger than GNR No. 251, though with a narrow firebox. From then on the NER concentrated on Atlantics of several classes for fast express work and built 4-6-os mainly for mixed traffic duties.

The 4-6-0 concept was expanded to much larger proportions when in 1903 J. F. McIntosh of the Caledonian Railway built his Nos 49 and 50, which were essentially the Dunalastair 4-4-0 expanded into a six-coupled design. They were claimed to be Britain's largest and most powerful express engines and were intended for the heavy west coast expresses over the Carlisle-Glasgow route, which included the formidable Beattock Bank with its 10 miles of 1 in 75. In 1906 he built a slightly larger version still, the 903 or Cardean class. No. 903 *Cardean* was used almost every day on the 2pm express from Glasgow on the first stage of its journey to Euston and back from Carlisle on the corresponding train down. In everyday work *Cardean's* performance was reliable rather than sensational, but on a test in 1909 over the LNWR line between Carlisle and Preston, she was fully extended uphill and with a load of 390 tons passed Shap Summit in 18 minutes 30 seconds for the 13.6 miles from the Penrith start, sustaining a speed of 44 mph up the 1 in 125 gradient. No other parallel British feat in hillclimbing was on record in 1909; it must have required an output of some 1500 indicated horsepower. In the higher speed ranges, however, the first GWR 4-6-os very comfortably surpassed *Cardean*.

These first six-coupled express engines of the twentieth century were the highly publicized pride of their owners. But in fact there was little further development potential in the saturated steam engine with short-lap short-travel valves so far as express passenger work was concerned. When fully extended an engine like *Cardean* was burning coal at a faster rate than it was reasonable to expect any fireman to sustain for a length of time. That alone explains the contrast between the test running and everyday performance experienced with *Cardean* and GNR Atlantic No. 251.

The prospect of electrification

Where to go next, then? Electric traction had become a practical possibility and with street tramways already eroding suburban railway revenue some people were looking to main line electrification. In 1903 a scheme was floated for a new electric railway between London and Brighton, to operate at speeds far in excess of anything possible with steam. To counter its appeal, the LB&SCR ran a number of test runs with their B4 class 4-4-0 locomotives, culminating in a run from Victoria to Brighton, 51½ miles, in 48

Right: To mark the centenary of Doncaster works, the two preserved Ivatt GN Atlantics, LNER Class C2 No. 990 Henry Oakley and Class C1 No. 251, were steamed on a London–Doncaster excursion. They are seen here climbing out of Kings Cross on 20 September 1953.

Below: With its 7 ft 1 in. driving wheels, Wilson Worsdell's Class Q 4-4-0 design of 1896 for the North Eastern was clearly intended for speed, but this class was displaced from East Coast main-line work within a few years by the NER Atlantics. No. 1878 simmers at Newcastle soon after its first appearance from Gateshead works.

Above: Britain's first Pacific, Churchward's No. 111 The Great Bear of 1908 for the GWR, heads an afternoon Cheltenham express out of London to Swindon. The reason for construction of this unique engine remains a mystery—Churchward himself had no liking for it. Basically an enlarged 'Star' 4-6-0, not a design properly exploiting the wheel arrangement's potential, its performance was unimpressive and its lengthy wheel-base enforced the Pacific's restriction to the London–Bristol main line. In 1924 it was theoretically rebuilt as 'Castle' 4-6-0 No. 111 Viscount Churchill, but precious little of the original was actually re-used.

minutes 41 seconds with a maximum speed of 90 mph at Haywards Heath. The load was only 130 tons and the high speed was dearly bought, as the moderately-sized 4-4-0 locomotive *Holyrood* burnt 60 lb of coal per mile against the norm of about 45 lb in everyday service on slower but heavier trains. But no more was heard of the electric railway project for nearly thirty years.

In 1901 another scheme envisaged an electric railway to serve the north-east suburbs of London in competition with the GER. Its backers cited the superiority of electric acceleration, asserting that to reach 30 mph in 30 seconds from a standing start was beyond any steam locomotive. To disprove this, the GER's James Holden built a three-cylinder 0-10-0 tank engine with a boiler even larger than that on GNR No. 251. It is alleged that this engine, nicknamed the Decapod, reached 30 mph in 30 seconds from rest with 300 tons, though some people believe this weight included the 80-ton locomotive itself. Politically the Decapod was certainly a success, since the bill for the electric railway was defeated, but the 0-10-0 was too heavy for everyday service over the GER track of the time, and was converted into a 0-8-0 goods engine.

Locomotive experiments
Although the demise of the steam engine was confidently predicted from the day the first

electric train ran, and although it had defects which made its ultimate end inevitable, it was nevertheless a most adaptable machine which lasted far longer than the experts predicted. A locomotive such as *Cardean* or the GNR Atlantic No. 251 would normally consume 5 lb of coal to make one drawbar horsepower available to haul its train; under test conditions this might be reduced to 4 lb, but by the end of the first decade of the twentieth century there were

engines which could produce one drawbar horsepower for $3-3\frac{1}{2}$ lb of coal as a matter of course.

The need to reduce coal consumption was recognized by F. W. Webb well back in the nineteenth century but his attempts with his compound locomotives (where steam was effectively 're-cycled') met only limited success. Some of his compounds reached the brink of success but others were near-failures. A number of these fiascos were not the fault of compounding as such, but were caused by the use of uncoupled driving wheels or valves of inadequate size. When Webb was replaced by his LNWR successor, George Whale swept away the compounds, replacing them with engines of monumental simplicity. The most successful was probably the Precursor 4-4-0 class, which had a great capacity for hard work. The Experiment 4-6-0 class was rather more temperamental, but

Above: Until the Southern ran Bulleid's Pacifics it did not deploy enough six-coupled types to cover all the summer traffic on the Kent Coast main lines. Hence this 1936 Victoria–Dover train is double-headed by two ex-South Eastern and Chatham 4-4-0s.

Above: In the Great Central's final years its mechanical chief, J. G. Robinson, built both inside and outside cylinder express and mixed traffic 4-6-0s; LNER Class B8 No. 5443 was one of the latter.

Below: A West Coast route express in Scottish territory headed by one of J. F. McIntosh's beautiful 'Cardean' class 4-6-0s of 1906, No. 907. This was the luckless engine destroyed in the horrific Quintinshill disaster of 1915, when 217 died in a double collision and fire in the worst rail disaster experienced in Britain.

one reached over 1250 horsepower when on test against the Caledonian *Cardean*.

Locomotive coal was cheap and plentiful in Britain before World War I, but was not so in France. There the incentive to perfect the compound locomotive was much stronger, and some of the finest locomotive work in the world was being performed daily on the Nord Railway of France by the De Glehn compound Atlantics. Among British designers impressed by these engines was G. J. Churchward of the GWR, perhaps the greatest locomotive engineer Britain produced in the twentieth century. Churchward took a long hard look at locomotive practice all over the world before grafting the best features of others on to engines suitable for his own line. In particular he studied the work of Professor Goss at Purdue University in the United States who had established values worthy of wider acceptance.

Churchward aimed to equal the theoretical efficiency of a compound cylinder arrangement by obtaining a better steam expansion ratio in the cylinders of a simple locomotive. With this in mind he used long-lap long-travel valves. He also perfected a correctly proportioned boiler and

solved earlier than most of his contemporaries the problem of steam leakage past pistons and valves. For test purposes he brought to the GWR a Nord-type four-cylinder compound Atlantic and later two larger Paris-Orleans-type 4-4-2s. These he tested against his own two-cylinder simple 4-4-2s and 4-6-0s.

Churchward's aim was a drawbar pull of two tons at 70 mph, which his own engines exceeded just as the French compounds did. The 4-6-0s also proved to be as fast as the imported French Atlantics.

However, the French compounds with their four cylinders and better balancing proved to be much more smooth-riding than the GWR 4-6-0s, with the powerful thrusts of their two outside cylinders with 30 in. piston strokes. Accordingly, Churchward built an experimental four-cylinder Atlantic named *North Star* and followed this in 1907 with ten four-cylinder 4-6-0s. From then on he built more of the four-cylinder 4-6-0s and these took over much of the heavier work on the West of England main line. The variously named four-cylinder engines were grouped together under the class title of Star, while the two-cylinder engines were grouped together under the class title 'Saints'. Many drivers considered the Saints superior for hard slogging in poor conditions, but they appreciated the smoother riding of the Stars at high speeds. Both classes had the same boiler. Later the GWR tended to use four cylinders for high-speed express designs and two cylinders for mixed traffic duties. The GWR Atlantics were subsequently rebuilt as 4-6-0s and only the French compounds remained as 4-4-2s.

The compound engine commended itself to several engineers, but few British railways acquired more than a handful of experimental machines. H. A. Ivatt on the GNR built two four-cylinder compound Atlantics and bought one from Vulcan Foundry. On the NER the chief draughtsman W. M. Smith was allowed to build an experimental three-cylinder compound 4-4-0, No. 1619, and two four-cylinder Atlantics, Nos 730 and 731. These produced some impressive test performances which surpassed the work of the two-cylinder simple Worsdell Atlantics. However, when Vincent Raven took over on the NER he built some three-cylinder simple Atlantics of his own design. These proved to be very fast engines on the level road, though they were inclined to slip at starting and were never very vigorous uphill.

The three-cylinder Smith system of compounding was the one which was most multiplied in Britain. J. G. Robinson built five compound

Atlantics of this kind for the Great Central, but the style achieved its greatest success on the Midland. In 1903 Johnson built five large 4-4-0 compounds on the Smith system and these were added to by his successor, W. M. Deeley. In 1924 the Midland compound 4-4-0 was chosen by the LMS as a standard type and many more were built.

As the end of the first decade of the twentieth century approached there were two ways of increasing locomotive efficiency – compounding, or building rationally designed, simple locomotives on the Churchward pattern. Most locomotive engineers shrank from either solution. Consequently several large 4-6-0 designs, such as the Sir Sam Fay class on the GCR, the Drummond Paddleboxes on the LSWR and the Hughes four-cylinder 4-6-os of the L&YR were impressive-looking machines which showed little advantage in performance over smaller four-coupled engines.

The invention of superheating

Salvation came to the British steam locomotive with the invention of superheating, which had been pioneered by Dr Schmidt in Germany. By passing steam through superheater elements placed inside the flue tubes between firebox and smokebox, steam could be dried and condensation reduced. It was found that a superheated engine used something in the region of 25 per cent less coal and water to do the same work as one of the same class using saturated steam. Problems of lubrication had to be overcome and this delayed the general adoption of superheating, but nevertheless the new invention made considerable progress during the second decade of the twentieth century. Some classes of engine were transformed into performers of a much higher order; among them – as already mentioned – were the Atlantics of the GNR, NER and NBR.

Churchward, whose engines were good in their original form, obtained a more modest improvement from superheating. He compromised by using a moderate degree of superheat which gave some benefit and avoided the worst lubrication troubles. For many years this policy was the best for the GWR, but towards the end of World War II Swindon had to make changes to adapt their engines to unfavourable operating conditions. The LNWR, however, adopted high-temperature superheat from the start. In 1910 C. J. Bowen Cooke built for them a superheated version of the Precursor 4-4-0, named *George the Fifth*. Dr Schmidt had been consulted about valve design in Germany, which

Above: Midland compound 4-4-0 No. 1013 heads a Bedford semi-fast at St Pancras in the dying days of the LMS before the 1948 nationalization.

Above: Bowen Cooke's four-cylinder 'Claughton' 4-6-0s for the LNWR *were comparatively unsuccessful, being difficult to steam, prone to run hot and heavy on maintenance costs.* LMS *No. 5964* Patriot *was the* LNWR's *War memorial engine; it was photographed at Birmingham New Street in 1930.*

was in advance of contemporary British standards on all lines but the GWR, and the result was a locomotive capable of work out of all proportion to its size. The 'Georges' regularly worked trains of 400 tons or over on start-to-stop bookings of 55 mph south of Preston and took loads of up to 400 tons unaided over Shap.

The 'Georges' were so good that the case for a large locomotive seemed to be not proven, but Bowen Cooke was planning one. In 1911 he had built a superheated version of the saturated Experiments, the first of which was named *Prince of Wales* and was the forerunner of a very large class; then in 1913 Crewe produced a four-cylinder 4-6-0 named *Sir Gilbert Claughton*. The aim was a 4-6-0 at least the equal of the GWR Stars. Bowen Cooke rejected the high boiler pressure of 225 lb used by Churchward, but used much higher steam temperatures with 175 lb pressure. On occasions, such as the 1600 hp recorded on test by the Claughton class engine *Ralph Brocklebank*, the performance of the Stars was matched or even slightly surpassed but if points were awarded for consistency and economy in everyday service the honours would rest with Swindon.

Other advanced express locomotives

An express locomotive larger and potentially more powerful than any 4-6-0 had been built at Swindon in 1908. This was the four-cylinder giant No. 111 *The Great Bear*, Britain's first example of the 4-6-2 Pacific type. No. 111 pointed the way to future development but was, in many ways, ahead of its time. The civil engineers restricted its use to the Paddington–Bristol main line, so that in practice it was less useful than a Star or Saint class 4-6-0.

Just before the 1923 grouping Nigel Gresley (later Sir Nigel) of the GNR had built two Pacific locomotives for express service, and shortly afterwards Sir Vincent Raven of the NER also introduced a Pacific design. These were both three-cylinder 4-6-2s and they differed from *The Great Bear* since they were intended as prototypes for new classes rather than as a purely experimental exercise. Gresley was appointed Chief Mechanical Engineer of the new LNER group and chose his own Pacific for new construction; the NER Pacific did quite well in comparative trials, but the GNR design had more promise for future development.

Swindon had been proud to claim for its

Pacific the title of 'Britain's largest and most powerful passenger locomotive'. Gresley's Pacific notwithstanding, the GWR in 1923 still insisted it had the 'most powerful' type – but in the shape of a new four-cylinder 4-6-0 little bigger than a Star. Named *Caerphilly Castle*, it was the first of the long line of Castle 4-6-0s to be built for decades to come. The GWR based its claim on the very controversial qualification of theoretical tractive effort, but the LNER protested that boiler size was the true criterion of power. The argument gained maximum publicity when a GWR Castle and a LNER Pacific were exhibited side by side at the 1924 Wembley Exhibition, so early in 1925 exchange trials were arranged. The result was a triumph for Swindon, as the smaller GWR engine did its work on less coal both on its own line and on the LNER. Its better modified valve gear made the engines more free-running and more economical, and this was later standardized. Gresley also tried a higher boiler pressure of 220 lb against 180 lb; this was adopted for all new Pacifics and it was one of these, Class A3 No. 2750 *Papyrus*, which in 1935 reached a maximum speed of 108 mph in trials preparatory to introduction of the streamlined Silver Jubilee.

The year 1927 was an interesting one. The stage had been set when towards the end of 1926 the Southern Railway built a large four-cylinder 4-6-0, No. 850 *Lord Nelson*, which had a tractive effort higher than that of a GWR Castle. The Southern were quite justified on this basis in claiming that they had Britain's most powerful passenger locomotive, though it is doubtful if a Lord Nelson could at that time excel a Castle on

Below: In BR *days* GWR *'King' 4-6-0 No. 6003* King George IV *heads a Bath–Swindon stopping train.*

the road. However, in the summer of 1927 the GWR carried the 4-6-0 arrangement to what must have been close to its maximum possible size within the British loading gauge, with No. 6000 *King George V*. The GWR publicity department exploited No. 6000's tractive effort of over 40,000 lb by advertising the new engine as 'Britain's mightiest passenger locomotive'. The 30 King class engines did good service on the GWR almost to the end of steam.

The largest of the British groups, the LMS, had the most troubled locomotive history. Pacific locomotives had been proposed – first a four-cylinder simple by G. Hughes, the LMR's first Chief Mechanical Engineer, then a four-cylinder compound by Sir Henry Fowler. But the operating department favoured the Midland policy of frequent short trains, each with a 4-4-0 compound. This was unsuitable for the traffic pattern on the LNWR section and in 1926 the LMS at last accepted that something bigger was essential. They shrank from the complication of Fowler's compound Pacific and wanted something nearer in size to a GWR Castle 4-6-0. A Castle was therefore borrowed for trial running on the LMS towards the end of 1926 and in 1927 the LMS introduced their own large 4-6-0 design, the three-cylinder Royal Scot class, which was destined to do much hard work over the next 40 years. Midway in size between a GWR Castle and a King, the Scots were rebuilt towards the end of World War II with a taper boiler and double chimney, and in their rebuilt form were very powerful for their size.

In 1930 Sir Henry Fowler retired and after a short interval was replaced by a Great Western man, William (later Sir William) Stanier. Under Churchward, Stanier had become Assistant Works Manager at Swindon, and in that post he struck up a close liasion with Churchward's successor as Chief Mechanical Engineer, C. B. Collett, to whom he had become Works Assistant when the LMS made its overture to him. The new chief soon decided that a Pacific was needed for the heavy west coast Scottish expresses, and in 1933 he built No. 6200 *The Princess Royal*, which was in effect a GWR King expanded into a Pacific. It took some time and various modifications before complete success was achieved, but by 1935 the Princess class were very capable machines.

An unusual express engine, indeed one designed for a specialised role, was built by the LNER in 1934 for the steeply graded Edinburgh–Aberdeen road. This was 2-8-2 No. 2001 *Cock o' the North*. The six engines of this Gresley design did not achieve complete success and rightly or

wrongly, Gresley's successor Edward Thompson rebuilt them as Pacifics, but if the valid criterion of locomotive power is ability to start a heavy train at the foot of a steep gradient, then these 2-8-2s really did rank as Britain's most powerful express engines. There the British express locomotive had reached its greatest size, but its zenith of performance was still to come from further development of the LNER and LMS Pacifics.

Revolutionary designs

Some mention must be made of the various attempts to make a sensational improvement to the steam locomotive by revolutionary design. In 1930 the LNER built a 4-6-2-2 express engine using an adaption of the Yarrow water tube boiler which had proved successful in ships. This boiler raised steam at 450 lb/in² and it was used in a four-cylinder locomotive numbered 10000 and nicknamed the 'Hush Hush Engine'. It did some unremarkable work in ordinary service, including a run on the non-stop London–Edinburgh 'Flying Scotsman'. The

LMS built a modified Royal Scot, No. 6399 *Fury*, with a Schmidt-Henschel high-pressure boiler of 900 lb/in² in a three-cylinder compound layout. Unfortunately a fatal accident marred its trials and it never ran in revenue-earning service. Both this and LNER No. 10000 were subsequently re-built as conventional locomotives.

The most successful experimental locomotive ran on the LMS from 1935 onwards. This was No. 6202, nicknamed the 'Turbomotive'; it was in essence a Princess class Pacific with cylinders replaced by a simplified non-condensing turbine drive. It ran more revenue-earning miles than any other unconventional locomotive and recorded a marginally lower coal consumption than a Princess. This was not, however, enough to justify the retooling of Crewe works to build turbine engines.

Mixed traffic locomotives

While the express engine set the pace of locomotive design it was the goods and mixed traffic locomotive which earned much of the revenue. Between the wars the mixed traffic

Below: A Fowler 'Royal Scot' 4-6-0 of the LMS as originally built, without smoke deflectors. No. 6143 Mail, later named The South Staffordshire Regiment *was one of those named after early LNWR locomotives until 1935-6; it heads a West Coast route express circa 1930.*

locomotive became increasingly important. In the 1920s the 2-6-0 or Mogul type was built by all four groups for fast goods and secondary passenger duties, but in 1924 the modern mixed traffic 4-6-0 was introduced when one of the Saint class 4-6-0s of the GWR, *Saint Martin*, was rebuilt with smaller driving wheels of 6 ft diameter instead of 6 ft 8 ins. The aim was to increase the drawbar horsepower at moderate speeds without seriously affecting its possible maximum pace on favourable grades. The success of *Saint Martin* in service led to the building in 1928 of the first of the Hall class, which finally reached a total of 330 machines capable of turning their hands to almost any job on the GWR. In an emergency in 1955 No. 7904 *Fountains Hall* took over the up Bristolian and ran from Little Somerford to Paddington, 89.7 miles, in 72 minutes 10 seconds with a pass-to-pass average of 80 mph for 71.6 miles.

On the LMS the Stanier Black Fives, similar in size to the GWR Halls but diferent in detail, were multiplied to a total of 842 engines. They were equally successful and after nationalization formed the basis of the BR standard 73000 class of 172 engines. On the LNER Gresley followed a different policy, building the very large 2-6-2s of the V2 or Green Arrow class. These were capable of deputizing for a Pacific and proved most valuable at the head of 18–20 coach trains during World War II. However, their axle loading limited them to the main lines, and to deal with secondary traffic Sir Nigel Gresley built two smaller 2-6-2s of the Bantam Cock class which would have run almost anywhere. Hardly had the first of these entered service than Sir Nigel's death was announced.

His successor, Edward Thompson, preferred a two-cylinder 4-6-0 more like a Stanier Black Five. He built the first of these, LNER Class B1, in 1942 and they were eventually extended to a class total of 410 locomotives. Their performance on the road was similar to that of the LMS and GWR mixed traffic 4-6-0s.

Goods locomotives

From the earliest days the 0-6-0 had done most of the goods work, but it was outclassed for the heaviest duties by the 0-8-0 and 2-8-0 mineral engine. Between the wars the freight engine reached its maximum size but its maximum efficiency had to await the standard BR 9F 2-10-0 of the 1950s. In 1925 Gresley built two 2-8-2 goods engines using a Pacific boiler; these could work 1700-ton trains, but they were not multiplied, possibly because of the industrial

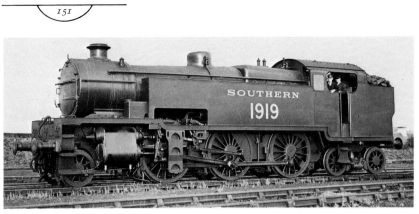

depression. He also built a 2-8-8-2 Garratt banking engine to assist coal trains up the very steep Worsborough bank in Yorkshire; this was definitely Britain's largest steam locomotive with a total weight of 178 tons. The LMS built some slightly smaller 2-6-6-2 Garratts for their Toton Brent coal trains, but with the decline of coal traffic in the depression they were frequently underemployed. The most generally useful freight engine proved to be the 2-8-0. During World War I the War Department built many 2-8-0s of the Great Central pattern for War Department use overseas, and in World War II the LMS Stanier pattern was similarly mass-produced along with an 'austerity' 2-8-0. A smaller number of 2-10-0s were also built, paving the way for a standard class in the post-war BR range.

Tank engines were always used for short-distance and suburban work, but for a brief period it seemed likely that they would perform a good deal of express work over moderate distances. Large express tank engines of the 4-6-4T or Baltic type were built by the LB&SC, LT&S, Furness, G&SW and L&Y Railways; these were in effect self-contained 4-6-0s. The 2-6-4T was the equivalent of the 2-6-0 mixed traffic engine. For a time this type was mistrusted for fast running following the derailment of an SR 2-6-4T of the River class at Sevenoaks in 1927, but later the 2-6-4T was held in high regard on the LMS, where maximum speeds of up to 90 mph were attained by engines of this wheel arrangement. Better valve and front end design made this fast running possible.

In the 39 years from 1900 to the outbreak of World War II the steam locomotive had doubled its maximum horsepower for only a 30 per cent increase in weight, and it had reduced its coal consumption per unit of work measured at the drawbar by about 40 per cent, yet it was still a wasteful user of fuel and it still demanded a great deal of dirty, unpleasant maintenance. Rival forms of power were becoming an increasing threat.

Above: Southern Class W 2-6-4T No. 1919, a three-cylinder type with high tractive effort built in 1931 to Maunsell's design for cross-London freight transfer duty.

Chapter 17

World War I and the grouping

Above: The coaching stock crest of the GWR- *one of the Big Four.*

THE STRATEGIC IMPORTANCE of Britain's railways was recognized at a fairly early stage, and in due course a railway line was considered to provide a reasonably secure route for the electric telegraph. In 1840 a Select Committee noted that 'the numerous servants of an established railway are available to protect the machinery required for this communication.' The Admiralty commissioned Cooke and Wheatstone to provide a telegraph line between the Admiralty and Gosport along the London and South Western Railway, and it shared the expense of the installation with the LSWR.

Since the Napoleonic wars ended in 1815

Britain had tried to avoid direct involvement in the turbulent affairs of the other great powers, except for a brief interlude in the Crimea. But by the turn of the century the rise and ambitions of the new German Empire were causing concern. As early as 1871, in fact, a section of the Regulation of the Forces Act empowered the government to take control of the railways in a national emergency, and 1912 saw the formulation of a Railway Executive Committee – consisting of the railway general managers – to run the railway as one system in case of need.

The need came swiftly in August 1914, and in one sustained effort over 16 days the railways

conveyed the British Expeditionary Force and its equipment to Southampton for the crossing to France. In eight days of August 69,000 men, 22,000 horses and 2500 guns with all their associated baggage passed through the port, and the flow continued on the same scale until the job was complete. On 4 August, when war was declared, plans were in existence for the conversion of rolling stock to form ambulance trains, but none had actually been built. By the end of the month twelve of these trains were ready. Lord Kitchener, the commander-in-chief, declared that the railway companies had more than justified the complete confidence placed in them by the War Office. Every unit had arrived in France 'well within the scheduled time'.

Below: The first of the controversial Highland Railway 'River' class 4-6-0s, originally named River Ness, *built in 1915. It is seen in the 1930s as* LMS *No. 14756. This engine was scrapped in 1939, but two of the class survived World War II.*

The Railway Executive Committee had under its control 130 railway companies or joint committees and 21,331 miles of route. The Irish railways were added in 1917. Railway staff at the outbreak of war numbered around 600,000 of whom more than 30 per cent joined the forces. To the shortage of men at home were added other problems created by wartime traffic requirements. The Highland Railway was sorely overtaxed by the special trains which had to be run to Thurso for provisioning the fleet at Scapa Flow, but under the centralized wartime management it was able to borrow locomotives from other companies and have its own repaired by outside contract.

The Highland locomotive shortage was the background to one of the puzzles of locomotive history. Shortly before the war the company had decided to introduce additional locomotives to supplement its 4-6-0s of the Castle class. A new 4-6-0 design was prepared by the company's locomotive, carriage and wagon Superintendent, F. G. Smith, and a contract for building six of the new class was awarded to Hawthorn, Leslie and Co. of Newcastle-upon-Tyne. While the locomotives were under construction it was decided to name them after Scottish rivers.

The first of the River class was delivered to Perth in 1915, by which time the Highland was in the thick of its wartime difficulties. The Board had already had a meeting with the Railway Executive Committee to ask for help from other companies. Far from helping to relieve the situation, the arrival of the first River plunged the company into a domestic crisis. When the locomotive was handed over to the engineer's department to calculate the stresses it would impose on bridges, the chief engineer, Alexander Newlands, refused to accept it because the axle load was higher than the one he

was led to expect. Smith was summoned before the Board. He admitted that he had failed to notice a draughtsman's omission in the drawings and took the entire blame on himself. The Board demanded his resignation, which he submitted without further ado. The six River class locomotives were sold to the Caledonian Railway – at a profit, it is said – and Smith left railway service, never to return.

The extent of the weight error and the true motives for Smith's dismissal remained in doubt for a long time. Evidence that has come to light in recent years suggests it was about $1\frac{3}{4}$ tons per driving axle. It seems probable that although Smith had communicated the original figure to Newlands, he had not discussed with him a revised figure received from the contractor when the design was gone through in detail. For its part, the Highland Board probably did not enjoy having to ask for help from the REC, particularly when the appeal revealed a serious backlog of heavy repairs in its own works, and they may have been tempted to put the whole blame for this situation as well as the River class weight error on Smith. He himself remained silent, but his wife continued to maintain that if he had had a 'Mac' in front of his name his treatment would have been different. Newlands became chief engineer of the London, Midland and Scottish Railway in 1927.

Assisted by motive power from other companies, the Highland nobly fulfilled the task of conveying fuel, materials and men for the fleet in its far northern anchorages, working heavy trains over its steeply graded main lines, much of them single-track. The lengthy coal trains to Thurso are remembered in the railway history of World War I as the 'Jellicoe Specials', after Admiral Jellicoe.

Passenger services were curtailed during the war and efforts were made to reduce civilian travel, but without much effect. Many restaurant cars were taken off but this amenity never disappeared entirely. As the climax approached in 1917 cheap fares were abolished, ordinary fares increased by 50 per cent, and train services drastically cut. Even these measures had relatively little effect in persuading the general public not to travel.

The aftermath – grouping
Government control of the railways continued after the Armistice of 11 November 1918 and was not removed until 15 August 1921. Grants were paid towards abnormal maintenance costs arising from wartime traffic, but the sums due

Above: The Far North of the LMS *in May 1928. No. 14676 Ballindalloch Castle, of Drummond's Highland Railway, enters The Mound, junction for the Dornoch branch.*

Below: The whole LNWR *class of 'Prince of Wales' 4-6-0s (totalling 245 engines) survived intact until 1933. In this 1930s picture* LMS *No. 25804 heads freight at Wavertree, Liverpool.*

were disbursed slowly and in the case of the North British Railway the sum claimed was challenged by the Ministry of Transport, which had been formed in 1919. The first Minister was Sir Eric Geddes, a former Deputy General Manager of the North Eastern Railway who had held several important government offices during the war. He now faced the North British Chairman, William Whitelaw, (later the first LNER Chairman), in a lengthy dispute which ended with the North British receiving £9,790,545 as against the sum of £10,681,243 which the railway had calculated was the total government debt. It was an expensive con-

frontation in terms of legal costs and certainly damaged the government's reputation in the eyes of other railways which had watched the argument pursue its slow and costly course. Eventually £60 million was allotted to be shared between the companies.

Demands for nationalization of the railways had been heard during the war, and the post-war government was aware of various useful measures of standardization and rationalization which centralized control had made it possible to implement. Politically, however, it was opposed to all-out nationalization in peacetime, and it envisaged instead wholesale amalgamations. Sir Eric Geddes was asked to prepare a scheme, which was embodied in the Railways Act of 1921. By this Act 120 railway companies found themselves reorganized as four groups and the change was to take effect on 1 January 1923.

The companies had not been consulted. If they had been, some of the anomalies of the grouping might have been removed, such as penetrations by one group into the territory of another, which were simply a leftover from early adventures by individual companies – for example the London and North Western to gain a foothold in south Wales, and the Great Central's meanderings through the south Midlands.

The principal members of the new groups were known as the 'constituent companies' and the others which joined with them as 'subsidiary companies'.

The London Midland and Scottish group

Largest of the groups was the London Midland and Scottish, whose eight constituents were the London and North Western; Midland; Lancashire and Yorkshire; North Staffordshire; Furness; Caledonian; Glasgow and South Western; and the Highland. With 27 subsidiary companies the group totalled about 7,500 route-miles, and it was always the senior of the major companies. Among the subsidiaries was the London, Tilbury and Southend, which joined the LMS because it had been taken over by the Midland in 1912.

The London and North Western and the Lancashire and Yorkshire had been close allies for years, and they anticipated the grouping by amalgamating on 1 January 1922. There were also close operating ties between the London and North Western and the North Staffordshire. Although the latter was a very distinct personality in its own territory, it is doubtful whether many travellers from Euston to Manchester in

an express routed via Stoke-on-Trent realized that at Colwich they passed on to North Staffordshire metals, rejoining the LNWR at Stockport. As a consequence of earlier London and North Western and Midland ventures in Ireland, the LMS also acquired the Northern Counties Committee and the Dundalk, Newry and Greenore Railways.

The London and North Eastern group

Just as the LMS was essentially built round the west coast route to Scotland, the London and North Eastern group had the east coast route as its backbone. Its seven constituent companies were the North Eastern; Great Northern; Great Eastern; Great Central; Hull and Barnsley; North British; and Great North of Scotland. With 26 subsidiaries its route mileage was around 6,700. Like the L&YR and the LNWR, the North Eastern and the Hull and Barnsley had merged on 1 January 1922. There had been some debate over what to do with the Great Central, whose cross-country main line in the north extended from LMS into LNE territory,

while its London main line served what were really the Midland preserves of Leicester, Nottingham and Sheffield. For the LNER it was something of a liability, although in the later 1930s it proved useful as a relief route for overnight reduced-fare services between London and the north-east.

The Great Western group

The Great Western Railway was the only line that effectively remained intact, retaining its name and its previous structure. The seven constituents were the parent company and the larger Welsh systems: Barry; Cambrian; Rhymney; Taff Vale; Cardiff; and the Alexandra (Newport and South Wales) Docks and Railways.

Twenty-six subsidiaries fell into the net, many of them long since 'Great Westernized' in appearance and practice. The cross-country lines which came into the group were the Didcot, Newbury and Southampton and the Midland and South Western Junction. The former had always been worked by the Great Western. It did not, in fact, reach Southampton, but after pass-

*Above: An early post-grouping view of Kings Cross, when carriage sidings still filled the centre of the departure side. Ex-*GC *Class B3 4-6-0 No. 1164* Earl Beatty *prepares to leave with the Harrogate Pullman. These engines were allegedly given the London–Leeds Pullman jobs in 1923-27 because the* LNER *appointed an ex-*GC *man as its Southern Area Running Superintendent.*

Above: This photograph was used for an SR *poster which became one of the best-known in British railway advertising history. Under Sir Herbert Walker the* SR *was, in 1924, the first railway to establish a Public Relations department. To head it, Walker appointed a Fleet Street journalist who later chaired the* BR *Railway Executive and London Transport– Sir John Elliot.*

ing through its own station in Winchester made an end-on junction with the LSWR near Shawford. The Midland and South Western Junction branched from the Midland at Andoversford, near Cheltenham, and ran southwards to join the LSWR near Andover Junction, passing through Swindon *en route*, where it had its own station, Swindon Town (Swindon GWR was officially Swindon Junction).

In 1875 the Great Western had been annoyed at the leasing of the Somerset and Dorset Joint line to the London and South Western and Midland Railways. Now it had its own link for through traffic between the LMS and the Southern. In its independent days the MSWJ had obtained running powers to Southampton, and its trains from Cheltenham conveyed through carriages originating in Sheffield, Manchester and Bradford. Similar services continued after grouping but never on the scale of the through trains over the Somerset and Dorset. In round figures the Great Western route mileage was 3,800.

The Southern group

The smallest group in route mileage (about 2,200 route-miles) was the Southern, whose constituents were the London and South Western; the South Eastern and Chatham; and the London, Brighton and South Coast, with 14 subsidiary companies to make up the group. The SECR was in fact a joint committee formed on 1 August 1899 to work the lines of the South Eastern and the London, Chatham and Dover Railways, both companies continuing in being until the grouping, after years of comical squabbling over the limited traffic available in Kent, which did neither the slightest good. The London and Greenwich Company, which had opened the first railway in London in 1836, actually survived until the 1923 grouping.

What the Southern lacked in mileage it made up for in its density traffic in the south-east of England and the ever-spreading London suburban area south of the Thames. All three constituent companies had suburban electrification in hand or in operation at the date of grouping, and under the new management this was pressed forward until the Southern electric system reached the coast. The group had its prestige services in the Continental boat trains and the Southern Belle all-Pullman express to Brighton. These SECR and LB&SCR services were relatively short-distance, but the London and South Western had a delightful main line to the West Country with trains giving a through service from Waterloo to a number of well-known resorts in Devon and Cornwall. In 1925 the 11.00 am from Waterloo was named the Atlantic Coast Express (ACE), giving the Southern a much more romantic image in the public mind than it could have hoped to acquire from its mundane commuter operations.

The effect of grouping

Transition from the old organizations to the new varied in smoothness from group to group. The Great Western was little affected. On the Southern the former General Manager of the LSWR, Sir Herbert Walker, filled the same post for the group and took the other constituents along with him in the policy of electrification he had already begun. The LB&SCR was obliged to drop the system of alternating current overhead electrification it had adopted, in order to conform with its new partners, but this was in line with the recommendations of various committees which had considered the future of railway electrification and been insistent on the need for through running between different lines.

The LNER chose a system of devolved management, dividing its system into Southern, North Eastern and Scottish areas with an area manager in each under the general direction of headquarters in London.

Things went less smoothly on the LMS, where rivalries between the constituent companies lasted for a decade. On the motive power side, George Hughes of the Lancashire and Yorkshire was appointed Chief Mechanical Engineer of the LMSR (largely as a compromise candidate between the LNWR and the Midland) but Crewe, Derby and St Rollox (on the Caledonian) carried on much as before. When Hughes retired in 1925, however, Sir Henry Fowler, who had been Chief Mechanical Engineer at Derby, took over and launched a programme of LMS locomotive standardization. As older and non-standard locomotives were discarded they were replaced by further models of what were considered the best of the remaining designs. In practice this meant that Midland types predominated, and the Midland had been a small-engine railway much given to double-heading with 4-4-0s.

In the end the LMS found itself lacking adequate power to work trains of increasing weight, and the need for a new six-coupled design became urgent. After a Castle class 4-6-0 was borrowed from the Great Western Railway in 1926 and had shown itself master of the work it was given, an LMS 4-6-0 design was

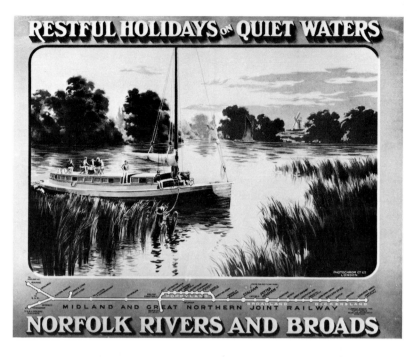

RESTFUL HOLIDAYS ON QUIET WATERS

MIDLAND AND GREAT NORTHERN JOINT RAILWAY

NORFOLK RIVERS AND BROADS

somewhat hastily put together and a contract for 50 locomotives placed with the North British Locomotive Co. Ltd. These were the three-cylinder Royal Scots, and they did much good work until with the appointment of W. A. (later Sir William) Stanier from Swindon as Chief Mechanical Engineer in 1932 a new era of LMS locomotive design began. From then on, withdrawals of the older locomotives were balanced by the introduction of new classes designed for the prevailing traffic conditions. The conflict between the small engine policy of the Midland and the large engine necessities of the 'Premier Line' was perhaps the most bitter in the history of 20th century railways. The two companies – two of the original 'big three' – were essentially incompatible and this was the great failure of the grouping.

The four main-line groups were soon popularly referred to as 'the Big Four'. Excluded at first were the Cheshire Lines Committee; the Midland and Great Northern; and the Somerset and Dorset, all of which were joint undertakings and not covered by the 1921 Act. The Cheshire Lines Committee remained as an undertaking even after nationalization, not losing its identity until 30 November 1948, but the Midland and Great Northern Railway was absorbed into the LNER in 1936. Up to grouping the Somerset and Dorset had been leased, but in 1923 Parliamentary powers were obtained for it to be transferred to the Southern and London Midland and Scottish companies jointly. Like the Midland and Great Northern, it therefore became a part of British Railways on 1 January 1948.

Above: A Midland and Great Northern Joint Railway poster. The M&GN was an 1895 amalgam of several small companies that mushroomed on the northern rim of the GER and eventually came under joint Midland and Great Northern ownership. This was perpetuated by LMS and LNER from 1923 to 1936, when the LNER assumed full control.

Chapter 18

Enter the electric railway

PUBLIC TRANSPORT BY electric railway in Great Britain began on the sea front at Brighton on 4 August 1883. The builder and operator of the line was Magnus Volk, an electrical engineer and inventor, and the project was begun by a chance combination of circumstances. In 1880 Volk had lit his house by electricity, installing a gas engine and dynamo to supply the power. In the following year he moved to a new house where mains electricity was available and his generating set went into store. Also in store was an electric motor which Volk had built for a London firm who had subsequently cancelled the order. In this equipment, prompted perhaps by memories of Werner von Siemens' demonstration of an electric line in Berlin in 1879, he saw the nucleus of an electric railway.

At the beginning of 1883, Volk applied to Brighton Council for permission to lay a line along the beach, next to the promenade, from the Brighton Aquarium to the old Chain Pier. He was given a trial period and had his little railway running in time for the Bank Holiday crowds. There were later extensions, and the local press commented approvingly that the railway was becoming a 'real means of locomotion and not a mere amusement'. It has continued to serve the

public ever since except for interruptions caused by weather or war.

Electrification in the north

The 1880s were a period of rapid electrical development. Volk, like Siemens, had generated power for his line at the low voltage used by the traction motor. This would have become uneconomic when power had to be transmitted over some distance, but very soon electricity was being distributed as alternating current at high voltage. This principle was used in all later electrifications by the main-line railway companies, most of whom installed sub-stations along their routes where the high-voltage AC was converted to low-voltage direct current before being fed to the trains. 'High' and 'low' are relative terms in this context. Volk's first electric car operated at 110 volts. Most of the later British electrified mileage was supplied at voltages between 600 and 700 volts.

The first of the main-line companies to introduce electric traction were the North Eastern and the Lancashire and Yorkshire. Both took the step, as others were to do later, because of tramway competition. The NER estimated that

Below: An impression of Magnus Volk's electric railway along the Brighton foreshore at its opening in 1883.

Above: Motor coach of the Midland's Lancaster, Morecambe and Heysham line of 1908, the first in Britain to use high-voltage AC electrification. The line later became a test-bed for BR's main-line AC electrification practice.

the Tyneside Tramways route between Gosforth, Wallsend and North Shields was taking about a third of the railway traffic in that area. The company therefore embarked on a scheme of electrifying its coastal and inland suburban lines north of the Tyne, and on 29 March 1904 inaugurated the first section, between New Bridge Street station, Newcastle, and Benton.

Electrification reached the coast on 1 July of the same year and eventually the North Tyneside electrified system formed a circular route from Newcastle to Wallsend, Tynemouth, Cullercoats, Whitley Bay and back via South Gosforth and Benton. A short section of the slow tracks of the east coast main line was included, which enabled the LNER to claim in later years that it owned the first electrified main line in the country. The North Tyneside lines were electrified at 600v DC. New Bridge Street station was later demolished and the station at Manors extended to take the electric trains.

On the other side of the country the Liverpool–Southport traffic of the Lancashire and Yorkshire Railway had reached the maximum which could be handled with steam traction at Liverpool Exchange station. A proposal to electrify the Liverpool–Southport line at 630v DC was approved in 1902, and a year later the section from Southport to Crossens was added to the scheme to serve a large residential area around the resort which had previously been dependent on a steam shuttle service to and from Southport. A partial electric service was begun in March 1904 but

steam trains were not withdrawn until May of that year. For a time, indeed, they had replaced the electrics completely while problems with the foundations at the generating station were being attended to.

In 1905 a connection was opened from Seaforth and Litherland to Seaforth Sands on the Liverpool Overhead Railway, and a service of L & Y trains of special lightweight stock was operated between Southport and Dingle at the southern end of the Liverpool Overhead Railway. Normally LOR trains did not run through to Southport, but terminated at Seaforth and Litherland L & Y station.

Between 1905 and 1913 electrification was extended over the main line to Preston as far as Ormskirk. A connection enabled LOR trains to join this route and from 1914 they worked through as far as Aintree on Grand National day, later adding a service to the course itself on 'Jump Sunday'.

Rolling stock and types of electrification

Although electric locomotives were used in the early days of London Underground electrification, the main-line railways worked their electric suburban services from the beginning with motorcoach stock. At first, all the traction motors in train formations with two motorcoaches were controlled directly from the controller in the leading driving cab, which carried the whole traction current. Later the multiple-unit system

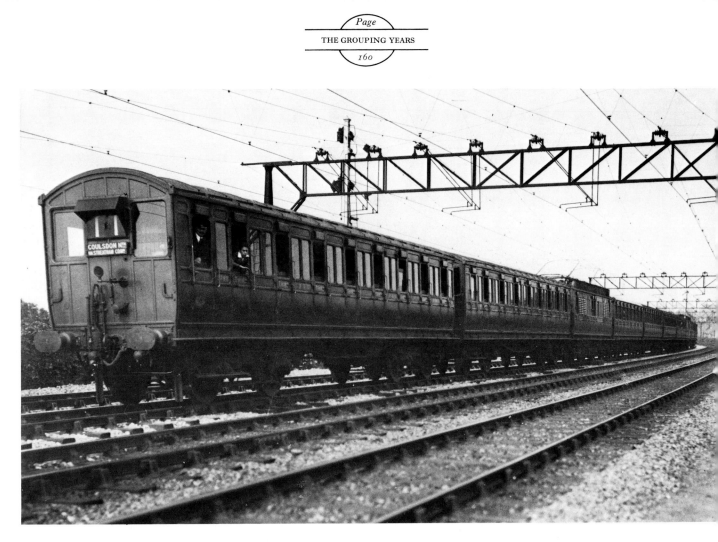

was introduced, in which the power equipments of every motorcoach were independent, but worked in unison, as they were interconnected by a low-voltage control circuit carrying electrical signals from the master controller in the cab of the leading vehicle. Because motorcoaches and trailers are usually assembled in fixed formations, or units, and trains may be composed of several of these units according to traffic requirements, this arrangement is called the 'multiple-unit system' and such a train is referred to for short as an 'emu' (electric multiple-unit).

Two electrifications which followed in 1908 and 1909 were on very different lines from those of the North Eastern and the Lancashire and Yorkshire. When the Midland Railway electrified its lines between Lancaster, Morecambe and Heysham it chose alternating current at 6,600V with collection from an overhead wire. The supply was transformed down to a lower voltage in the motorcoaches and fed, still as alternating current, to the traction motors (high-voltage AC electrification of this kind was being developed successfully on the Continent and in the United States at the time). The traction motors were similar to those in DC trains, although a little more complicated mechanically. If it had been possible to use alternating current at the same

frequency as the supplies generated for industrial and domestic users this system would no doubt have gone ahead rapidly, but for good traction motor performance in low speed and high current conditions it was necessary to use a frequency below the standard of 50 cycles per second (now referred to as 50 Hertz, contracted to Hz). The Midland Railway therefore generated its own supply at 25 Hz.

Throughout the later history of electric traction the relative advantages of generating a special-frequency AC supply at high voltage, with resulting economy in distribution, or using an industrial frequency supply and rectifying it to provide DC have been debated at length. Continuous technical development in both systems has held the balance even. Even now that main lines can be electrified with AC at 50 Hz drawn from national electricity supply systems, countries with established low-frequency AC systems have generally retained them.

The Lancaster–Morecambe–Heysham electrification opened in April 1908. This first British attempt at alternating-current traction was followed by a similar but eventually much larger undertaking. The London, Brighton and South Coast Railway decided to respond to tramway competition by electrifying its South London line between London Bridge and Victoria. The railway also had in mind eventual electrification of its main line to Brighton, and for that reason chose 6,700v AC at 25Hz with overhead collection. Electric services between London Bridge and Victoria began on 1 December 1909. From 1903 to 1908 the number of passengers on the South London line had fallen from eight million to three million, but the impact of electrification was swift and by 1910 the numbers had already risen again to eight million, attracted by the new, efficient, 'clean' system.

The South London line was an inner area electrification, serving places such as Brixton and Denmark Hill. The next stage, coming into operation on 12 May 1911, made a wider sweep through Clapham Junction, Balham and Crystal Palace, later reaching Norwood Junction and Selhurst. Further extensions were deferred on the outbreak of World War I. They were eventually carried out after grouping, reaching Coulsdon on the main line to Brighton, and Sutton on the line to Dorking and Horsham. By that time the days of the AC system in southern England were numbered.

Other schemes around London continued slowly in the war years. The London and North Western Railway began its 630v DC electrification with the opening of the Willesden to Earls Court electrification on 1 May 1914 and completed Broad Street to Richmond on the old North London line in October 1916. In the previous year the London Electric Railway (better known as the Bakerloo tube) had extended its service from Baker Street to Willesden via Queens Park. Electrification continued northward alongside the main line to Watford, and in 1917 the LER and the LNWR began a joint service over this section, which is still in existence today. Electrification throughout between Euston, Broad Street and Watford was completed in July 1922, including the branch from Watford to Croxley Green. The Rickmansworth branch was electrified in 1927.

The start of electric locomotive traction
Over the years various committees discussed electrification in Great Britain, but in terms of which DC voltages to adopt as standard rather than choice between DC or AC system. Although for many years the electrified lines were widely scattered, the committees were much concerned with inter-running in the future, and in general terms favoured a higher voltage for main-line use which should be a convenient multiple of the voltage used on suburban systems – for example 1,500v and 750v.

In 1915 the North Eastern Railway had opened a 1,500v DC electrification with overhead contact wire between Shildon and Newport, Co. Durham. Its purpose was to transport coal from the Bishop Auckland area to the Erimus marshalling yard at Newport and it was the first major example of electric locomotive traction in the country. Ten four-axle locomotives of 1,100 hp were built to a design that included a central cab and 'bonnets' fore and aft under which the control gear was housed. One of the locomotives on test hauled a 1,400-ton train on the level at 25 mph and averaged 23 mph up a 1 in 230 gradient with 800 tons; a stop-and-restart test with the 800 tons load on an up-grade of 1 in 103 showed a maximum drawbar pull of 16 tons.

Unusually for electric locomotives at that period, the Newport–Shildon units were provided with step-by-step control plus automatic acceleration. Instead of advancing his controller notch by notch and watching his meters to maintain a steady current, the driver could move the handle straight to full power. This action wound a spring which made the control drum follow the handle, but it could only do so in steps because it was restrained by an escapement mechanism. The escapement was controlled by

Above: Original LNWR *open saloon multiple-units, still in* LNWR *livery, form a Broad Street–Richmond train near Acton in August 1925.*

Above: The NER *aimed
to electrify its main line
from York to Newcastle
and as a test-bed it
opened electric working
at* 1.5kv DC *overhead
between its West
Durham, Shildon, and
Erimus, Teesside, yards
in* 1915. *The line's locomotives are congregated
in their Shildon depot
in* 1927.

a relay. Each time the motor current during acceleration fell to a pre-set value, the relay operated to release the escapement and allow the drum to move one step. A switch in the relay coil circuit gave the driver the choice of a higher rate of acceleration when load and rail conditions were suitable.

The Shildon–Newport locomotives trundled their heavy loads efficiently for 20 years accepted in their environment but attracting surprisingly little notice elsewhere. For photographers, in particular, they seem to have had little appeal and to the average traveller on the east coast main line the Newport–Shildon line was little more than a brief glimpse of gantries at an overbridge near Aycliffe. Coal traffic on the line was badly hit by the coal strike of 1921 and did not resume its former levels. Electric working was abandoned in 1935.

Newport–Shildon was not the first NER line worked by electric locomotives. In 1905 the company electrified its short and steep branch from Newcastle Central to quays below alongside the Tyne, using 600v DC as on the suburban lines. Two small four-axle locomotives were built for transfer traffic and shunting on the quays, and one of them has been preserved in the National Railway Museum at York. The longest-lived survivor of the Newport–Shildon locomotives

was one which was reconditioned after World War II for shunting duties at Ilford car sheds; it was withdrawn in 1964 and scrapped.

The technical success of electric traction on the Newport–Shildon line encouraged the North Eastern Railway to consider electrifying its main line from York to Newcastle. Provisional approval was given in 1919. By this time a 1,200v DC system with current collection from a protected third rail was operating on the Lancashire and Yorkshire Railway between Manchester and Bury, and there have been suggestions that the NER also envisaged at one time a third-rail system but at 1,500v.

Eventually, however, orthodox overhead current collection was decided upon and an express passenger locomotive was built at Darlington to the designs of the NER Chief Mechanical Engineer, Vincent (later Sir Vincent) Raven. The locomotive, No. 13, was completed in 1922, but Grouping was pending and the main line project was shelved. The first CME of the LNER, H. N. (later Sir Nigel) Gresley, was less of an enthusiast for electrification than Raven, who had entered deeply into the question with the electrical industry of his day.

The Quayside and Newport–Shildon locomotives had been power-bogie designs with axle-hung motors. No. 13 was an electric locomotive in the grand manner with a fixed driving wheelbase and traction motors inside the body. The wheel arrangement corresponded to a 4-6-4 in steam notation and the 6 ft-8 in. diameter driving wheels had a distinctly steam locomotive look. The six 300hp traction motors were mounted in pairs, each pair geared to a hollow shaft enclosing the corresponding driving axle. Torque was transmitted from the shaft to the driving wheels by springs pressing against the spokes. With this arrangement the driving axles could move vertically or laterally with the action of the suspension without disturbing the meshing of the gears. It has been picturesquely said of No. 13 that: 'On starting the giant helical springs which pressed on the spokes would suddenly compress. Then she would move away with startling acceleration – thrilling, occult and swift.'

Unfortunately there were few opportunities to enjoy the spectacle. There were some trial runs on the Newport–Shildon line in 1922, and in 1925 No. 13 took part in the procession of motive power at the railway centenary celebrations, when she was propelled by a steam locomotive. Those splendid 6 ft 8 in. driving wheels were not to spin again under their own power, for No. 13

went into store. Proposals that it should re-emerge in the 1950s for the Manchester–Sheffield–Wath electrification were unfulfilled. Renumbering as LNER No. 6999 in 1946 had been a mere formality, as was the further re-numbering as BR No. 26600, under which insignia the erstwhile No. 13 was towed to a breaker's yard for scrapping in 1950.

Third-rail systems

A break with the usual pattern of DC electrification in Britain occurred in 1913 when the Holcombe Brook branch of the Lancashire and Yorkshire Railway was electrified between Bury and Holcombe Brook at 3,500v overhead by the firm of Dick, Kerr, which was looking for experience with high-voltage DC in the light of a possible contract in South America. Two 800hp motorcoaches and two trailers were built and equipped for the service, which began on 29 July 1913. The LYR described the trains as 'much more comfortable and airy than a tram' – evidently with a sidelong glance at the opposition – and traffic built up well.

The LYR was planning electrification of several lines in the Manchester area, but it

Below: In June 1927 a mineral train leaves Shildon behind one of the 10 ex-NER 1100hp Bo-Bo locomotives. A coal slump made electric working uneconomic and steam returned to the line in 1935. The locomotives were stored by the LNER but scrapped by BR without resuming work.

considered that overhead construction would be unduly complicated in the network of lines near the city. It therefore chose a third-rail system, but adopted 1,200v instead of going into the more usual 600–700v range. At this voltage the live rail had to be protected by a continuous wooden casing with a gap through which the current collector shoe could make contact with the rail. The shoe was a plate projecting downward from the motorcoach bogie through the gap contacting the rail at the side instead of riding on top of it, as was the usual practice with an unprotected rail. In top-contact systems the shoes normally rely on their own weight for effective contact pressure, but in the Manchester –Bury arrangement the pressure had to be provided by a spring.

Electric operation between Manchester Victoria and Bury began on 7 April 1916. The Bury–Holcombe Brook line was converted to the same system, and third-rail working at 1,200v began on 29 March 1918. Although Bury–Holcombe Brook saw its last electric trains on 24 March 1951, and was closed entirely on 4 May 1952 after a period of steam operation, the Manchester–Bury line has retained its non-standard DC system. There were thoughts of changing it to high-voltage AC after

British Railways adopted that system as the future standard in 1956, but new rolling stock was urgently needed and it was decided to build more trains for the existing system rather than undertake conversion and redesign.

In the south-east of England the ever-spreading suburbs, with much of their population working in London, began to be served by a network of electrified lines which contrasted with the pattern of widely dispersed and self-contained systems elsewhere in the country. The LBSCR had made a start in 1909, and on 25 October 1915 the London and South Western Railway electrified from Waterloo to East Putney as the first step in a widespread conversion of its suburban services. Before the work was undertaken, the Electrical Engineer of the LSWR had visited the United States to study how it was done over there, and after further consultation with British experts on his return he recommended third-rail electrification at 660v DC. It was a momentous choice, for it settled the form of the post-war Southern Railway electrification. Under its General Manager, Sir Herbert Walker, the LSWR pushed rapidly ahead with its network of electrified suburban lines, and when in 1923 Sir Herbert became General Manager of the Southern

Below: For the inaug-uration of the SR's Brighton main line electrification in 1933, the Pullman Car Com-pany had three five-car all-Pullman multiple-units built for the 'Brighton Belle' service, One is seen here south of Quarry Tunnel, Merstham.

Left: The interior of an early twentieth century coach on the City and South London Railway, which was opened in 1890. It was the first practical underground electric Tube railway in the world.

Railway he pursued a similar policy for all sections of the Group.

A committee under Sir Alexander Kennedy had reported on railway electrification in 1920. It had before it detailed proposals from the LBSCR for extending its AC system to Brighton, but grouping was impending and in the light of the extent of the LSWR third-rail electrification, and the fact that installation of a similar system on the South Eastern and Chatham lines was imminent, the committee recommended reconsideration of the Brighton company's plans, stressing the need for inter-running between different electrified sections of the Southern Group. Although after grouping the LBSCR section of the Southern Railway opened further extensions of its AC electrification, the Southern management decreed in 1926 that the whole of the overhead system should be converted to third rail. The last AC trains on the Brighton section ran in 1929. Under Sir Herbert Walker the Brighton's aim of an electrified main line to the coast was achieved, but the work was done on the LWSR third-rail system.

Post-grouping electrification

Grouping brought yet another electrification committee, this time headed by Sir John Pringle. Its report in 1927 endorsed most of the findings of the pre-grouping Kennedy Committee, but it suggested standardizing voltages of 750 or 1,500 volts for future work, whereas the Kennedy Report had proposed allowing lines already working at voltages between 600 and 660 to continue in that range. The Southern's representative on the Pringle Committee dissented from the 750v standard, and that company continued with 660v in all the major schemes up to World War II. The increase to 750v did not come until extensive modernization of power supplies took place in the late 1950s, when the change was executed in stages.

There was another 'special case' on Merseyside in 1938 when the London Midland and Scottish Railway electified its lines in the Wirral at 650v DC for compatibility with the existing electrification of the Mersey Railway, over which the LMS trains ran into Liverpool from Birkenhead Park. In the same year the LNER also had a reason for staying outside the Pringle recommendations in electrifying its South Tyneside suburban lines from Newcastle Central to South Shields at 600v – this time for compatibility with the existing North Tyneside electrification.

The first new electrification after publication of the Pringle Report was conversion of the Manchester South Junction and Altrincham joint line, and here a Pringle recommendation was followed in the use of 1,500v DC with overhead contact wire. This was the first 1,500v

Right: The Metropolitan Railway bought locomotives to haul its longer-distance trains that had to take on steam power to finish their journey beyond conductor rail limits. No. 10 W. E. Gladstone, one of the final 1922 series, approaches Northwood with an Aylesbury–Baker Street train in 1947, under LPTB ownership.

Right: The District Railway had locomotives to run through trains between Ealing and the London Tilbury and Southend line as far as Barking. One of 10 built in 1905 nears Acton with an Ealing–Pitsea train of LT&S coaches in May 1925.

DC passenger-carrying line in the country. The system was accepted as the standard for main-line electrification in Great Britain until the change to 25,000v AC at 50Hz in 1956.

By 1930 the Southern Railway had virtually completed its electrification plans in the London suburban area, and with nearly 900 track miles was able to claim 'the world's greatest suburban electrification'. At the company's annual general meeting in that year the chairman announced that the main line to Brighton was to be electrified from Coulsdon, which was then the limit of the third rail, to Brighton and along the coast to Worthing. The company viewed this as an extended suburban electrification rather than a main-line scheme and therefore kept the existing 660v DC system. By this means it could reduce the amount of new rolling stock required by using existing stock to supplement its sources at weekends and holiday periods. By the end of December 1932 the work was com-

pleted and the formal inauguration took place on 30 December with a special train from Victoria to Worthing and back to Brighton for luncheon and speeches.

Multiple-unit stock was used for all services. Brighton non-stops, making the run 'on the hour in the hour' (a 55-minute schedule came later) were formed of six-car units, each with a Pullman car. The Pullman Car Company built three five-car all-Pullman sets for the Southern Belle service, the only electric multiple-unit Pullman trains in the world. The last Belle ran on 30 April 1972.

Between 1933 and 1938 the main lines of the former LBSCR were electrified, but other sections of the Southern came into the programme as well. On the eastern section the live rail reached Sevenoaks early in 1935, and the Medway towns in July 1939 – two pointers towards eventual electrification to the Kent coast, although this was not to come until after nationalization and the railway modernization plan of 1955. In July 1937 the Southern completed electrification of the route from Waterloo and Portsmouth Harbour specifically for the Isle of Wight traffic. On New Year's Day 1939 electric working began between Waterloo and Reading via Ascot, where the trains divided and a portion was detached for Guildford via Aldershot. The various extensions of the live rail necessary for these services brought the extent of the Southern electric system up to 655 route miles on the eve of World War II and the many changes in railway organization which followed it.

Southern electric was an institution in its own part of the country. The geography of the system ruled out dramatic improvements in journey times, but the regular interval services and standardized departure times were a better selling point to the general public than a few crack high-speed trains. All the routes electrified had a good commuter potential both from their terminal points and at intermediate stations, and although attractive timetables throughout the off-peak hours could not entirely dispose of the problem of stock under-utilization for much of the day, they at least kept up a reasonable patronage. It was entirely a multiple-unit operation; freight traffic and passenger trains to and from other parts of the railway system continued to be steam-hauled. In 1942 the Southern introduced the first of three mixed-traffic 1,470hp electric locomotives to help out the ageing steam locomotive stock of the former LBSCR lines, but the multiple-unit policy persisted for passenger services and was refined technically in various directions which have proved their value in the further development of the system since nationalization.

Although a comprehensive programme of

Below: Metropolitan Railway multiple-unit stock of 1905 on Hammersmith and City line service at Praed Street. Two-class travel survived on LPTB trains (Tubes excepted) till February 1940: note the hanging sign on the near platform reading 'Wait here for third class.'

Above: London Transport earned widespread acclaim for the surface architecture of the stations added in the suburban extensions of the Tube lines in the 1930s. Wood Green was part of the Piccadilly Line projection to Cockfosters, finished in 1933. Note the taxi on the left.

electrification had been recommended in 1929 by the Weir Committee, which based its economic calculations on the 1,500V DC system recommended by Pringle, only the Southern undertook anything of the kind. The depression years of the 1930s were unfavourable and the other main lines did not have a similar densely populated area to draw upon for medium- and longer-distance commuting, although the Great Western considered electrification, as described later. In 1935 government aid was made available for electrification schemes and the LNER brought Liverpool Street–Shenfield and Manchester–Sheffield out of the files again. A start had been made on both by the time war intervened.

The London Underground

Outside the Southern Railway, the most active area of electrification in the first half of the twentieth century was the London Underground. At first the system was operated by individual companies, of which the pioneer City and South London has already been mentioned. In 1900 the Central London Railway was opened between Shepherds Bush and the Bank, starting a decade of rapid development. The Bakerloo began operations between Baker Street and Waterloo in 1906, and a year later a tube line from Charing Cross to Euston and Hampstead foreshadowed the Northern Line of today.

In 1910 a number of lines amalgamated to form the London Electric Railway, and by the outbreak of World War I the Underground system in central London was much as we know it now. In later years there were extensions into the

suburbs which were carried further by new works financed under the government aid measures of 1935. Certain branches of the main-line railways in the London area were electrified and tube trains projected over them. Tube trains were seen as far afield as Ongar, Mill Hill East and High Barnet on lines formerly worked by the 'Big Four', and extra tracks were laid for Central Line trains to serve Great Western suburban stations out to West Ruislip on the Birmingham main line from Paddington. In November 1939 a short section of tube line was opened from Baker Street to Finchley Road which enabled Bakerloo trains to join the Metropolitan and run via Wembley Park to Stanmore, replacing the former Metropolitan service on the Stanmore branch.

From 1933 the London Underground system was operated by the London Passenger Transport Board. One tube line, however, remained outside the organization. This was the line from Waterloo SR to the Bank which had been opened in 1898 as the Waterloo and City Electric Railway, with the backing of the London and South Western. Originally the LSWR had planned to have a terminus near London Bridge, making Waterloo a through station. This plan was abandoned, but the Waterloo and City gave LSWR commuters access to the 'Square Mile' and in 1907 the company took it over. Thus in later years British Railways acquired a tube, actually the second tube line to be opened in this country. Its appointments are austere and its habitués call it 'the Drain', but for the City-bound it is a useful alternative to buses in the swarming traffic overhead, or to the long haul round London Transport's Circle Line.

Chapter 19

Getting to grips with the motor

Below: The GWR bought its first road motor buses in 1903. As the Chairman told GWR shareholders: 'Independent persons run motor-car services . . . to our railway stations. We do not see why we should not feed our railway ourselves by means of motor cars'.

AFTER THE REPEAL of the 'Red Flag' Act in 1896, private motoring remained for some time primarily a hobby for the well-to-do. Magnetos were not introduced until 1901. Fiddling with the methylated spirit burners of hot tube ignition, perhaps pumping petrol by hand, and then whirling a starting handle with no certainty of the outcome could only be contemplated by those with leisure or a chauffeur. Mass motoring on a scale large enough to affect railway passenger traffic did not begin until the 1930s. The motorbus, on the other hand, had arrived at the beginning of the century.

In the early days of commercial road transport, some railways found it a useful auxiliary and indulged in it themselves to provide a new and flexible form of feeder to their main lines which avoided the costly construction of new branches. The pioneer in this respect was the narrow gauge Lynton and Barnstaple Railway in its efforts to improve communication between Lynton and Ilfracombe. At first a service of horsedrawn coaches had been run between Ilfracombe and Blackmoor station on the L&B, but in 1903 the company's Chairman, Sir George Newnes, bought two Milnes-Daimler wagonettes and formed a subsidiary company to operate them over the same route. The service began in June of the same year, but was short-lived. In an area where the horse-drawn vehicle was deeply entrenched, the motor vehicles were not as popular as had been hoped, and there were problems with the local police. They alleged that vehicles were 'speeding' at more than 8 mph.

Above: As an economical means of rural passenger service the push-pull method with a locomotive, besides simplifying turnrounds, had the advantage that the power could be released for other work. It remained a widespread technique on the GWR until the Beeching closures of the BR era. This is a 1964 photograph of 2-6-2T No. 4564 and the Chalford push-pull, or auto-train, at Gloucester Central.

Newnes disposed of the wagonettes to the Great Western Railway, which was at that time being pressed to build a line from its branch terminus at Helston to the Lizard. Here was a cheaper alternative, and one which would test the market. The Helston–Lizard bus service began on 17 August 1903 – the first of many.

In referring to the company's road activities at its half-yearly meeting in 1903, the GWR Chairman said: 'We have been considering the cases in which independent persons run motor-car services along the roads to our railway stations. We do not see why we should not feed our own railway ourselves by means of motor-cars.' Some railways intending to operate road services at this period applied for powers to do so, but the Great Western evidently considered its bus activities its own affair and it was never challenged. In 1904 it extended into Devon with a service connecting Modbury with the Yealmpton branch; another operator was working on this route and eventually his undertaking was acquired by the Great Western – probably the first example of a railway taking over a bus com-

pany. The success of the railway-owned buses was variable, and quite a number of GWR routes were closed down after a short time, but by 1911 the GWR was operating some 31 services.

The Helston–Lizard service was watched with interest by the Great Eastern Railway, which immediately applied for road powers and began a bus service between Lowestoft and Southwold in 1904. In the meantime the North Eastern had started a service between Beverley and Beeford only three weeks after the pioneer GWR enterprise. The Great North of Scotland Railway was active with bus services in the Deeside area from 1904 onwards, beginning with a route from Ballater to Braemar. Not to be outdone by its Great Western competitor in the West Country, the London and South Western began operating steam buses between Exeter and Chagford in 1904. The London and North Western started bus operations with a service between Connah's Quay and Mold in 1905, and by 1914 this company was running nearly 40 buses fairly evenly divided between North Wales and the Watford area. These early services foreshadowed the rail/bus interchange stations of the present day, when congestion on the roads has reawakened appreciation of the role of the bus as a feeder to the train.

World War 1 accelerated the development of motor transport and created a reservoir of manpower trained to drive and maintain motor vehicles. After 1918 some started their own haulage businesses, but many more were absorbed into an expanding bus and coach industry. The railways' own bus activities had been feeders to their stations or extensions of service beyond the limits of their tracks. They were now confronted with point-to-point competition along their routes and in 1921 sought to offset lost revenue by applying for powers to invest in road transport undertakings. Their request was refused at first, but in the next few years the erosion of their short-distance passenger traffic prompted a change of heart at the Ministry of Transport and in 1928 Acts were passed which enabled each of the four main-line railway groups to make co-ordination agreements with provincial bus companies and to acquire large shareholdings in them, although the holdings were not to be so great that they would give the railways a controlling interest. By 1931 they had an interest in 19,500 buses out of 14,500 then running on British roads.

Competition from long-distance coaches
A railway strike in 1919 opened the door to another challenge to the railways from the roads. During the strike a weekend express coach service was opened between Bournemouth and London, and this was extended to daily operation in the years that followed. These 'Royal Blue' services made no intermediate stops, but in 1925 'Greyhound' coaches inaugurated a service between Bristol and London that picked up and set down at scheduled points *en route*.

The spread of this principle attracted many passengers from the railways, particularly in the London area where they could board a coach locally direct to their destination, instead of having to take a train to the London terminus before beginning their journey; at the same time they enjoyed the advantage of very cheap fares. These two factors offset the longer journey time.

At this period outer suburban stations around London were poorly served by long-distance trains. In the Second World War calls were scheduled at points like Watford Junction so that passengers could reach their suburban homes without travelling into central London and running the gauntlet of air raids. The practice was discontinued after the war, then sporadically revived, generally with some reluctance because of the time it took steam locomotives to regain speed after the stop. Diesel and electric traction removed objections to the outer suburban stop, which is now recognized as a means of attracting traffic that would otherwise go by road, although today the competition comes from the private car rather than the long-distance coach.

Mass motoring versus cheap fares
In spite of economic depression, passenger journeys by land transport in Great Britain increased by 48 per cent between 1920 and 1938, but almost all this increase was on the roads by public or private transport. A boom in the demand for private cars in the immediate post-war years threw some parts of the infant motor industry into confusion and a number of hopeful small firms went out of business because their production was uneconomic. But one manufacturer in particular, W. R. Morris, weathered the

Below: The one-piece steam railcar was more economical of power, but an inflexible tool. GWR No. 15 was built in 1905, two years after the GWR's first steam rail-motors had been introduced between Stonehouse and Chalford.

SOUTHERN RAILWAY
"SAVE TO TRAVEL" SCHEME

8 9 10

FOR SUNSHINE
HOLIDAYS
AND DAY OUTINGS

VOUCHERS 10/-
5% INTEREST

STAMPS 1/-

ASK AT ANY STATION OR OFFICE
FOR FULL DETAILS
AND SAVINGS STAMP CARD

Right: One of the ideas conceived by the 'Big Four' in the 1930s when they were fighting for their holiday and day excursion passenger business against the encroaching private car and charabanc.

losses of the bad years which followed the boom and took the risk of reducing prices to broaden the basis of his market when buying resumed. His gamble, as many thought it, paid him handsomely, and since his manufacturing methods had been planned to meet demand, he saw the annual sales of Morris cars increase from 3,076 in 1921 to 55,582 in 1925. Car prices fell all round and when the Austin Seven appeared in 1922 the age of mass motoring had begun. Motorways were still unknown but bypasses multiplied. 'In my little wheeled abode I rush along the by-pass road' wrote a contemporary contributor to *Punch*, contemplating the weekend motoring scene and noting how, at a given hour, 'Each one pushes out the clutch/Of his tiny moving hutch', to pull up for a wayside picnic.

The railways had various responses to this competition for recreational travel. Special rolling stock was built for tourist trains by the LNER, and in general the Sunday half-day excursion train became comparable in accommodation and speed with the average weekday service. Regular trips were run from London to quite distant seaside resorts, such as Skegness, with bottled beer and pork pies in the buffet car

to round off the day. Some excursion fares included a motorcoach trip to stately homes in the Dukeries or the Peak District. Special evening fares to resorts close to large inland towns offered relaxation by the sea for a few coppers; Exeter enjoyed a sixpenny return fare to Dawlish available by a train popularly called the 'Woolworth', and there were similar travel bargains from Newcastle Central to stations on the electric coastal line.

Some very low fares were offered for longer-distance trips. In 1935, for instance, the LNER advertised a return excursion from Ipswich to London at three shillings for the 137 miles. For an agricultural show at Birmingham in the same year, visitors from Bath were provided with a special train which took them the 187 miles to New Street and back for two shillings and ninepence, which works out at nearly six miles for one old penny. Various reduced fare inducements were available on ordinary scheduled services as well, notably three-day return tickets at single fare which were introduced in 1935.

All the railway groups ran 'save to travel' schemes. The GWR began one in the spring of 1935, and in 1936 the LMS, LNER and Southern launched a scheme of their own, outbidding the Great Western by adding interest at the rate of a halfpenny a month for a year on each complete ten shillings saved. In 1938 some 85 per cent of passenger receipts were derived from reduced fares compared with only 34.4 per cent in 1924. As one might expect, average receipts per passenger mile fell from 0.86 pence to 0.6 pence in the same period, a trend which contributed significantly to the decline of more than a quarter in passenger receipts.

Competition fathers some railway novelties
In 1932 the LMSR reconstructed its commercial department and encouraged its representatives to seek out new traffic, both passenger and freight, by means of an inter-district competition called the Quota Scheme. Its creators hoped that 'egoism and the love of sport' would be the inducements which 'through the game of quota hunting impel every salesman on the LMSR to give of his best'. Results, achievements and new ideas were reported in a staff periodical, *Quota News*. Quota calendars were displayed showing how the various districts had fared month by month, with humorous drawings of 'quota men' climbing towards their goal or tumbling down in disarray after a setback. The scheme aroused enough interest and response to encourage the

LMSR to introduce a similar campaign in 1934, with punctuality figures as the goal.

Considerable thought was given to improving economy of operation and the attractiveness of secondary services. The Great Western again had recourse to the internal combustion engine, but this time on rails. In 1934 it placed a 130hp diesel railcar in service between Slough, Reading, Didcot and Oxford. The body was streamlined to follow the modern fashion set by high-speed diesel trains in Germany, although the streamlining of the GWR vehicle was simply for the sake of appearance. At the GWR meeting on 27 February 1935 the Chairman reported that the experiment of running the car on local services where there was not enough traffic to justify running an ordinary train, or even a steam railcar, had proved quite satisfactory. By the beginning of February 1935 the vehicle had carried 136,000 passengers and run over 60,000 miles; it had proved very popular with the public, and many passengers had been attracted by the novelty of this first opportunity of 'motoring' on the railway, perhaps with a seat behind the driver and for the first time a view of the line ahead.

In the meantime the GWR had ordered three twin-engined railcars of similar design but of 260hp for fast services with too little traffic to operate a conventional train economically. The new vehicles provided buffet and lavatory accommodation and were first put to work between Birmingham and Cardiff. This time there was a definite service improvement – the journey was made at an overall average speed of 50 mph and saved 34 minutes compared with the existing best timing between the two cities.

Sixteen of the 260hp railcars were ordered and services expanded further. One of the cars which had been working between Birmingham and Cardiff was put on the route between Birmingham and Stratford-on-Avon on 1 April 1935, making intermediate calls at Earlswood Lakes and Henley-in-Arden. Of the new orders, one car was for parcels traffic and started work between Paddington and Oxford on 4 May 1936. A seventeenth vehicle was added to the series, similar to the other 260hp units, but with a strengthened underframe enabling it to haul passenger or goods vehicles up to a trailing load of 60 tons. Delivered in 1937, it was put to work on the Lambourn Valley branch.

The top speed of the 260hp cars was 75–80 mph; one of them in 1937 ran 40 miles at an average speed of 68 mph on a journey from Oxford to Paddington. In 1936 the cars were running about 3,600 miles a day on routes serving places as far apart on the Great Western system as Tenby in the west, West Bromwich in the north, and Weymouth in the south.

A short-lived experiment with a vehicle able to run on rails or on the road was undertaken by

Below: In the 1930-1 winter the LMS tested on the Harpenden-Hemel Hempstead branch the 'Ro-Railer', an amphibious vehicle built by Karrier to the LMS Road Motor Engineer's specification with interchangeable road and rail wheels. After a period of public service between railway and the LMS Welcombe Hotel at Stratford-on-Avon, the 'Ro-Railer' ended up as an engineer's service vehicle on the LNER West Highland line.

the LMSR in 1932. The company's Welcombe Hotel at Stratford-on-Avon was some distance from the Stratford terminus of the branch from the main line at Blisworth. Between 23 April and 2 July in that year the road-rail venture – called the Ro-Railer – operated between Blisworth and Stratford in connection with expresses to and from Euston. Previously the Ro-Railer had been tested on the Harpenden–Hemel Hempstead branch. In the mid-1930s the LMS had three 130hp diesel railcars in service on various local routes and also operated a 200hp diesel-electric vehicle belonging to the English Electric Company. A further diesel experiment took place in 1939 with a three-car diesel unit which ran at first on the cross-country Oxford–Cambridge line and later worked out of St Pancras on services to Bedford, Leicester and Nottingham.

All these ventures were intended to cut costs and make the service more attractive in a period of severe competition from the roads. It has been estimated that by 1937 the railways were losing between 250 and 300 million journeys a year on short-distance services alone. Even at the zenith of steam it was felt that internal combustion operation could reduce the costs and enhance the attractiveness of some types of service worst hit by road competition.

Another LMSR experiment involved borrowing a rubber-tyred Michelin railcar from France. Early in 1935 this vehicle made a test run from Leighton Buzzard to Euston, covering the 40.2 miles in $42\frac{1}{2}$ minutes, and impressing

observers as 'very steady and silent'. The car was powered by a 240hp engine and the rubber tyres had steel flanges. Loss of air pressure sounded a warning buzzer in the driver's cab and a rim inside the tyre prevented more than a very small loss in diameter even if air pressure were lost completely. After the trials it was returned and future railcar ventures followed the conventional practice of steel wheel on steel rail.

The railways enter road haulage

With the powers conferred by the Acts of 1928 the railways went into road cartage by the purchase of Pickfords and Carter Paterson, but expansion in this area was slow and by 1938 the railways owned only 10,000 goods vehicles out of a total in Britain of nearly 495,000. The Road Traffic Act of 1930 overhauled the system of licensing public service passenger vehicles and protected the railways from some of the more extreme and unregulated competition, but in freight the railways were still at a disadvantage.

A deputation from the railways saw the Minister of Transport in January 1932 to ask that a system of licensing goods vehicles should be introduced. A conference of road and rail representatives was called, and produced a report on the situation which became the basis of the Road and Rail Traffic Act 1933. Under this legislation a licence was necessary to carry goods commercially by road. There were three classes of licence: the A licence for the regular road haulier operating as a public carrier; the B

Below: By the end of World War I both petrol and steam road goods vehicles were in widespread use and the Lancashire and Yorkshire was one railway which operated a fleet of Sentinel steam lorries. It built the trailers for them in its own works.

licence for those using their vehicles partly for their own purposes and partly for those of others; and the c licence for the private carrier whose vehicles were used exclusively for his own business.

Railways and roads were now on rather more equal terms, but severe problems remained from the early years of the railway age in the shape of old obligations as common carriers which had then been laid upon them, and the complicated rules on which the prices they could charge were based. From 1933 a system of 'agreed charges' permitted the railways to make annual contracts with traders to carry the latter's goods, but some onerous provisions regarding the quotation of special rates remained in force from the Railways Act of 1921. The legislators who set up the Railway Rates Tribunal to administer these matters could not foresee at that time how road transport would mushroom in the years ahead and how it would affect railway revenues.

The inter-wars entrepeneurs

In the final years before World War II the railways were transport entrepreneurs in all three elements. The Sealink division of today's British Rail, the biggest short-sea shipping operator in the world, is an amalgam of the activity of the pre-1948 Big Four, which in turn had assembled their fleets from shipping activity developed by their pre-Grouping constituents. In the mid-1930s the combined fleets of the Big Four totalled over 140 ships, some sailing further afield than Sealink's vessels do now; both LMS and LNER, for instance, operated cargo ships to Hamburg, the former from Goole, the latter from Grimsby. Besides their seagoing ships, the LMS and LNER ran extensive steamer services up and down the Clyde and to Bute and Arran; the LMS also had steamers on some of the English lakes.

In 1929 the Big Four gained parliamentary powers to operate their own air services too. The first to take positive action was the Great Western, which on 12 April 1931 went into partnership with Imperial Airways, using one of the latter's six-seater Westland Wessex planes (repainted chocolate and cream!) to operate a daily service from Cardiff to Haldon, near Torquay in Devon; a year later the flights were extended from Cardiff to Castle Bromwich, for Birmingham. From 1934 this venture came under the auspices of the Railway Air Services, a company formed jointly by the Big Four and Imperial Airways. For the most part the company's activity was confined to special charters. Under the Civil Aviation Act of August 1946 it was absorbed by the new-born British European Airways.

Above: Holyhead harbour circa 1880. In that year the Prince of Wales, later King Edward VII, opened an extension of the inner harbour, a new station and a new hotel.

Chapter 20

The heavy freight business

THE MIXED FREIGHT train with its miscellaneous assortment of open wagons and vans used to be one of the most familiar railway sights. The variety of its loads reflected the long-standing principle, stated in the Railway and Canal Traffic Act of 1854, of the railways' 'obligation to carry' all the articles offered to them for transport. For many years most stations had their goods shed and sidings, which were visited daily by the local goods train – the 'pick-up' – to detach and collect wagons. The 'pick-up' took its wagons to a yard, where they were sorted and marshalled into long-distance goods trains, each of which concentrated onward movement to a specific group of destinations.

By their nature the railways could not provide door-to-door transport without the help of road cartage. Sir Francis Head visited the good department of the still young London and North Western Railway at Camden in the late 1840s and noted that the company undertook th 'vexatious and intricate business of collecting and delivering these goods from and to all part of London, as also throughout the various town on their line, excepting Liverpool'. For hand ling a certain proportion of the merchandise th company had 'with great prudence availe themselves of the practical experience of Messr Pickford and Messrs Chaplin & Horne, whon they have engaged as their agents at Camden station'. Arriving wagons were addressed to on or other of these undertakings, and Head note with approval that between them 'a wholesom competition exists, highly advantageous to th public'.

Below: Rural freight: a pick-up freight on the remote Wenford Bridge branch of the SR in Cornwall, with ex-LSWR Beattie 2-4-0 well tank No. 30587 in charge in 1959.

Left: A trans-shipment shed for less-than-wagonload merchandise at Birmingham Moor Street in the 1920s, before the days of mechanical aids to sorting and loading.

After arriving wagons had been uncoupled at Camden in the late 1840s, railway horses positioned them in sidings, from which they were removed by horses belonging to the two agents and manoeuvred so that each class of goods could be unloaded into its own store, from which delivery to the final destination was made by spring wagon. The cartage agents also had receiving sheds where they loaded rail wagons, fitted tarpaulins and handed them over, duly labelled, to the railway company's goods department. The wagons were then drawn by horses over the weighbridge and on to the turntables, by which they were distributed among the 13 tracks on which outgoing trains were made up, some of them loading up to 80 or 90 wagons. Nearby was the engine shed housing 'twenty five of the largest class engines . . . capable of drawing 600 tons at the rate of twelve miles an hour'. Head described the variety of merchandise passing through the sheds in equally lively fashion:

Here lies a waggonload of beer from Chester, there another of sugar-loaves, in blue paper, from Northampton, of groceries for Buckingham, cheeses, millinery and gas-pipes for Peterborough, a vanload of empty hosiery skips to return to Leicester, empties to Glasgow, filberts for Birmingham, &c: and as the goods are coming in as fast as they are going out, the colours of this kaleidoscopic scene are constantly changing.

This summed up the whole problem of the railway business in general merchandise.

The mineral business

The other and traditional side of railway freight was the mineral business, which had been the reason for building the Stockton and Darlington Railway in 1825, and other lines subsequently laid down in the north-east to carry coal and ore. In the 100 years from 1850 to 1950 the tonnage of coal carried was always well over half the total volume of freight traffic, although revenue was not proportionately high – it was about 45 per cent of the total received from freight in the years before World War I. Coal and mineral traffic are both sensitive to changes in business activity, and during the depression years of the early 1930s total British railway goods revenue ranged between £99 million and £81 million compared with nearly £127 million in 1920.

The problems of private ownership

One of the obstacles to economic freight working was the widespread use of open wagons of 7 or 10 tons capacity, which were the largest that could be handled on most private colliery lines. Trials with a bogie wagon of bigger capacity were carried out on the Great Western Railway in

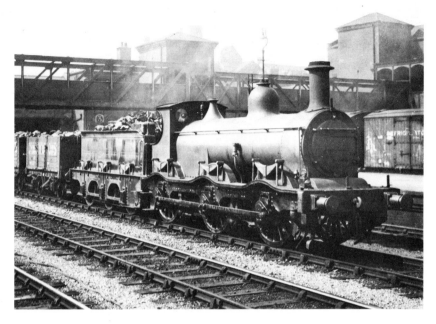

Above: A typical un-braked coal train of the 1920s and 1930s. Ex-Midland outside-frame 0-6-0 No. 2704 trundles tonnage from the East Midlands pits through Nottingham en route from the LMS Toton yard to the south.

1888, and a batch of bogie wagons was built by the Caledonian in 1903, but the sharp curvature of the colliery lines restricted their use so much that no more were ordered. Another characteristic of freight working in Britain was the large number of private owners' wagons, of which there were eventually more than 600,000. One lesson of railway operating learned in World War I was the advantage of common user of wagon stock. In 1913 60 per cent of the wagon mileage was run empty, but by the end of the war empty mileage had been reduced to 20 per cent, with a saving in running costs of nearly £500,000 a year. A similar transformation occurred in World War II.

The Ministry of Transport Act of 1919 gave the minister powers to restrict or prohibit the use of private owners' wagons, but the powers were not exercised and some 544,000 wagons remained privately owned until they were taken over by British Railways in 1948. Some steps towards wagon standardization were taken in 1920 by the Railway Companies Association, which agreed on a specification for a 12-ton wagon. Again its use was restricted by the capacity of existing cranes, hoists and sidings, so the wagon stock retained its inconvenient variety throughout the years between the two world wars. Sir John Aspinall, when Consulting Mechanical Engineer to the Ministry of Transport, compared the sorting of wagons made necessary by the variety of designs and ownership with 'the perpetual piecing together of a jig-saw puzzle with all the disadvantages of waste work'; he once branded the private wagon as 'the bane of the railways'.

The beginnings of centralized control

Freight working had one important influence on railway working in general. A scheme introduced by the Midland Railway in 1907 to provide relief crews to prevent enginemen in the Masborough area having to work excessive hours was later developed to become a traffic control system of general usefulness. It was a natural evolution, for the overtime problem stemmed in part from late running of freight trains, which could be reduced by centralized supervision of their movements. In 1909 the Midland extended control to freight and mineral trains throughout the Toton–Cudworth area. District control offices were set up at Cudworth, Masborough, Staveley, Westhouses and Toton; each district had reporting stations from which the passage of freight trains was reported by telegraph to the district office, and a central office at Derby exercised general supervision over the work of the districts, particularly in respect of rolling stock and motive power distribution.

Each district office made out a card for every train passing through its area. On the card was shown the description of the train; the driver and guard (with times of booking on duty); the engine; and the number of wagons. A diagram of the lines in the district was shown on a 'train board' to which the cards were attached. As messages reporting the progress of a train were received, its card was moved along the diagram, which showed at a glance the latest reported positions of all trains in the district. Many of the goods services were unscheduled and had to be superimposed on the regular timetable. The train board showed where paths were available and these were first cleared with Derby and then allocated.

Watching the general pattern of traffic as displayed on the board, the district controllers could also advise signalmen on the best way of handling regularly scheduled trains. Derby was kept informed of wagon movements, and the system as a whole contributed to the reduction of empty mileage and the availability of rolling stock and locomotives where and when required. Trains were identified at first by code letters displayed on the guards' vans, but it was later found that the large numerals which the Midland characteristically applied to its locomotives were easily read by the reporting stations.

On 1 January 1917 control was extended to express passenger trains, and later to express freight trains. Eventually 26 important stations reported train movement direct to Derby, where the train board was an inch-to-the-mile diagram of the main lines. The individual boards in dis-

Below: Another LMS *freight scene in the 1920s: the exterior of the former Midland Railway freight depot at Nottingham. Note the advanced sliding roof van in the left foreground.*

trict offices remained in use, but Derby now had its own picture of the overall traffic pattern to help it organize the distribution of vehicles and the allocation of pilot locomotives if necessary.

Traffic control was adopted on other lines and its usefulness grew with the development of communications. The telegraph gave place to the telephone, at first with shared lines and code ringing on many circuits. Later came selective calling with dial-type telephones, but much clerical work was still involved in recording passing times and writing down lists of loaded and empty wagons telephoned at regular intervals from yards and stations. Today high-speed data transmission has taken over, and the information once transcribed by hand now flows into and out of the stores of the TOPS (Total Operations Processing Systems) computers.

Advances in goods train organization

In the marshalling yards where wagons coming from many different places were assembled into trains, shunting locomotives used to run many miles in the to-and-fro movements involved in this complex sorting operation. An improve-

ment was achieved by the 'hump' yard where wagons were propelled slowly to the summit of the hump, there uncoupled by shunters into 'cuts' (one wagon or several coupled together for the same destination) and left to run by gravity down the other side into their appropriate sorting siding. A typical hump, as in the Feltham yard opened by the London and South-Western Railway in 1922, was graded at 1 in 40 on the approach side and at 1 in 50 from the summit towards the sidings.

Hump shunting underwent various stages of mechanization, the most important being the use of railbrakes to check the speed of wagons descending the hump, an operation once performed by shunters running alongside and operating the wagon brakes with their poles. At first the control tower operators in the yards used their judgment in applying pressure from the rail-brakes to the flanges of the wagon wheels passing through them, but eventually electronic methods of detecting speed and assessing wagon 'rollability' enabled the braking pressure to be adjusted automatically, so that the wagons rolled gently to a standstill in the sidings to which they were directed, avoiding violent collision with those already standing there.

With power-worked points a route into any siding could be set by pressing a single pushbutton. Later, wagon destinations were

MIDLAND RAILWAY GRAIN WAREHOUSE

MIDLAND RAILWAY GOODS AND GRAIN WAREHOUSE.

recorded on punched tape which was passed through a tape reader in the control tower and set the routes in sequence as each 'cut' of wagons came over the hump. In these days the punched cards generated by the TOPS computers can perform the same function, but with the changing pattern of goods traffic many yards have been closed and a growing proportion of rail borne freight now travels in 'block' trains direct from point of origin to destination.

Idiosyncrasies of braking

For many years one of the unusual characteristics of freight operation on the railway of Great Britain was the small proportion of wagons fitted with vacuum or air brakes under the control of the driver. Vehicles equipped in this way were used mainly for perishable traffic on freight trains running at express speeds. For the most part the wagons only had a mechanical brake which had to be applied individually to stop before descending a gradient so that the brakes could be 'pinned down'. While the train was moving it had to depend on the braking power of the locomotive and the brake van at the rear. The unbraked wagons were coupled by chain-link couplings which slackened when the vehicles were running downhill or slowing down, and considerable driving skill was needed to avoid a severe shock and possible fractured couplings when power was reapplied and the chains tautened. Braked and unbraked wagons might be found in the same train, the unbraked vehicles being fitted with pipes to maintain continuity of the vacuum.

Locomotives

From the earliest days the railway freight business produced some distinctive locomotive types. In the period when one or two pairs of large-diameter driving wheels were normal for passenger locomotives, goods engines were built with three coupled axles and small wheels to give good adhesion and high tractive effort, speed being unimportant. The 0-6-0 wheel arrangement was seen in the 1820s on the Stockton and Darlington Railway, but not until 1848 did it attain the form in which it remained for many years afterwards, the classic British goods engine.

For the heaviest freight traffic the pre-grouping and group companies built eight-coupled locomotives with the 0-8-0 and 2-8-0 wheel arrangements, also 4-8-0 and 0-8-2 locomotives specifically for hump shunting. The ten-coupled locomotive was not seen, except for the Great Eastern Decapod (see Chapter 16) and an 0-10-0 banking locomotive for the Lickey incline on the Midland, until the 'austerity' 2-10-0s of World War II in 1944, which were a development of the earlier 'austerity' 2-8-0s, and like them were built for the War Department with overseas use in mind. The 2-10-0 reappeared as the last of the British Railways standard steam locomotive types in 1954, designated Class 9F. The last steam locomotive built by British Railways was in fact a 9F 2-10-0, No. 92220 *Evening Star*. Sixty years had then elapsed since the 'Big Goods' on the Highland. Both classes took their turn on passenger work, but by 1954 the division between passenger and goods locomotives had become blurred by the 'mixed traffic' concept, and the 9Fs were specifically intended for mixed traffic as well as heavy freight. There are two authenticated records of their having reached 90 mph when working express passenger trains in an emergency.

The Midland division of the LMS remained faithful for some years to the Midland tradition of double-heading heavy freight trains with 0-6-0s, but in 1927 Garratt articulated locomotives with the 2-6-6-2 wheel arrangement were introduced for coal trains from Toton Yard, near Nottingham, to London (Cricklewood). The average speed of the loaded trains was raised from 18 to 21 mph by these locomotives, with a saving in fuel of some 15 per cent.

The most lasting contribution to railway motive power proceeding from the freight business was made by the diesel shunting locomotive. The LMS tested several prototypes in 1934 and from them evolved the 350hp diesel-electric unit which eventually was adopted as the British Railways standard shunter. The LMS diesel shunter represented the first large-scale use of diesel power on the railways of Great Britain, and convincingly demonstrated the advantages of a motive power unit which was always available for use, consumed no fuel except when actually working, and could be handled easily in comfortable conditions, with a good all-round view for the driver which was an important safety factor when shunting.

Below: The 2-8-0 became the favoured heavy freight type of all the 'Big Four' except the Southern. No. 3822 was a representative of Churchward's 1903 2800 class design for the GWR.

The fight for a square deal

In the late 1930s heavier road competition made the railways increasingly resentful of the disadvantages under which they operated in the freight business. Although the 1933 Road and Rail Traffic Act had given the railways some freedom in negotiating charges for carrying traders' merchandise, the basis of charging was still in broad terms the value of the service rendered, which in turn depended on the value of the articles moved. A vast number of rates was quoted in the Classification of Merchandise Book and a road haulier could undercut the railways in quoting for transport of high-rated goods, leaving the railways to return the empty packing cases at the lowest rates in the book, which as common carriers they were obliged to do. Another difficulty was mentioned by the Chairman of the Great Western at the company's meeting in 1937. The preceding year had seen very big fluctuations in the requirements for wagons, which varied sometimes by as much as 4,600 from day to day. The Chairman pointed out that while their road transport competitors were able to secure fairly constant use of their vehicles, being able to compete for any of the railways' traffic and carry only the most profitable, the railways had to carry any traffic that was offered to them and thus had to bear the expense of making provision for the peaks.

Lord Stamp, Chairman of the LMSR, spoke in a similar vein, pointing to the ability of road hauliers to pick and choose traffic and to make

rates and charges without any responsibility for transport as a whole. The railways had opposed granting of licences to some road hauliers and had been attacked for it, but these objections had been made only when the traffics concerned were of a kind which had been originally, and still were, carried by rail, and where the rail facilities were substantially equivalent and adequate, and where the length and directness of the haul reduced the particular advantages of road service.

These broadsides from boardrooms were followed in November 1938 by a press, poster and banner campaign in which the railways asked for public support in pressing for a 'Square Deal'. A message addressed to every member of the public read:

If you think the railways are doing their job

If you want them to go on giving a vital service to your interests as they have done for over a hundred years

If you think they ought not to be tied hand and foot by out-of-date restrictions on their charges for merchandise

Support their claim to Parliament for equality

Other literature in the 'Square Deal' campaign insisted that all the railways were seeking was freedom to charge appropriate rates for the goods they were bound to carry under the Carriers' Acts. Two million copies of a booklet entitled *Clear the lines*, setting out the companies' case, were distributed to the public.

On 24 May 1939 the Minister of Transport announced that the government had decided to accept in principle the recommendations made by the Transport Advisory Council, and that it intended to introduce appropriate legislation as soon as possible in the next session of Parliament. Crises and war intervened, however, and when at length the anomalies of which the railways had complained were removed by the Transport Act of 1953 a very different situation existed.

Dealing with small loads

In the years between the end of World War II and nationalization efforts were made to improve the handling of the thousands of small consignments handed in to the railways for transport every day. The railways operated their own road vehicles for collection and delivery and now introduced a zonal scheme to put them to better use. The Great Western and the LMSR were both active in this direction in the late 1940s. The aim of the scheme was to divide the country into zones, each with one station as a centre and a number of sub-rail-

heads. A number of stations at which goods trains used to call became simply receiving offices at which goods were handed in for collection by railway road motors.

A package handed in at one of these stations would be taken first to a sub-railhead where similar packages came in by road from many other receiving stations. At this point it might be possible to make up full wagonloads of packages bound for the same destinations. Packages that could not be consolidated into full wagonloads were taken on by a railway road motor 'trunk' service to the railhead of the zone. A package for a destination served by the railhead's local road delivery network might then finish its journey without travelling in a train at all. If its destination was in another zone, it might find a place in a wagon being forwarded to a sub-railhead in that zone, from which it would be delivered by road. The flow of packages arriving at a railhead increased the possibility of full wagonloads being made up. If a package could not be sent direct from a railhead to a sub-railhead near its destination, it would go to the railhead in its destination zone and be forwarded from there by trunk motor to the sub-railhead, finishing its journey by local C&D (collection and delivery) motor.

The zonal system improved both the economy and speed of handling 'smalls' traffic – it concentrated packages so that the possibility of making up wagon loads was increased, and it kept packages on the move. If a consignment could not go by wagon to its destination at once, it was not held in a goods shed until a wagonload could be made up but despatched by trunk road motor.

A zonal scheme was introduced by the Great Western as early as December 1945. The time saved was considerable. For example, under the old system a consignment from Windsor to Llantrisant in South Wales would have gone first to Paddington and perhaps not be forwarded until the next day. Under the zonal system it would be taken to Slough railhead and travel either to Llantrisant sub-railhead for local delivery the next morning, or to Cardiff railhead and on to Llantrisant by trunk motor, again with delivery next morning.

Other zonal schemes followed on the LMS, and after nationalization the principle was extended throughout British Railways. Soon, however, the changes in the role of the railways as a freight carrier led to a new organization which greatly diminished the volume of the 'smalls' traffic which had for so long been a problem of railway freight handling.

Right: Shortly before the grouping, in 1921-2, Urie created for the LSWR *this heavy 4-6-2T to perform transfer freight working across London between Nine Elms and Feltham and Brent and Willesden yards. As* SR *Class H16, No. 30516 heads a goods out of Guildford in November 1949.*

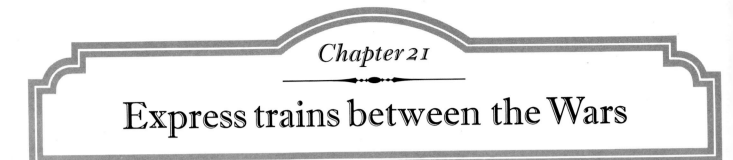

Chapter 21

Express trains between the Wars

*Below: In 1904 the
LNWR and LBSCR ex-
perimented with a
through coach service
between Manchester and
Brighton to meet growing
demand for a holiday
facility that avoided
cross-London
interchange. Immediate
popularity saw the ser-
vice expanded in 1905
into a full train using
LNWR coaches linking
Liverpool, Manchester,
Brighton and Eastbourne.
Titled the 'Sunny South
Special', it is seen here in
1910 approaching
Clapham Junction behind
LBSC Class B2X 4-4-0
No. 210.*

AFTER 1918 THE railways were slow to regain pre-war standards of express passenger train speed. Only the Great Western seemed to have been able to reserve enough energy during the war to keep its express engines in good enough condition for restoration of 1914 timings on all the principal trunk routes from Paddington as early as 1921. On all but the Birmingham route, however, there was a wide gap between the end-to-end schedule of the day's fastest train and the rest of the pack.

The effects of the 1923 grouping

The 1923 grouping into the Big Four made early impact on the services of only one of the quartet. On the Southern and LMS the newly assembled motive power departments were in some disarray. Only one of the Southern's constituents had yielded the new company any six-coupled tender locomotives, so that until a modern express passenger design could be

formulated heavier train loadings there could make no advance; as late as 1925, in fact, standards on the Southern's south-eastern and south-western main lines were still lagging behind those of 1914.

The LMS was riven by the jealousies and the diametrically opposed policies of its major constituents which, so far as its locomotive affairs were concerned, no one had the power to override until the LMS President, Sir Josiah (later Lord) Stamp appointed William Stanier Chief Mechanical Engineer at the start of 1932 with a categorical mandate to put the unruly house in order. Until then little had been done to weed out the 393 different locomotive classes which the LMS inherited in 1923; the main pre-grouping locomotive works and design offices had been left much of their pre-1923 independence; and with Midland voices dominant in operating councils new express locomotive construction was limited to Midland compound 4-4-0s in line with the traditional Derby 'small-engine-and-

double-head-if-necessary' philosophy. One LMS man of the 1920s pithily summed up the situation this way:

At Derby the nice little engines were made pets of. They were housed in nice clean sheds and were very lightly loaded . . . At Horwich [the former Lancashire and Yorkshire works] they had all gone scientific and talked in 'thous' [thousandths], although apparently some of their work was to the nearest half-inch. At Crewe they just didn't care so long as their engines could roar and rattle along with a good paying load, which they usually did.

For much of the 1920s all this left the LMS Commercial Department with little scope for enhancing its express trains beyond giving them names; a number of LMS titles were born in 1927, Royal Scot among them.

The LNER started life with a commanding Chief Mechanical Engineer, Nigel Gresley, with his first Pacifics already in existence. In its first grouping year the company quickened the Flying Scotsman by 40 minutes, restored 1914 timings on the West Riding and Great Central routes, and improved upon them on the East Anglian lines from Liverpool Street.

Pullman experiments

The most significant LNER development of the early 1920s, however, was its innovation of all-Pullman trains north of the Thames. The Midland had run the first Pullmans (day and sleeper) to Scotland at the opening of the Settle–Carlisle line in 1876; the Highland had operated Pullman sleepers between Glasgow and Inverness from 1885 to 1907; and the Caledonian had contracted with the Pullman company in 1914 for them to cover all its restaurant car requirements – but in each of these instances the Pullmans had been marshalled individually in trains completed by ordinary stock. *Force majeure* prompted the LNER enterprise, since it had inherited a stock of Pullmans and an unexpired Pullman contract from the Great Eastern's American-born General Manager, Henry Thornton, who had incredibly – it was the only serious misjudgment of an otherwise brilliant and broadly based rail executive – expected East Anglians to patronize Pullman as enthusiastically as his compatriots. Except on the Liverpool Street–Parkeston Quay (Harwich) boat trains, they didn't; so the LNER naturally sought more profitable routes for the cars.

After abortive attempts in 1924 to interest Nottingham, Sheffield and Manchester in a daily Pullman train from Kings Cross, the East Coast main line Pullman operation settled down in 1925 to a pattern of two services: one from London to Scotland via Leeds and Harrogate – it was named the Queen of Scots in

Above: A Bristol–Birmingham express of 1924 mounts the 1 in 37¾ Lickey Incline on the outskirts of Birmingham, double-headed by an ex-Midland Johnson 4-2-2, No. 614, and a Class 2 4-4-0, with rear-end assistance from 'Big Bertha', the unique 0-10-0 Lickey banker No. 2290.

1928. The other ran from London to the West Riding; until 1935 it carried on beyond Harrogate to Newcastle, and finally bore cars for Hull as well as Halifax; it was called the West Riding Pullman from 1928, and the Yorkshire Pullman after 1935.

Some LNER Pullmans were retained on the Great Eastern line for the Harwich boat trains and also for a remarkable summer excursion launched in 1929 and continued until the outbreak of World War II – the Eastern Belle. Each week in high summer the all-Pullman Eastern Belle went from Liverpool Street to a different East Anglian holiday resort and back daily, and moreover to timings equalling those of each route's best normal service trains. The full summer's programme was publicized in advance and the public was encouraged to take out a season ticket covering a whole week's round. The fares were a bargain – as late as 1939 a whole week's trips, Pullman surcharge included, cost no more than £1.97 first, £1.32 third class – and so were the cut-price meals served at all seats from Pullman kitchens.

Even when ordinary East Coast route expresses had been re-equipped with coaches as luxurious, but innocent of supplementary fare, and were as fast or faster than the Pullman trains, the Pullman still prospered. They had a distinctive club atmosphere, a *corps* of waiters always hovering at the passenger's elbow and primed to anticipate his wants if he were a regular, which attracted an unshakeably loyal clientèle. No less distinctive were the Pullman menus which had a ring all their own; soup would always come with 'golden croûtons', the entrée with characterized vegetables ('carrots Crécy', for example, never plain 'carrots'), the dessert with 'double Devon cream'; the savoury would be euphoniously billed as the 'English County Cheese Tray' and cigarettes and cigars would be 'specially selected by the Pullman Car Company'. More practically important, the chief conductor of a Pullman car train was far more the fully-fledged restaurant manager than his dining car counterpart, for he had the entire responsibility for ordering his kitchen's raw materials as well as supervising their output. In the 1930s the Pullman company operated a reserved 'Road Motor Saloon' between Kings Cross and Victoria for the exclusive use of passengers booked Pullman on both LNER and SR legs of a journey between the north and the Channel ports.

Inter-war Pullman ventures were not totally successful. The Southern did well with the Golden Arrow, the name bestowed in 1929 on the train which Pullman's energetic Chairman, Lord Dalziel, had persuaded the SR to inaugurate to connect via the Calais–Paris Flèche d'Or with his expanding network of mainland European Pullman trains. As rewarding as the London–Brighton Southern Belle had been since its 1907 debut was the companion Bournemouth Belle, which the SR introduced in 1931 (whereupon the pioneer Belle was retitled the Brighton Belle). But the Great Western belly-

Below: From the mid-1920s until the early 1930s the LNER Pullman workings between Kings Cross and Leeds were monopolized by the ex-GN Ivatt Class C1 Atlantics, which put up remarkable performances for their size. No. 4459 heads the down 'West Riding Pullman' in this 1920s scene.

lopped with the Torquay Pullman it was coaxed into launching in 1929, after Dalziel had won a Paddington bridgehead by getting Pullmans included in the GWR's Plymouth–Paddington transatlantic boat trains. The train ran in full for one summer only; then, because of poor patronage, it was truncated in 1930 to become a five-car section of an ordinary train, and never reappeared, as the GWR cleared out all its Pullmans to the SR early in 1931.

Trials of speed

By then the express passenger scene was much livelier. Back in 1923 the GWR, equipped with the first of Collett's Castle 4-6-0s, which both epitomized the genius of Collett's great Swindon predecessor, G. J. Churchward, and prefigured the culminating features of British steam locomotive design, decided to bid for the British speed title. At the time the only mile-a-minute average runs in the timetables were on the LNER, between Darlington and York, and on the Great Central main line between Leicester and Nottingham's Arkwright Street (the only non-island station on the whole Great Central main line). The GWR had yet fully to exploit one of the country's most inviting rail racecourses, Brunel's superbly engineered main line from Swindon to London. In 1923 it did so by picking a thoroughly obscure early afternoon train from Cheltenham to Paddington and cutting its time from Swindon by ten minutes to secure an average schedule from Swindon to London of 61.8 mph start to stop. One major advantage was that the route was relatively quiet at the time and fast scheduling was therefore possible. The Cheltenham Flyer was born.

Only one regular timetabled train in the world, between Camden and Atlantic City on the Philadelphia and Reading RR in the USA, was known to have a faster schedule. In 1929 the GWR cut another five minutes from its Flyer schedule and took the crown from the Americans with a 66.3 mph average. Within two years a fresh challenge was mounted by Canadian Pacific in the Montreal–Toronto corridor, but the GWR quickly rebuffed it by fresh acceleration in autumn 1931 to a 69.2 mph average. Oddly, although the GWR placarded the Cheltenham Flyer engine's smoke-box door with the train's name and its claim to be 'The World's Fastest Train', the title was never shown in the public timetable.

Before the war dismissed the Flyer to history, the GWR had not only, in September 1932,

trimmed its 77.3-mile Swindon–Paddington to a final 65 minutes for a start-to-stop average of 71.4 mph, but on 5 June that year staged the fastest journey – in terms of end-to-end speed – ever recorded with British steam, when No. 5006 *Tregenna Castle* cut over eight minutes from the schedule to average 81.7 mph start to stop. In the later 1930s, however, the Flyer was kicked far down the table of the world's fastest daily trains by the upcoming diesel streamliners of North America and Germany; and in June 1937 it surrendered even its British crown to the 71.9-mph Kings Cross–York booking of the LNER's Kings Cross–Edinburgh Coronation streamliner.

Advances in design, comfort and entertainment

The late 1920s witnessed some striking advances in coach design and comfort. In 1927, for instance, the LMS pioneered the modern style of inter-city coach with a new series that eliminated compartment doors, at first in first-class vehicles only, but for third-class as well from the start of the 1930s. More impressively still, the first-class coaches of this order, built for the newly named Royal Scot and other front-rank expresses, were generously arranged for only two-a-side seating in their elegantly upholstered compartments, while the passenger space in some brake-end firsts was laid out as a lounge, with 10 seats comprising individual leather armchairs and a settee. Unexpectedly this last type of accommodation was none

Above: The northbound 'Royal Scot' takes on passengers at Euston's No. 13 platform in 1933. The train's overall schedule from London to both Glasgow and Edinburgh was 7 hours 40 minutes at the time.

too popular, probably because the armchairs were too low for a decent view through the still quite shallow windows.

In 1930 the LNER also cosseted first-class clients with two-a-side compartment seating when it further refined the handsome new Flying Scotsman train-sets it had built in 1928. An eminent interior designer of the day, Sir Charles Allom, was commissioned to create a new rail travel ambience in these trains and he succeeded stunningly in the restaurant cars – integrally furnished in Louis XIV style, with loose, patterned armchairs, concealed lighting behind translucent pelmets and hand-painted wall decor, they are still the most memorable British diners of this century. Gresley, who

had pioneered electric cooking on British trains in 1921, installed the first train-borne electric refrigerators in the adjoining kitchen cars. In 1929 the LNER added to the Scotsman's services' distinctions a unisex hairdressing salon and a ladies' retiring room, both staffed throughout the journey, and three years later the vehicles incorporating these amenities were further rebuilt with cocktail bars in the chromium-lined style beloved of the period.

Generally speaking, the first-class market and only front-rank trains benefited significantly from refinements in coach design until well into the 1930s. Until 1935, for instance, the only GWR coaches to display marked interior origin-ality were the Pullman-like 'Super-Saloons' o

1931 (it has been alleged, in fact, that Swindon based them on measured drawings of the Torquay Pullman cars which the London Old Oak depot staff were bidden surreptitiously to make before the Pullmans were shipped out to the Southern). But the Super-Saloons, with their two-a-side armchair seating at tables in an expensively panelled setting, were essentially for the first-class transatlantic traffic of the Plymouth boat trains; and the GWR, moreover, added a 50p surcharge to the full first-class fare for their use – a very hefty extra for the early 1930s, higher than the Pullman supplement for a comparable mileage and twice the contemporary price of a full restaurant car dinner on inter-city expresses.

Both LMS and LNER produced the first sleeping cars for second-class passengers in 1928, and the GWR followed suit in 1929. Until then night travel in a berth had been a first-class preserve and the railways were uncertain of the lower-level market response. Consequently the early second-class sleepers were a dual-purpose equivalent of the later Continental European *couchette* – day coaches with compartment seats convertible into lower berths, and hinged upper berths which could be folded into the walls when out of use. Occupants got only a pillow and a rug for their berth fee of 30p or 35p (according to distance) and there were no individual lights at the bedheads. Even so, the second-class berths quickly pulled in such business that before 1929

Above: On 27 April 1928, three days before the LNER's start of scheduled non-stop London–Edinburgh operation, the LMS stole the publicity limelight by running the 'Royal Scot's' Edinburgh and Glasgow sections non-stop from Euston. The Edinburgh train, here climbing Shap, was run the whole 399.7 miles by 4-4-0 No. 1054.

Above: SR *'Lord Nelson'*
class 4-6-0 No. 861
Lord Anson *attacks the*
climb out of Victoria to
Grosvenor Bridge with
a Dover Continental
boat train in the late
1930s. Pullman cars were
included in several of the
regular boat trains to the
Channel ports.

was out the LNER had ordered a new batch with all four berths in each compartment fixed.

As early as 1924 the LNER had laid on a silent feature film show in a luggage van of the Flying Scotsman as a one-day experiment, but in the early 1930s the company's Commercial Department set out determinedly to broaden the entertainment appeal of train travel. In 1930 the coaches forming the main morning Kings Cross–Leeds service and the afternoon express back were fitted with headphone sockets at every seat and connected to a radio set and record player in one of the brake vans (the record player took over whenever a tunnel blotted out radio reception); the train staff issued passengers with headphones in the same way that stewardesses do on a modern jetliner, except that use on the 1930 train was free. Two years later the mid-day Kings Cross–Edinburgh train-sets were similarly equipped, but the LNER went no further and in fact abandoned this interesting and imagin-

ative service in 1935.

Meanwhile, though, it had fitted the Leeds trains with a full luggage brake converted into a cinema, which presented an hour-long programme of newsreels, travelogues and cartoons (for 5p), just like the news cinemas which were popular in London and provincial cities at the time (a few at the main stations). In its first year this Pathé cinema attracted more than 35,000 patrons, but only one more was operated, on Leeds–Edinburgh expresses from 1936, and the concept died with the war.

I'll take the high road . . .

The thrust and counter-thrust of the LMS–LNER contest in Anglo-Scottish non-stop running during the late 1920s were typical of the railway's absorption with one-off spectaculars from which there was scant spin-off for the express service as a whole. In the Anglo-Scottish case, however one must concede that the two companies were still bound to keep their overall speed within the limits which the East and West Coast confederations had set themselves after the 1888 and 1895 races to the north. Not until 1932, with road transport a real menace, did the LMS and LNER mutually agree that the pact was an anachronism and that from then on each company should do as it pleased, provided only that it kept the other informed of its plans.

Advance briefing between Kings Cross and Euston was not a feature of the non-stop contest. The starting gun was the LNER's 1927 launch of non-stop running from Kings Cross to Newcastle by the 9.50 advance portion of the Flying Scotsman; immediately the LMS gave its newly-named Royal Scot the public timetable appearance of non-stop operation all the way to Glasgow. In fact the Royal Scot had to stop both at Carnforth to change engines and at Syminton to separate its Glasgow and Edinburgh portions (the LMS maintained a competitive, restaurant car service from Euston to Edinburgh Princes Street by both Royal Scot and Mid-day Scot right up to 1939; in the last pre-war summers, in fact, there were two complete Royal Scot trains each way daily, one to and from Edinburgh, the other to and from Glasgow). With the delivery (at last) of modern six-coupled express engines, the Royal Scot 4-6-0s, the LMS was soon able to advance the engine-changing point to Carlisle Kingmoor, 301 miles from Euston, and proclaim a new British non-stop record.

The LNER immediately re-set its non-stop

Left: First-class berth of an LNER sleeping car in the late 1920s. No third-class sleepers were built until 1928 and, at first, these were no better than present-day couchettes on Continental European railways.

sights to Edinburgh, 393 miles from Kings Cross. That was beyond the physical compass of a single engine crew, so Gresley devised a new version of his eight-wheeled Pacific tender with a narrow side corridor through which the engine crew could be relieved at the half-way point by another pair who had been riding 'on the cushions' in the train (each non-stop crew, by the way, got a free restaurant car meal and was also paid double-time). The construction of the first corridor tenders was pushed through Doncaster works in only seven weeks to achieve a non-stop

Below: The 'Cheltenham Flyer' accelerates past Shrivenham in 1931 with 4-6-0 No. 5004 Llanstephan Castle in charge. The LNER-style engine headboard was soon replaced by one proclaiming the 'Flyer' as the 'World's Fastest Train', but by 1933 the German diesel 'Fliegende Hamburger' had seized that title.

Above: The 'Cornish Riviera Express' in the BR era, heading west near Pewsey behind 4-6-0 No. 6026 King John *in March 1953. Throughout its history the train's title has wavered between 'Limited' and 'Express' as a suffix: the BR-style engine headboard took no chances, omitting both.*

premiere on May Day, 1928.

But the LMS had secretly laid plans to muffle the LNER's publicity drums. Only essential operating staff knew what was happening on 27 April, three days earlier, when – unusally for a spring weekday – the down Royal Scot set out as two separate trains, one for Glasgow behind Royal Scot 4-6-0 No. 6113 *Cameronian*, the other for Edinburgh with only a compound 4-4-0, No. 1054. The presence on each locomotive's footplate of an extra engineman and the fact that each engine had shed its usual tender for one of greater coal capacity should have primed any knowledgeable spectator as to what was on, but it wasn't until both trains were under way that the true intent rippled down the West Coast main line. That gathered welcoming parties at each Scottish terminal to salute the arriving trains for record non-stop runs: 401.4 miles to Glasgow Central by *Cameronian* and an extraordinary 399.7 miles to Edinburgh Princes Street by No. 1054, the latter a quite unrivalled feat by a British four-coupled engine. But the exploits were unrepeatable as a routine, whereas the Flying Scotsman at once claimed and clung to the world record for length of regular daily non-stop working.

High days and holidays

At the start of the 1930s the train was still the natural medium for a leisure journey of any length. At any time of the year an event of national interest was guaranteed to fill a fleet of excursion trains. The St Leger race meeting at Doncaster, for instance, would pull in upwards of 50 specials from as far afield as St Albans, Cambridge, Blackpool, Chester, Sunderland and Newcastle, enthralling local railway enthusiasts with a day's parade of unlikely locomotive power and a mis-shapen mix of vintage coaching stock.

High summer weekends would pack the main lines to the popular coastal areas with so many extras for outgoing and incoming holidaymakers that not only was freight traffic crowded off the tracks but often local passenger services would have to be curtailed. The wakes week exodus from northern industrial towns and the fairs holiday flight from Glasgow was almost exclusively by train.

In winter the GWR's Cornish Riviera Limited could serve eight destinations with one train: Weymouth by two slip-coaches detached on the approach to Westbury; Ilfracombe and Minehead by two more slip-coaches detached as a pair before Taunton; the Kingsbridge, Newquay

Falmouth and St Ives branches by through coach; and Penzance with the remaining five coaches, including the restaurant car. But on summer Saturdays the traffic demanded four separate departures from Paddington at five-minute intervals from 10.25 to 10.40. The Southern's Atlantic Coast Express spawned an even bigger summer Saturday shoal. On normal weekdays this was another train of many parts, for Ilfracombe, Torrington, Plymouth, Padstow, Bude, Exeter, Exmouth and Sidmouth, but on summer Saturdays almost every town had a train to itself, six in all (the total had risen to eight by 1938). In the 1930s, moreover, cross-country trains like the Sunny South Express from the north-west and the Midlands to Brighton, Eastbourne and Hastings, the Pines Express from the north-west to Bournemouth via the Somerset and Dorset Joint line, and the Devonian from the West Riding to Torbay, despite pedestrian end-to-end speed, all needed their own relief trains to aggravate the holiday area congestion when they merged with the flows from London.

But if the road motor had yet to make its full impact on long-haul leisure travel it had begun to threaten the shorter-distance business, by both regular and excursion trains (whether all that 1930s excursion traffic was really profitable one doubts: but in those days cost allocation was futuristic science, the pursuit of volume was all.) From now on the Big Four showed growing concern for the overall standard of their express passenger services, for upgrading of their second-rank and shorter-haul operations, and for product appeal in the third-class market.

Advances on the buffet car front

A symbol of changing attitudes was the LNER's unveiling in 1932 of what the timetables prosaically billed as the Garden Cities and Cambridge Buffet Expresses, though to Cantabrians they were always the 'Beer Trains'. Liverpool Street was the traditional London starting-point for Cambridge, but because of the tortuous GE route exit from the capital and the weight of train necessary to serve East Anglia beyond Cambridge the express service that way was wretchedly slow. So the LNER switched to Kings Cross and the Hitchin–Cambridge branch, putting on a daily sequence of short, fast trains serving intermediately the garden cities of Letchworth and Welwyn, and embodying two novelties: three-a-side second-class seating with armrests, and a buffet car. It was above all the new experience of being able to drink their way

through a 58½-mile journey, of course, which had undergraduates immediately hang the 'Beer Train' tag on the new service.

The first buffet cars were improvizations. The same year, 1932, the GWR sketchily rebuilt two of its very first, 36-year-old clerestory-roof diners with a fairly crude counter in one half of the saloon, and introduced them as 'café cars' on the Paddington–Oxford–Birmingham and Paddington–Bristol routes. Neither GWR or LMS acquired more than a handful of custom-built buffet cars before 1939, but the LNER steadily developed the idea on short-distance routes which were being deprecated by road competition – Newcastle–Carlisle, Hull–Liverpool, London Liverpool Street–Cambridge (which got its own 'Beer Trains' in 1937), Newcastle–Stockton–Middlesbrough and Leeds–Scarborough. The LNER was also careful to price its buffet wares attractively below its contemporary restaurant car tariffs. Another feature of this period was keener interest in open-saloon layouts, partly because they were thought to have third-class market appeal but chiefly because they accommodated more passengers for a given coach weight. Only the LMS was a convinced advocate, however: the GWR quaintly regarded open saloons as fit only for excursion trains and barred them from scheduled services.

The pre-World War II apotheosis of the buffet car was the Southern's modish design, with a ten-stool bar and saloon of unusual window-facing tables, for its Mid-Sussex electric express train-sets of 1938. Far more significant, though, was the character of the train service which employed them. Twenty years later the nationalized British Railways would recognize and confirm as the most potent

Below: To counter road transport's erosion of its excursion business, in 1933 the LNER introduced special green-and-cream liveried 12-coach 'Tourist' train-sets, entirely third-class, in open saloons laid out with high-capacity bucket seating at tables, and with two buffet cars in each formation. The patently posed pictures used by the PR departments of the railway companies were often highly amusing. This coach appears to be floating in mid-air.

weapon to counter far more virulent road competition the standardized, intensive, regular-interval main-line service with uniform train-sets which the Southern, under Sir Herbert Walker's perceptive management, pioneered in its Brighton electrification of 1933, its extension to Eastbourne in 1935 and then the Mid-Sussex scheme. The last of these projects, incidentally, was undertaken with the stimulus of the low-interest funds which the government made available to the railways from 1929 onwards for capital investment projects which would relieve unemployment.

General speed improvements

The Great Western came to the brink of main-line electrification in the 1930s, but balked at the cost. Back in 1925 its General Manager, Sir Felix Pole, had initiated conversion studies with his Bristol or Birmingham main lines in mind, but his colleagues were cool and diverted the exercise into a consideration of the Taunton–Penzance area. A fully worked out 3,000v DC overhead scheme involving over 160 electric locomotives was eventually formulated, but pigeonholed by the GWR Board in the spring of 1939 on grounds of inadequate return. If Walker had been in command at Paddington and the study had been pinned to the more suitable Birmingham line the future history of British railways could have been profoundly altered; the case for making electrification of the London Midland main line a priority in the 1960s could

Below: Gresley's Class A4 Pacific No. 2509 Silver Link *forges north across Welwyn Viaduct on the 'Silver Jubilee' press demonstration run of 27 September 1935 when 112.5 mph was touched in the course of running 25 miles on end at 100 mph or more.*

have been weakened in favour of the Eastern.

The late 1930s are naturally best remembered for the feats of the LNER's streamliners, the Kings Cross–Newcastle Silver Jubilee of 1935, then the Kings Cross–Edinburgh Coronation and Kings Cross–Leeds and Bradford West Riding Limited of 1937, and to a lesser extent for the achievements of the LMS Euston–Glasgow Coronation Scot, which was not set timings so far in advance of ordinary services as the LNER trains (see Chapter 22). Of far greater importance to the travelling public, however, was the general raising of speed standards. Here the LNER was clearly outshone by the LMS and GWR.

The LMS set to work in 1932, even before the first of Stanier's modern six-coupled passenger and mixed traffic locomotive types had taken the tracks. The 1932 accelerations on both the West Coast and the Midland main line from London in October that year were probably the most widespread in any single timetable change of the steam era. By the outbreak of war the LMS books showed twice as much daily mileage scheduled in excess of 58 mph average as the LNER's.

LMS policy was exemplified by its London–Manchester service; the best train of the day was only a quarter of an hour faster than the front runner in 1913, but each weekday's tally of seven trains from Euston was on average 35 minutes quicker. Illuminating, too, was the contrast in trends between the East and West Coast Anglo-Scottish services; the LMS had reduced the average weekday Euston–Glasgow transit time by 48 minutes to 8 hours 10 minutes compared with 1913, whereas the LNER's Kings Cross–Edinburgh average cut over the same period – notwithstanding the six-hour schedule of the streamlined Coronation – was a mere 18 minutes, down to a norm of 8 hours 2 minutes.

The GWR had singled out another train for special speed attention in 1935, when it marked its centenary with the introduction of the Bristolian between Paddington and Bristol on a 1¾-hour schedule demanding an average speed of over 67 mph, but with five other weekday trains on a two-hour timing between the two cities the overall average of the 10 trains-a-day service was 11 minutes faster than in 1913. In terms of mileage scheduled at 58 mph average or more set against total express train mileage, the GWR in fact ended the inter-war period at the top of the British league. The only disappointment of the 1930s speed-up – and it was serious – was that the improvement was almost entirely concentrated on the radial routes from London. The best journey average from Liverpool to Bristol, for instance, was a miserable 36.3 mph.

Chapter 22

The development of the streamliners

THE DEVELOPMENT IN the mid-1920s of pneumatic tyres large enough for buses and lorries sharpened road competition considerably. Road vehicles became fast and comfortable enough, even in those pre-motorway years, to attract some long-distance passengers from the railways. Air competition had not made the same headway in a small country like Britain, but the long-term threat was already recognized. In the early 1930s, therefore, the acceleration of main line railway services was made a priority, and existing types of conventional steam locomotive were coaxed to reveal reserves of speed and power never realized before. At the start of the 1930s rate of acceleration was faster in Britain than anywhere else in Europe. Not only that, but from 8 July 1929 the GWR could claim to run the world's fastest daily service with its Castle 4-6-0s, when the train later known as the Cheltenham Flyer was put on a 66.3 mph start-to-stop timing from Swindon to London, as described in the preceding chapter.

Below: Gresley's first LNER Pacific type, the Class A1 of 1922, is exemplified by No. 4472 Flying Scotsman, seen at Kings Cross shed in 1935. No. 4472 was later modified to Class A3.

Alternatives to steam

Anxious about the long-term competitive position of the railways, British managements were themselves studying the newer forms of traction. In 1931 the government-appointed Weir Committee issued a report advocating large-scale electrification of the 1.5kv DC overhead system, but in the weak economic state of Britain at the time the recommendation was only of academic interest, given the high cost of setting up the current supply system.

Diesel traction, on the other hand, needed no overhead wires or third rails .The diesel-electric main line locomotive was still in its early and crude development stage, but the Americans and the Germans were already achieving startling results with lightweight diesel railcars, to which diesel power units were best suited at their early period of development for rail use.

The first of these to go into regular daily service was the German Reichsbahn's 'Flying Hamburger', a twin-coach streamlined diesel unit which ran between Berlin and Hamburg at

an average start-to-stop speed of 77 mph. Launched in May 1933, it was the fastest train in the world and the object of much national pride. The 'Flying Hamburger' attracted the attention of railways all over the world and the LNER asked the German builders to estimate the possible timings for similar units between Kings Cross and Leeds or Newcastle. The reply was disappointing because the gradients and slack of the LNER route contrasted with the much easier running conditions of the 'Flying Hamburger' route. So the LNER decided to see what could be done with an ordinary Gresley Pacific locomotive and a light train or ordinary stock.

Steam competes

On a misty morning of 30 November 1934 the 11-year-old Gresley Pacific No. 4472 *Flying Scotsman*, driven by Driver Sparshatt, who had a reputation for fast running, left Kings Cross with a four-coach special and stopped at Leeds Central Station, 185.7 miles away, only 2 hours 31 minutes 56 seconds later. Stoke Summit, usually passed at 45–50 mph by the express trains of those days, was topped at 81 mph. On the return journey two more coaches were added, bringing up the seating to double that of the German unit. In 157 minutes 17 seconds *Flying Scotsman* was back in Kings Cross, having attained 100 mph on the descent of Stoke Bank. This was the first time a 100 mph claim had the support of a dynamometer car recording. However, coal consumption had been heavy for so light a load and would not have been acceptable in ordinary daily service.

On 5 March 1935 the more modern 220lb/in.^{2} pressure A3 class Pacific No. 2750 *Papyrus* in the hands of Driver Gutteridge was sent out on a similar trial run to Newcastle. Despite some delays *Papyrus* was at Newcastle in 237 minutes 7 seconds, compared with the German diesel builders' estimate of $4\frac{1}{4}$ hours – and the steam train had twice the seating capacity. After $2\frac{1}{2}$ hours' rest *Papyrus* started back with Driver Sparshatt in charge, and Kings Cross was reached in 231 minutes 48 seconds for the 268.3 miles after a maximum speed of 108 mph on the descent from Stoke. In the course of the day *Papyrus* had covered 300 miles at an average of 80 mph, but the most significant figure was the coal consumption of 43 lb per mile compared with 54 lb by *Flying Scotsman* on the Leeds trip. In ordinary service at moderate speeds there was no significant difference in the coal/dbhp/hr figures of the A3 Pacifics with 220 lb pressure and those which retained their 180lb boilers but had the valve gear modification ordered after the 1925 exchange. It may well be that the later engines were better in the higher speed ranges, but the locomotive handling on the Newcastle trip had been improved by experience on the earlier trial.

Streamlining

As a result of these successful tests the LNER decided to introduce a high-speed train on a four-hour booking to Newcastle in the autumn of 1935. Named Silver Jubilee in honour of King George V's 25 years on the throne, it was fully streamlined. Streamlining was a feature of the age but its benefits are now thought to have been less for a train than for a racing car or an aeroplane. Modern theory holds that aerodynamic drag on the coaches is more influential than the shape of the engine front. The LNER publicity department welcomed the streamlined shape as showing that the steam locomotive was able to adapt itself to the fashion of the 1930s rather than becoming as obsolescent as the steam traction engine and the tramcar.

The silver-grey livery and the different shape of Gresley's Pacific certainly attracted attention. The wedge-shaped front also helped to carry smoke and exhaust steam clear of the cab windows. Under the casing, however, the new A4 class Pacific was not greatly different. One of the greatest advances in locomotive practice had been made by André Chapelon in France. Chapelon had found that many compound engines had not been able to make full use of the steam generated in the boiler owing to the restricted steam passages, ports and valves. Some of Chapelon's ideas for the free passage of steam were incorporated by Gresley in his new A4s.

The Silver Jubilee train

On 27 September 1935 the new Silver Jubilee train, hauled by the first of the new A4 class Pacifics, No. 2509 *Silver Link* driven by Driver Taylor, set off from Kings Cross with specially invited guests for a demonstration run. They also wanted to test how much reserve power and speed would be available in ordinary service. Peterborough, 76.4 miles from Kings Cross, was passed in 55 minutes 2 seconds after covering 70 miles at an average of 91.8 mph, 43 miles at 100 mph, 25 miles at 107.5 mph and twice attaining a maximum of $112\frac{1}{2}$ mph. These remained British records for sustained speed with steam, and it is only in comparatively recent times that all these remarkable records have been surpassed with modern motive power.

In ordinary daily service the Silver Jubilee could keep time with a maximum speed no higher than 90 mph, and was still far faster than any other British train running over comparable distances. The small supplementary fare was good value, for an hour was saved on the journey. Time-keeping and loading were both satisfactory and the train boosted the railway's internal morale and their public esteem.

High-speed trains to Glasgow

Inevitably the success of the Newcastle streamliner raised demands for a similar service to Edinburgh, and this disturbed the LMS whose philosophy was different. The LMS preferred a general improvement in the standards of the whole service, rather than concentrating on one crack train as did the LNER and the GWR. Both policies can be justified, but when a high-speed service to Edinburgh was likely the LMS had to consider something similar to Glasgow. So it was that on 16 November 1936 the Stanier Pacific locomotive No. 6201 *Princess Elizabeth* set out from Euston at the head of a seven-coach train to make a fast test trip to Glasgow. The 900ft summit at Shap was topped at 57 mph and the 1000ft Beattock bank was climbed at nothing lower than 56 mph. Today the electrics climb these banks at such a speed that the ordinary passenger is unaware he is climbing, but for hand-fired steam the performance of *Princess Elizabeth* was sensational. Glasgow was reached in 353 minutes 38 seconds for 401.3 miles, and the greatest caution had been exercised on all the curves.

The success of the down run encouraged the LMS to add another coach to the return train the next day, yet *Princess Elizabeth* ran even better

Below: Class A4 Pacific No. 4466 Herring Gull eases the up 'Silver Jubilee' into Kings Cross at the conclusion of the four-hour run from Newcastle. In 1938 demand had forced the addition of an eighth coach to the train-set's original seven.

Above: Stainer streamlined Pacific No. 6200 Coronation *heads out of London past Kilburn on the pre-launch press run of the* LMS 'Coronation Scot' *on 29 June 1937. On this day 114 mph was touched for a new record but so close to Crewe that the train all but derailed on the station's approaches.*

Opposite: Yielding to the streamline fad, the GWR *directors in 1935 asked for a 'King' and a 'Castle' to be dressed up. Collett, their* CME, *dutifully moulded plasticine around models as a basis for the fairings, which served no aerodynamic purpose. The various excrescences were gradually removed from both engines, starting as early as 1935 with the cylinder fairings, which were a cause of over-heating.*

and reached Euston in 344 minutes 14 seconds with an average start-to-stop speed of 70 mph over 400 miles. No attempt had been made at high downhill maxima, but the peak of 95 mph attained near Crewe on level track with no help from gravity was of equal merit to downhill speeds of well over 100 mph. The coal consumption of 46.8 lb/mile northbound and 44.8 lb/mile southbound was moderate.

It was decided, on the results of these tests, to introduce a high-speed train to Glasgow in the summer of 1937 using a larger streamlined Pacific locomotive. The train was called the Coronation Scot but its schedule of six and a half hours was modest and many considered it unduly cautious compared with the LNER proposal of six hours to Edinburgh for its Coronation. The LMS, however, intended to feel their way gradually and to increase the load rather than the speed with further experience. At first the load was nine coaches, as was that of the LNER Coronation. The LNER ran a beaver-tail observation coach as their last vehicle.

The first new LMS streamlined Pacific was named *Coronation* and was larger then the LNER A4, having a grate area of 50 ft² as against 41½ ft² for the A4, and four cylinders against the three used on the Gresley Pacifics. The LMS engine needed to be larger on account of the

heavier gradients of the West Coast route, but in terms of high-speed capacity it was well matched. The new LMS Pacific had a rounded streamlined nose which may have been aerodynamically better than the wedge-shaped front of the A4, but it was less effective in carrying smoke clear of the cab. The engine and train were painted mid-blue with silver lines extending from engine front to brake end. The LNER A4s intended for the *Coronation* were also blue with red wheels, while the coaches were finished in Garter blue below the waistline and lighter Marlborough blue above. With two such handsome trains coming into service in coronation year, 1937, the hearts of railway enthusiasts were high, except that the worsening international situation raised doubts as to how long the good things would survive.

Coronation rivalry of LMS and LNER

On 29 June 1937 the new streamlined Pacific *Coronation*, in the hands of Driver Tom Clarke, the hero of the Glasgow test runs of 1936, left Euston for a demonstration run of the Coronation Scot to Crewe and back. The LMS was very anxious to share in the favourable publicity gained by the LNER with the 112½ mph of *Silver Link* in 1935 and then 113 mph by *Silver Fox*

(on the up Silver Jubilee) in 1936, but they had no stretch of line quite as suitable as the LNER's Stoke Bank for a maximum speed record. Their best stretch was the descent from Whitmore to Crewe, but that left little space in which to stop. The intention was to run fairly gently as far as Stafford and then to give *Coronation* a run. The climb to Tring Summit, with its minimum of 82 mph, broke all known records with steam, but then the running was relatively easy as far as Stafford, when No. 6220 *Coronation* was opened out to pass Whitmore at 85 mph. Speed then rose rapidly until near milepost 156 the stopwatch records estimated speed to be 113 mph, a dead heat with *Silver Fox*. But the speedometer on the engine recorded 114 mph and while a speedometer should not in itself be regarded as final proof, there were few who begrudge the LMS their claim for a record, especially as the engine still seemed to be accelerating when steam was shut off.

At milepost 156 there remained only two miles to Crewe station and with flames coming from the brake blocks the train tore past Crewe Sorting Sidings and Crewe South Shed, finally coming to rest at Platform 3 still safely on the rails with the crockery in the dining car smashed to smithereens. From passing Whitmore to the dead stop in Crewe 10½ miles had taken just 6 minutes 58 seconds! The LMS publicity people made good use of the 114 mph, but wisely no further high speed attempts were made at that spot. The return journey was in real merit terms a better run. Here the aim was a high sustained average speed, and the return journey to Euston, 158.1 miles, was made in 119 minutes with no higher maximum speeds than 100 mph at Castlethorpe; 150 miles had been run at an average of 83.2 mph and 72 miles at 88.9 mph.

The rival Coronation had a demonstration run on the following day and despite LNER protests that it was not intending to break records, it would have been happy to have done so. The maximum was only 109½ mph, but with a heavier full train load of 325 tons, whereas the LMS had cut one kitchen car out of the Coronation Scot, leaving 270 tons; so faces were saved. The late Cecil J. Allen described the situation as 'honours easy', and the worst competitive excesses of the 1895 races to Scotland were avoided.

In everyday service, however, there was no doubt that the LNER had the more exciting train. While the Coronation Scot could keep time with

no higher maximum than 83–85 mph, Coronation had to travel at up to 90 mph and occasionally topped the three-figure mark up to a maximum of 107 mph recorded in ordinary service. The daily booking of 157 minutes start-to-stop from Kings Cross to York was the fastest ever performed by steam in Britain. Timekeeping was generally very good, but the margin was a slender one. This was no defect of the A4 design but a measure of the limitations of a large, hand-fired engine. A firing rate easy enough at 60 mph was much more difficult when each mile took only 40–45 seconds.

In the autumn of 1937 the LNER added a third streamliner, the West Riding Limited from Kings Cross to Leeds, 185.7 miles, in 163 minutes down and 164 minutes up. This was an eight-coach train like the Coronation, but without the beaver-tail. In 1938 increasing patronage led to strengthening of the Silver Jubilee from seven to eight coaches. The LMS made no attempt to introduce Coronation Scot-type trains to Liverpool or Manchester, but planned instead a gradual improvement of ordinary services. Had there been no war the Coronation Scot would have been increased to 11 coaches in 1940, and design work had started on a giant, mechanically-fired 4-6-4 which would have timed the Coronation Scot with 15 coaches. World War II put an end to all such hopes.

The GWR made some half-hearted and un-convincing attempts in 1935 at streamlining a King and a Castle class engine with a bulbous front to the smokebox, but thanks to Brunel's excellent main line it was able to run some quite fast trains with ordinary 4-6-0 engines, and so experimented no further. In 1938 the LMS built two more large Pacifics, but ten of these were not streamlined. It was the non-streamlined form which was destined later to be standardized.

Streamlining abroad

The streamlined steam train made further headway abroad as steam engineers reacted against the advance of the diesel. In Germany a large fully streamlined 4-6-4 with 7 ft 6 in. driving wheels reached a speed of 124½ mph in 1936, but the most courageous exploitation of steam for high-speed service was that of the American Hiawatha express from Chicago to the twin cities of St Paul and Minneapolis. Some streamlined oil-burning Atlantics were built for this train by the Milwaukee Road in 1935, but increasing patronage led to their being super-seded by some very large semi-streamlined 4-6-4 Hudsons in 1938. These were coal-burning with mechanical firing. One of them on test went over the 120 mph mark for five miles. In ordin-ary service during the war years 4-6-4 No. 101

Below: Twilight of the Gresley A4 Pacifics: superseded by diesels on the East Coast main line, No. 60009 Union of South Africa *heads the 7.10 am Aberdeen–Glasgow out of Stone-haven in March 1965.*

hauling 680 tons covered 47.8 miles at a pass-to-pass average of 104.9 mph while another with 780 tons covered 62 miles at an average of over 100 mhp. The Hiawatha performed the fastest start-to-stop booking ever given to steam anywhere, with a scheduled 81 mph start-to-stop from Sparta to Portage. Its Atlantics and Hudsons maintained a punctuality record of 93 per cent in all weathers. But even this could not prevent Hiawatha and other American high-speed trains going over to diesel power.

British steam records

The two last precarious years of peace were enlivened in Britain by two outstanding locomotive performances. These were destined to become the twin peaks of British steam achievement. On 3 July 1938, in the course of some brake tests down Stoke Bank, the LNER A4 class engine *Mallard*, hauling 240 tons, reached a maximum speed of 125 mph for 900 ft with a momentary maximum of 126 mph. This was a world record for steam and although it was

attained downhill, *Mallard* was a smaller engine than the German 4-6-4 and the American Hiawatha Atlantics and Hudsons, the only other types for which credible claims of two miles a minute may be accepted.

A performance of a very different nature was recorded in February 1939 when the LMS non-streamlined Pacific No. 6234 *Duchess of Abercorn* was tested over the difficult Crewe–Glasgow main line with a load of 20 coaches weighing 610 tons. This was a test of power rather than speed, and record drawbar horsepower of over 2500 were recorded in the dynamometer car. The official calculated indicated horsepower was over 3500, which was a British record, even if short-lived.

The speed of *Mallard* and the horsepower of *Duchess of Abercorn* remained British records, though postwar tests on the stationary rollers of British Rail's Rugby test plant and on the road of LMR No. 46225 *Duchess of Gloucester* were more significant because they were longer sustained. One design feature common to both *Mallard* and *Duchess of Abercorn* was that both

Below: Sunset of the steam age at the buffer-stops of Kings Cross in May 1960. On the left is the front end of a Gresley Class A3 Pacific in its final form, with double chimney and smoke deflectors; in the background Class A4 Pacific No, 60010 Dominion of Canada.

had double chimneys. *Mallard* had the French Kylchap type and the Duchess had the more simple LMS type of double chimney. Double chimneys improved performance in two ways – they enabled better draughting which raised more steam, and they reduced back pressure because of the greater freedom with which exhaust steam escaped. The double chimney was destined to be used to good effect both during and after the war to adapt engines to lower-grade coals.

The everyday standards of steam performance after the war never quite recovered to the pre-1939 level, though individual runs of equal or sometimes greater merit were recorded on rare occasions. Diesel traction by 1939 had progressed far beyond the experimental rail cars of the early 1930s, especially in the US.

The Bulleid Pacifics

In Britain, despite the war, O.V.S. Bulleid of the Southern Railway made a courageous attempt to adapt the steam locomotive to changing conditions. He combined a boiler of high steam-raising capacity with three cylinders and a chain-driven valve gear enclosed in an oil bath. The whole engine was shrouded in a sheet-metal casing described as being 'air-smoothed' rather than 'streamlined'. The main aim was to simplify cleaning by allowing the engine to pass through carriage washing plants, rather than to assist its passage through the air.

The first Bulleid Pacific was ready in February 1941, and because of its 6 ft-2 in. driving wheels it was officially described as being 'mixed traffic', which made its construction acceptable in wartime. The short piston stroke and piston valves, large in relation to cylinder size, made the engine capable of the highest speeds required in normal service. The larger Bulleid Pacifics were named the Merchant Navy class in honour of the heroic efforts of merchant seamen in the national interest. They were joined in 1945 by a smaller, lighter version which could work over most of the Southern Railway; these became the West Country and Battle of Britain class.

These Pacifics did not represent the end of the ingenuity of the designer. After the war Bulleid built an experimental tank engine named the *Leader*, which was an attempt to build a steam locomotive with all its weight available for adhesion and to give the driver a lookout as clear as that on a diesel or electric locomotive. The engine was carried on two six-wheeled bogies with chain drive between the axles. Each

bogie was driven by a three-cylinder sleeve-valved engine. Unfortunately it gave considerable trouble; the engine never ran in revenue-earning service, and BR had little alternative but to scrap it in the 1950s.

The Bulleid Pacifics did a lot of excellent running, but their repair costs were high and mileages were disappointing. In the 1948 locomotive exchanges, which were intended to suggest design features worthy of incorporation in future BR standard designs, the Bulleid Pacifics produced some of the highest horse-powers but also the highest coal consumption figures. This was confirmed by longer, more detailed tests at the Rugby plant in 1954, and the decision was made to rebuild them on more conventional lines without the oil bath lubrication and the air-smoothed casing. In course of time all the records of the originals were equalled or surpassed by the rebuilds and coal consumption and repair costs were reduced. All the larger Pacifics were rebuilt, and about half of the lighter version.

All new postwar Pacifics were built without streamlining and the casings were removed from the LMS engines, leaving only the Gresley A4s as a memory of the days when streamlining was the fashion. In due course square-ended electrics were to be seen, and diesels with only rudimentary streamlining, running at speeds well in excess of the fastest of the pre-war trains. Today, in the high-speed trains on the Western and East Coast main lines and in the Advanced Passenger Train developed for the West Coast route, there is a revival of streamlining on a more scientific basis. While the streamliners of the 1930s were to some extent examples of the caprice of fashion, their effect on the contemporary railway image should not be underestimated.

Above: Two of Bulleid's light Pacifics on shed at London's Nine Elms in the 1950s. The air-smoothed casings were removed in subsequent BR rebuilding.

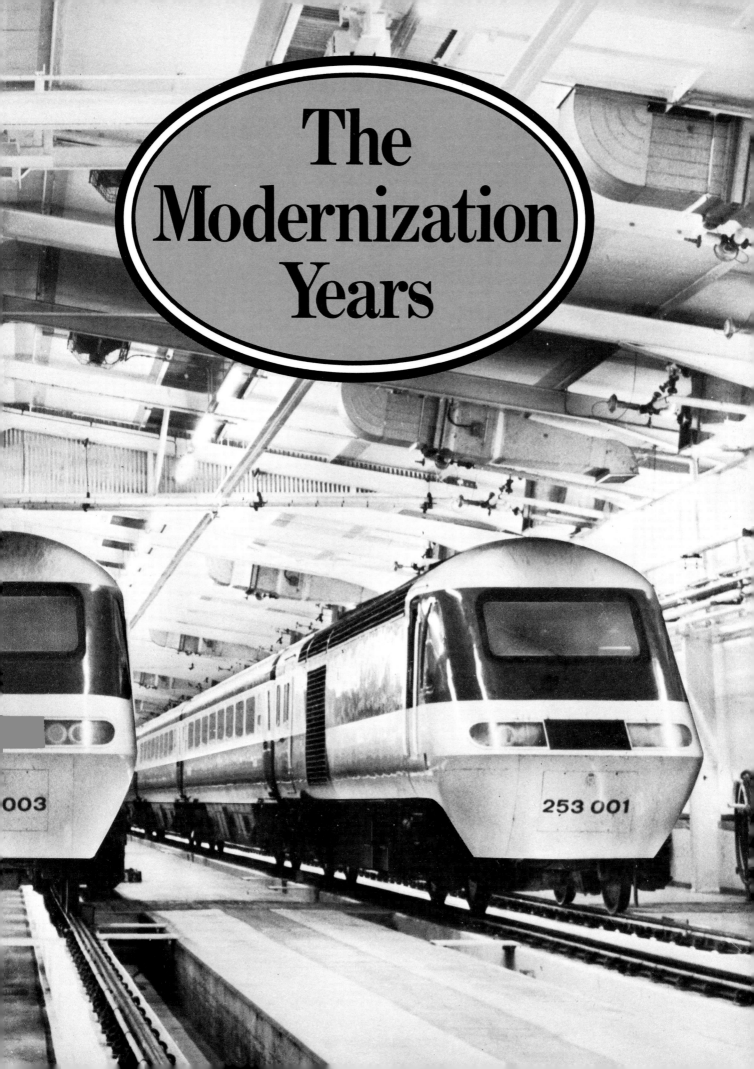

The Modernization Years

253 001

003

Chapter 23

World War II and nationalization

Previous pages: The 'Inter-City 125' diesel train-sets of Classes 253 and 254 are serviced at custom-built maintenance depots. This is one of the first of the two establish-ed on the Western Region —at London's Old Oak Common and Bristol's St Philips Marsh. Each unit carries enough fuel for 1400 miles' running, and returns to its depot every two days for routine examination.

I N THE SECOND half of the 1930s a new European war looked more of a certainty each year, and by 1937 the British government and railway managements were once more planning against a likely emergency. The fear of unheralded attack from the air was widespread, so evacuation planning and protection of railways and railwaymen was as important a topic in the 1937–8 discussions as preparation of the railways for military supply service. At that time only half-hatched, the evacuation schemes were very nearly put into action at the height of the 1938 Munich crisis over Nazi Germany's demand for Czechoslovakia's Sudetenland. Had the button been pushed then, things would have been chaotic, but thanks to meticulous planning it was near faultless when the crisis did arrive.

With war inevitable, on 1 September 1939 the government formally took control of all four main-line railways, the London Passenger Transport Board and five minor railways, acting as in the 1914–18 war through a Railway Executive Committee (REC), this time comprising the Big Four and LPTB general managers chaired by the LNER's Sir Ralph Wedgwood. The REC operated from offices carved out of a disused Piccadilly tube station at Down Street, under London's West End (from early 1941 Prime Minister Churchill took advantage of its security as an office during the heaviest air raids), so as to be at the government's right hand, but in a superhuman operation the Big Four headquarters' offices were each moved, staff, files and all to Home Counties retreats in the course of that first September weekend. And over the same first four days of September the railways carried out with scarcely a hitch one of the most remarkable mass passenger transport exercises in their history, the evacuation from London of over 600,000 civilians – mostly children – in

1,577 special trains, and of well over 700,000 more in a further 2,246 trains from 17 other conurbations in England and Scotland.

Emergency passenger timetables drastically pruned and slowed down services – in some cases to slower times than in the grimmest years of World War 1 – and a system-wide speed limit of 60 mph was enforced to reduce maintenance requirements. Crack trains like the streamliners were abandoned for the duration (forever, it turned out, in the case of the streamliners), and at first only the Southern was allowed to retain any sort of train catering. With the Germans deceptively quiet in the west, however, the draconian restrictions were relaxed, and with the speed limit raised to 75 mph many long-haul passenger services were accelerated in December 1939. As Whitsun 1940 approached the railways were even scheduling extra trains for holiday-makers.

But there was no Whitsun holiday. The German invasion of the Low Countries and the Dunkirk evacuation suddenly and terrifyingly supervened. Expecting at first to retrieve only about 30,000 British officers and men through the Channel ports, the railways had abruptly to set up trains for nearly 300,000. That was the total shifted by 565 specials, 327 of them from Dover, between 27 May and 4 June 1940 in the most extraordinary instant improvization in British railway operating history. In early June

200 more specials were needed to carry survivors who had been evacuated from western French ports to ones in the West Country, principally Plymouth.

From now on the railways came under intensifying strain. A reduced passenger service swollen by service movement generated massive trainloads, especially on the LNER's East Coast main line, where on at least one occasion Kings Cross loaded a 25-coach train of which not only the engine but the first coach as well were not merely beyond the platform but standing *inside* Gasworks Tunnel before departure.

The freight burden steadily mounted, not entirely in terms of trains to be moved – until some new construction in 1943 available wagon stock was running down for lack of repair capacity – but to a significant extent through pressure for more efficient wagon loading. The true measure of the railways' freight effort is their net ton mileage graph, which by 1943 had risen a sensational 43 per cent above its peacetime level. This, moreover, had been achieved despite the surrender of over 100,000 staff to National Service; a desperate shortage of materials, manpower and plant to maintain equipment adequately (most railway workshops had been co-opted for munitions and armaments manufacture of all kinds, from guns to ammunition to, eventually, aircraft assemblies, tanks and landing craft); and the hazards and difficulties of

Above: To provide motive power for war-damaged European railways in the wake of the Allied invasion the Ministry of Supply had R.A. Riddles design simple and easily maintained 2-8-0 and 2-10-0 types. Of the 2-8-0s no fewer than 935 were built; 733 of them returned to peacetime service in Britain and were among the last BR steam engines to be scrapped. Officially known as one of Class WD, popularly as an 'Austerity', No. 90364 heads freight over the Settle-Carlisle line.

Left: Gresley's three-cylinder, 6 ft 2 in. driving wheel Class V2 2-6-2s were one of the most versatile mixed traffic designs. Capable on all types of freight, they could also put up 90 mph-plus on East Coast expresses. One wartime March 1940 day, a V2 lifted a 26-coach train out of Kings Cross. Here, No. 60879 passes Potters Bar with empty stock in 1951.

Above: Many an elegant nineteenth-century station train-shed lost its roof glass through bomb blast in the 1939-45 war. One was the former New Street Station, Birmingham, seen here. Former Midland compound 4-4-0 No. 1025 is backing on to a Stanier Class 5 4-6-0 to double-head an express to Bristol.

night-time operation under blackout conditions.

On top of all this the Germans piled the bombs of the 1940–1 blitz, and subsequently their V1 flying bombs and V2 rockets. Like their compatriots in the Civil Defence services, railwaymen were on the scene of any bomb incident as soon as it had been reported, often getting repair work under way while bombs were still falling around them. In many instances the damage was made good before the next night, though if bridges or viaducts had been destroyed they inevitably took longer to clear and repair or replace.

Photographs of direct-hit damage to some key railways structures, such as Kings Cross, Paddington and St Pancras terminals or York Station, have become familiar since the war, but a sharper impression of the problems confronting railwaymen after a major air attack comes from a situation report on the morning after the Coventry blitz of 14–15 November 1940. In the whole history of the London blitz the LMS never had to contend with more than 23 incidents in a single night in its territory around the capital. After the Coventry attack it faced the aftermath

of 122 in and around the city; with the exception of one remote avoiding line, every rail route touching this busy traffic centre was blocked and the city's station itself was unusable. Because of the total disruption, clearing and repairs could only be started at sites it was possible to reach with a work train, so the restoration of much of the city's rail network within a week speaks for itself.

The post-Dunkirk transformation of England's entire southern shore from Essex to Cornwall into a battlefront, and of all southern England into its rear area; the inflow from North America, first of lend-lease supplies and then of armies of Americans themselves and their equipment; and the development of key war material production in areas whose peacetime transportation demands had been far less intensive – all this significantly reoriented the historic flows of the railway system.

Improvement of cross-country routes became imperative and from early 1940 some important new construction was ordered. On the edges of the London area, in particular, new junctions were laid to create circular bypasses which accelerated north–south through traffic and kept more out of the city centre. One of the biggest route widenings in the country was the quadrupling of the Bristol–Birmingham main line between Gloucester and Cheltenham (a sector since returned to double track under British Rail's slimming of operating capacity) to smooth the flow of armaments from South Wales factories and of American imports through the Bristol Channel ports.

Preparations for the day and night air offensive from British bases saddled the railways with new burdens. In 1943, when the crash construction programme of some 150 bomber airfields in East Anglia and many new fighter bases in Kent and Sussex was at its peak, country stations near the sites were coping manfully with ten times their daily peacetime flow of freight as trains streamed in with building materials and rubble from bombed areas. When the airfields were completed, they had to be populated; the LNER reckoned that it took 460 special trains to assemble all the men at the new East Anglian bases. Railways had a key role in the eventual operations, too; a 1000-bomber raid on average meant 28 trains of fuel and 8 of bombs.

Needless to say, D-Day imposed the severest strain on the railways. In the two months from the start of troop movement on 26 March to invasion day itself, 6 June 1944, 24,459 special trains had to be scheduled and of these 3,636 were run in just one week immediately preceding D-Day. In the following four weeks the demands on the railways were heavier still; including forces mail trains, ambulance trains and others transporting the inflow of German

POWs to inland camps, the special train total in that period soared to over 18,000.

Throughout this critical season the government had strictly forbidden the railways to run any extra trains for civilian or non-essential traffic, and a number of scheduled main-line passenger services had been cancelled to release men and rolling stock for military business. But with the Germans' new V1 flying bomb assault on the south–east a fresh evacuation of children was authorized. The government now accepted too, that war-weary adults must be allowed to snatch a few days' respite in the country from the relentless wail of sirens as the V1s droned inland day and night. Without any of the special provisions made to cover a similar situation in 1939, the railways came to their only operational breaking-point of the war on the last Saturday of July 1944. Almost all London termini were suffocating with masses of humanity unable to find train space, and at Paddington the pressure was so threatening that the station had to close every entrance for three hours. As the *Daily Mail* editorial commented the next day, 'We hesitate to think what the casualty list might have been had a flying bomb fallen there.'

The aftermath of war

The railways emerged from the war physically and materially exhausted and miserably run down. Fixed structures and rolling stock had received no more than the minimum maintenance needed to keep them mobile. One of the Big Four alone – the LMS – calculated that it would have to spend £14 million (in the money

Left: When the SR demanded more 0-6-0s in 1941, Bulleid gave them his strange-looking Class Q1 of 1942. Undoubtedly Bulleid took the elimination of usual detail, such as splashers, to deliberate extremes, but a good deal was sensibly sacrificed to allow the use of a big boiler and to increase power without excessive axle loading. In BR ownership No. 33007 heads a stone train past Herne Bay.

Right: At the end of World War II the GWR *management fancied that gas-turbine electric traction would perform well over the gradients of Devon and Cornwall. A 2500hp locomotive was ordered from Brown Boveri and delivered in 1949; it is pictured here leaving Paddington. A British-built locomotive followed in 1951. Neither, however, showed superior thermal efficiency to steam.*

values of 1945) merely to catch up with arrears of track and signalling maintenance, and £26 million more to bring its track up to acceptable peacetime standards; in the money terms of the late 1930s the two figures would aggregate at least £200 million.

But the railways were financially drained too. The slump of the 1930s, road transport's erosion of rail freight largely because of its freedom from the ancient statutes which hamstrung the railways' competitive manoeuvrability, and heavy 1930s investment in express passenger equipment had combined to impoverish the Big Four in the pre-war years. In 1938 only the GWR could muster a dividend – and that a miserable one – for its ordinary shareholders; the LNER's wretched investors had seen no return on their money for four years.

Before the war the government had promised the railways that in the event of war they would receive a measure of the revenue they could have expected in a reasonably successful peacetime year. But when war came the government reneged on its promise and the railways ended up far more shabbily treated than in 1919. Under a retrospective agreement backdated to 1 December 1940 the railways ended up sharing amongst themselves less than half the revenue they officially earned – and it needs to be remembered that much of the traffic was carried at substandard rates; apart from servicemen and others travelling at concessionary fare rates

government freight had to be charged at 10–33⅓ per cent less than the scheduled scales. The balance of the railways' theoretical wartime earnings totalling over £176 million at the money values of the period was pocketed by the Treasury. Moreover the railways were far from adequately compensated for damage by enemy action.

Even if the railways had had the financial resources it would have made scant difference to their rate of recovery. For the first post-war decade successive governments all took the view that railways had a very low priority in the queue for scarce raw materials and industrial capacity as well as capital investment. The railways were conceded a handful of sizeable improvement schemes such as the completion of the 1.5kv DC London Liverpool Street–Shenfield and Manchester–Woodhead–Sheffield electrifications which had been deferred because of the war. But for the most part the British system, since it was still usable unlike the ravaged railways of mainland Europe, had to renovate on the cheap or else make do and mend. Long before those ten years of parsimony were up the huge post-war flow of new motor transport had begun to flood the roads.

Nationalization and its effects

With the 1945 election of a Labour government commanding a large House of Commons

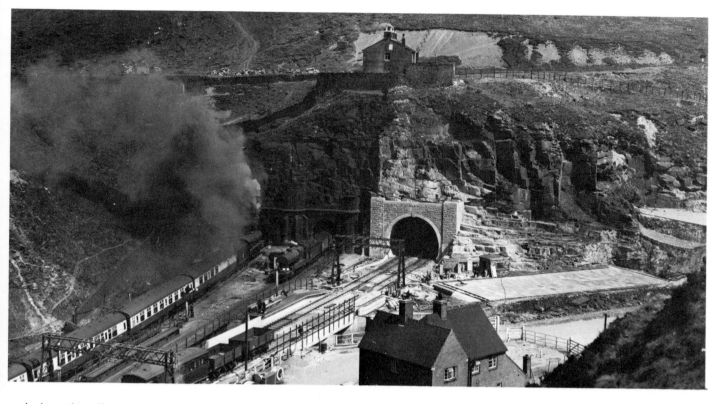

majority, the all-embracing nationalization of British railways threatened in World War II had become a certainty. Interestingly, a committee which the railways' boards themselves set up in the 1940s to consider post-war organization had recommended fusion into one corporate system, though one that remained in private ownership. The railway boards, however, rejected this conclusion and requested the Ministry of Transport to restore the companies to their 1939 constitution as separate entities.

The railway directors told Churchill's National Government:

The nationalization of railways in other countries has not resulted in a better service being provided than that afforded by British railways and has generally necessitated assistance having to be given by their national exchequers.

As soon as the incoming Labour administration reaffirmed its nationalization intention, the four railway boards launched a vigorous but quite abortive campaign to fend off the takeover. A number of officers opted for early retirement rather than submersion in a state undertaking; the most important of these was the Great Western's General Manager, Sir James Milne, a particularly strenuous opponent of nationalization, who declined an invitation to chair the Railway Executive of the new British Transport Commission (BTC).

Almost to a man, however, the rank and file of the railways greeted nationalization as the millenium. The old Labour-associated newspaper, the *Daily Herald*, not only proclaimed 1 January 1948 – the vesting date established by Attlee's nationalizing Transport Act – as 'Railway Sunday', but reported moves to have the date enshrined in the national calendar of high days and holidays for evermore.

The Labour government's objective was state control and co-ordination of all public transport. In theory the Attlee administration's 1947 Act was substantially founded on a 1938 pamphlet, *British Transport at Britain's Service*, written by Herbert (later Lord) Morrison, who as Transport Minister in the 1929 Labour government had welded London's underground rail and bus operations into the London Passenger Transport Board structure. Advocating a National Transport Board to control not only the railways but all long-distance and some other categories of road transport, Morrison saw this as ending:

. . . the destructive war between road and rail. It does not follow that there would be no duplication of road and rail services; public taste and preferences must be taken into account. It would, however, be a duty of the Transport Board to build up a complete co-ordinated system and see that the most efficient means of transport are available for appropriate classes of traffic.

The BTC was never given time enough to

Above: Deterioration of the original GC single-bore Woodhead Tunnels under the Pennines forced postwar construction of a new double-track tunnel before the pre-war Manchester–Sheffield 1.5kV DC electrification scheme could be finished in 1954. This photograph shows old and new tunnel mouths early that year.

achieve that end; Labour's instant theory was one thing, acquisition of practical knowhow something else. Forty years and more on, an economically beleaguered Britain is still trying to reconcile due account of 'public taste and preferences' with pursuit of a maximally cost-effective but optimally efficient national transport system.

The 1947 Transport Act's approach was to establish the BTC as corporate overlord of subordinate Executives severally charged with day-to-day management of the main-line railways, public road transport, docks, canals and London Transport. Of the pre-war Big Four, the Southern and Great Western suffered little physical mutilation in their transmutation to Southern and Western Regions, but the LMS and LNER were deemed too far-flung for effective control under the new order. The LMS remained largely intact south of the border as the London Midland Region, but besides surrendering its Scottish territory, as did the LMS, to a new Scottish Region, the LNER's English system was bisected into Eastern and North-Eastern Regions (they were reunited as one Eastern Region, with headquarters at York, in 1967).

The headquarters of these regions had little of the power of the pre-war railway managements. In those early nationalization years the Railway Executive exercised a strict functional control down to ground level in every department of engineering and operation. The Chief Regional Officers, as the regions' heads were first called, were figureheads, unable to authorize projects costing more than £2,000 or appointments carrying a salary in excess of £600 without the Railway Executive's rubber stamp.

Of all the decisions taken by the Railway Executive the most momentous was to persist with steam traction. Gresley's steam streamliner achievements from 1935 onwards had blinded all Big Four managements to the rapid refinement of diesel traction in Germany and North America, but after the war both LMS and LNER had been persuaded by the diesel's sweep of US railroads to embark on pilot main-line dieselization schemes. The LNER's was the more ambitious proposal, envisaging an order for 25 1,600hp locomotives to take up East Coast main-line haulage.

The Railway Executive, however, decided to write a fresh chapter of steam locomotive history with a new range of standard and mainly mixed traffic types in seven power ranges from light tender and tank engines up to an express passenger Pacific equivalent to the later products of the Big Four. The LMS did produce two proto-

type main line diesels of 1,600hp and the Southern three more while the Western, exercising the independence it fought bitterly to preserve until Paddington met its match in Beeching, experimented with two gas turbine-electric locomotives, one Swiss and the other British.

No other major railway in the industrialized west committed itself so heavily to steam traction in the post-war period as the new-born British Railways. The cost of the decision, which squandered the opportunity for leisurely evaluation of alternative diesel designs and a carefully phased transition from steam, was not to be realized until BR was forced into the most hectic dieselization a national railway system had ever attempted.

Persistence with steam was one of the reasons – but by no means the only one – for BR's depressingly slow recovery of pre-war train service standards. Good steam coal was scarce. Post-war full employment in an inflationary wage situation reduced the pre-war attractiveness of railway service as a secure job, especially if it involved filthy work with steam locomotives. Steam locomotive depot staffs dropped below establishment and locomotive maintenance suffered; and that, coupled with unpredictable fuel quality, made unreliable performance common. The BR standard locomotives had been specifically designed to overcome these handicaps but

Below: One of the late efforts to improve steam locomotive efficiency: No. 44755, heading an express over the Leeds–Carlisle main line, came from a batch of Class 5 4-6-0s built to Stanier's LMS design. This group was built in 1948 with double chimneys and Caprotti valve gear for more efficient use of steam, and with Timken roller bearings to cheapen maintenance.

even they were not entirely immune to the effects.

Meanwhile it was clear that the BTC was not achieving the aims of its creators. Apart from inability to reduce accumulating deficits – the BTC blamed only the historic pricing restraints placed on railways when they had a transport monopoly, but modern critics would attribute much more to blinkered thinking about the kind of railway needed in the post-war world – the Commission could only make halting progress on the co-ordination front. The BTC was at loggerheads with its Railway Executive, which regarded itself as the fount of all wisdom on railway management, and railwaymen down the line increasingly resented their subjugation to the Executive.

To the Conservative party decentralization of power was the panacea. So, when Churchill and the Tories were returned to power late in 1951, a new Transport Act was again a certainty. Heady expectations of a return to the pre-1939 Big Four indulged by some popular newspapers of the Right were not fulfilled, but the Tories, in their 1953 Act, did abolish their principal Aunt Sallies, the BTC's Executives, including the Railway Executive. Both the stature and power of the Regional heads, now redesignated Chief Regional Managers, were greatly enhanced; and now the BTC dealt with them directly through what was named its Railway Division. This was

the period when Western Region pushed its independence to the point of reviving the old Great Western rolling stock liveries.

The 1953 Act also began the abolition of BR's statutory charging and common carrier obligations, opening the door to today's market pricing and traffic selectivity freedom, which was completed by the Tories' 1962 Transport Act. This, as we shall see, finally killed off the BTC itself and sent London Transport, canals, most of the former railway docks and other BTC subsidiaries off on their own.

Above: The LSWR *survives almost unchanged as late as 1965 on the Isle of Wight as Class 02 0-4-4T No. 16* Ventnor *climbs between Shanklin and Wroxall with a Ryde—Ventnor train.*

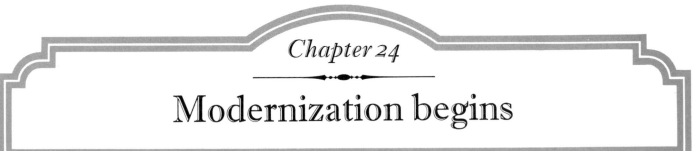

Chapter 24

Modernization begins

Above: General Sir Brian Robertson (later Lord Robertson), Chairman of the British Transport Commission from 1953 until 1962.

THE BRITISH TRANSPORT Commission was at last let off the financial leash in 1955 and allowed to embark on a massive re-investment in railways. That year a Moderniz-ation Plan adding up to a capital expenditure of £1,240 million (at 1955 money values) was authorized by the government and announced by the Chairman, General Sir Brian (later Lord) Robertson. Both Whitehall and the BTC insisted that from 1970 onwards progressive repayment with interest of the cash loaned to execute the scheme would be a comfortable formality, so surely would the requipment increase BR's efficiency and – in the words of the published Plan – 'recover the ground that has been lost to

other forms of transport over the past thirty years'.

The bulk of the money would go on traction and rolling stock. Electrification was program-med for the East Coast main line from Kings Cross to Doncaster, Leeds and possibly York; for the London Kings Cross suburban system; for the London Midland main lines from Euston to Birmingham, Liverpool and Manchester; for the Eastern Region ex GE line beyond Chelmsford to Ipswich, including the Clacton, Harwich and Felixstowe branches; for the Liverpool Street-north-east London suburban network; and for the Southern Kent coast lines and the rest of the Southern's then unelectrified

Right: The shape of the future – one of the cumbersome diesel-electric types of BR's aborted dieselization scheme pilot, a Class 45 1-Co-Co-1, under scrutiny at Leicester. The photograph was taken in June 1977.

Below: Fading steam: 'Jubilee' class 4-6-0 No. 45581 Bihar and Orissa starts an express from Liverpool Lime Street.

main routes east of a line drawn from Reading to Portsmouth.

Over the rest of the system steam was to be eliminated by large-scale dieselization with both locomotives and multiple-unit railcars. Diesel traction, the BTC emphasized, was second choice for the most heavily trafficked routes; if the technical and financial capacity to undertake more electrification emerged as the Plan unfolded, then the diesel traction orders would be reduced.

The Plan's other major areas of expenditure were track reconstruction, to overtake the skimped maintenance of wartime years; resignalling; and the freight business, for which more than a quarter of the total investment money was earmarked. Most of the freight cash was to be spent on new wagons, building or rebuilding over fifty marshalling yards, and equipping all goods wagons with continuous brakes operable from the locomotive.

The pitifully small proportion of BR's wagon fleet with continuous brakes – or 'fitted wagons' in common railway parlance – was a crippling handicap in the competitive post-war freight market. When brakepower was available only on the locomotive of a 500-ton-plus goods train, or on the engine and a handful of fitted wagons coupled immediately behind it, speed had to be severely restricted. In this respect British railways were medieval by comparison with the rest of the world's major systems, which had long

ago taken continuous braking of all freight wagons for granted.

Unhappily, this long overdue modernization was emasculated by the BTC's faint-hearted retention of the vacuum brake system inherited from most of the pre-nationalization railway network, instead of seizing the opportunity to switch to the more efficient air brake. Regional managements of BR lobbied strenuously to spare their operators the short-term harassments of a changeover, which admittedly would have been formidable, though they must have realized that the higher average speeds envisaged by the Plan would compel their successors to change to air braking.

Within a decade air braking had been standardized for new construction, but in the meantime not only had huge quantities of new passenger and freight stock been built with vacuum braking, but also a big fleet of new locomotives, which were particularly costly to modify for a different braking system. In the late 1970s, although all front-rank inter-city passenger and freight services were air-braked, a considerable quantity of stock, in the freight sector especially, was still vacuum-fitted, or else lacked any continuous braking.

The really glaring fault of the 1955 Modernization Plan was its assumption that Britain's economy would stand still for the next 15 years: that the railways could take their time to re-equip, then step back into a competitively unaltered arena and mop up as of right all the traffic, long-distance and local, passenger and freight, which they had lost since end of the war. No one recognized the fact that the gradual disappearance of this business – even though BR prices were getting cheaper in relative terms – was a damning reflection on the validity of traditional railway practice in the post-war transport market.

The Plan saw no reason to modify the size of the system or the way it was run, except to aim for a speed-up of every operation through diesel or electric traction, electrically-controlled colour-light instead of mechanical semaphore signalling, mechanized shunting and rehabilitated track, stations and depots. Some of the Plan's projects had in fact been drafted before the war and had now been dusted off with scanty modification by BR regions and engineering departments scrambling for their share of goodies in the great shopping spree. These

drafts were hastily edited into a finished document by a small group of officers who had been secluded in BTC headquarters to cobble everyone's greed into coherence as soon as the government had hinted it would give re-investment in railways the nod.

The 1950s had not faded away before it became obvious that the plan was not soundly based. Except on urban or inter-urban routes, the new diesel railcar multiple-units could not gain enough passengers from buses and rapidly increasing private cars to cover their direct running costs. On the freight side, the roads' share of the expanding traffic in general consumer goods enlarged by the month. This was brought about partly as a result of the 1953 Transport Act's relaxation of own-account road haulage restrictions; partly through an upsurge of heavy road freight vehicle capacity (between 1958 and 1962 the roads saw a 60 per cent upsurge in lorries of over three tons unladen

weight and one of nearly 50 per cent in vehicles of five tons unladen weight or more); and partly because of road operators' increasing proficiency in economical door-to-door movement via the improving trunk road system. Meanwhile BR was still dealing in wagons or containers of restricted pre-war capacity, and wasting far too much of their own and the customer's time and money in shunting vehicles from train to train in the marshalling yards, where, moreover, connections between services were very unreliable. Consequently, uncompetitively slow transits were often made still less attractive. BR's situation deteriorated to the extent that between 1958 and 1962, when the volume of inland goods transport rose by 13 per cent, the railways' share fell by 12 per cent. Although heavy lorries accounted for only a fifth of Britain's total freight transport vehicles, they were now responsible for more than three-quarters of the total road freight ton-mileage; and half of them were only three years old or less.

Below: The final flowering of the Western Region diesel-hydraulic, the 2700hp Class 52 C-C which emerged in 1961. No. D1061 Western Envoy *eases an express from South Wales into Paddington in the 1960s.*

Reappraisal

The Plan had sanguinely assumed a substantial degree of wage and price stability, but as early as 1956 pay rises and inflating material costs had outstripped BR's ability to cover working expenses, let alone repay borrowed modernization funds. In 1958 the BTC nervously reappraised the Plan and managed to persuade itself that the projections were off course only because the rest of the world was not following the scenario as sketched out by the BTC. The national economy was not growing fast enough; industry was not burning enough coal to fulfil BR's forecast loads (South Wales coal forwardings, for instance, were running a third below the worst recorded at the depth of the 1931-3 Depression); the government was not allowing BR to raise fares fast enough; and railwaymen would not accept anything less than the wage levels that other industrial workers were winning for themselves. The likeliest remedy was to accelerate modernization. If that were done, the BTC predicted with supreme optimism, the railways would by 1963 be reporting an annual working surplus of £50 to 100 million.

Within a year that became still more improbable when, confronting a strike threat over pay, the government appointed the Guillebaud Committee to consider railwaymen's wage grievances. Guillebaud advocated an immediate, substantial increase, stating as a principle that the railways' notoriously laggard pay scales should keep pace with those of other basic industries. It was no more than a reaffirmation of Lord Cameron's oft-quoted dictum in an earlier BR wage arbitration, that having willed a state railway system the nation must also will the means to run it properly; and it was no more than stark realism, if the railways were to recruit and keep good-calibre staff in a prosperous economy. But Guillebaud set off a merry-go-round of wage rises trailed by despairing attempts to cover them with increased revenue that intensified the railways' financial crisis.

The rush to dieselize

Problems were multiplying, too, on the re-equipment front. The BTC's Railway Executive had originally intended to conduct a protracted pilot scheme evaluation of 174 diesel locomotives of various manufacturers' designs in three broad power ranges. They were to be grouped around carefully selected depots to build up a file of experience in handling and operating diesels, so that each class could be assessed as a candidate for mass production.

Apart from BR's own lack of diesel know-how, this cautious approach was dictated by the dearth of any proven models on the shelves of British industry, whose diesel business up till then had very largely consisted of small, custom-built orders for overseas railways of a type not quickly adaptable to BR's traffic requirements. The highly developed American diesel locomotive industry had a wide, service-hardened range that was the rational answer, but fierce political pressure by British industry put that out of bounds; British builders were desperate for a home market as a base from which to mount their own attack on main-line dieselization markets overseas.

Nevertheless Western Region pressed for and eventually secured grudging BTC agreement to build to a German pattern under licence. This created a sharp distinction between the Western's first main-line diesels and those elsewhere on BR.

There are three main ways of transmitting a diesel engine's power to a traction unit's road wheels: mechanical, through a fluid coupling, a gearbox and a final drive, which is practical only for a modest power output, as in the lowest-powered of BR's first generation of multiple-unit railcars, with their bus-type engines; electrical, in which the engine direct-powers a generator of current for DC electric traction motors (or more recently, as in BR's Inter-City 125 High Speed Trains, produces the traction current via an

Right: Birmingham Snow Hill in June 1958, with two Swindon-built cross-country type diesel multiple-units, plus a strengthening locomotive-hauled coach forming an evening Hereford–Cardiff departure at Platform 5. The decline of Snow Hill began with the start of the Euston–Birmingham electric service in 1967; lingering death became final in March 1972.

alternator and a rectifier); and hydraulic, through one or more torque converters, where the link between drive and driven mechanism is fluid, so that it can transmit and multiply smoothly much higher power than a mechanical transmission.

For main-line locomotives electric transmission had by far the longest and best documented record of service. From the start of their dieselization in the 1930s the American railroad industry had plumped for it exclusively, in association with hefty but rugged medium-rpm diesel engines. All but the Western of BR's regions preferred to take on diesel-electrics because, with the electric lines they operated, they had the experience and the workshop apparatus to maintain electric traction equipment.

The Western's management, however, was also greatly impressed by German industry's alliance of lightweight, but complex, high-rpm engines with hydraulic transmissions – much less bulky than all the trappings of an electric transmission – to achieve a 2,000hp locomotive 40 tons lighter than the unwieldy first-generation diesel-electrics which the BTC's Railway Executive was contemplating. Looking ahead, Western's management foresaw that if all freight vehicles were to be brake-fitted as promised, the case for extra locomotive weight to strengthen the braking restraint on unfitted goods trains would go. Additionally, the passenger-freight speed band would narrow, which would open up opportunities for extremely intensive daily use

of a multi-purpose locomotive with high power/weight ratio like the German hydraulic. And so orders were placed for prototypes of the German design, scaled down to the more constricted BR loading gauge, alongside the several diesel-electric types for the rest of the system. At the start engines and transmissions for the Western diesel-hydraulics were imported from the German manufacturers.

The pilot scheme for evaluating diesels never got off the ground. Faced from the mid-1950s with a fast deteriorating financial situation, the BTC concluded that getting rid of steam was the immediate way to trim operating costs. The basis of the decision to go for rapid dieselization was the diesel traction unit's theoretically superior running characteristics and greater availability for work (steam needed substantial time off for servicing between every sizeable journey). A faster and more reliable train service should be capable of the same coverage with far fewer traction units.

Other inducements were the growing shortage and escalating price of good steam coal and the difficulty in many industrial areas of recruiting good steam footplate and maintenance staff, for want of whom all too many steam locomotives were in poor condition. At this time modern factories were steadily improving the general environment of industrial life, quite apart from their lure of higher wage rates. So in the second half of 1957 the BTC placed orders for mass production of several of the types that were to have been tested under the pilot scheme, in some cases before the prototypes had rolled off the assembly lines.

The hectic pace of dieselization can be gauged from a comparison of BR's motive power in 1958 and 1963. At the close of 1958 BR was operating 16,108 steam locomotives, 105 main-line diesel locomotives and 2,417 diesel multiple-unit railcars (mass production of the railcars had begun in 1956). Five years later the steam stud had been butchered down to 7,050, main-line diesel locomotives numbered 2,051, and the diesel railcar and shunting locomotives fleet were virtually complete at 4,145 and 2,009 units respectively. The last of the world's major railways to embark on dieselization, BR was attempting to catch up at a speed and on a scale without precedent.

Traumas were inevitable. A steam locomotive can be built, maintained and kept going, almost literally, by moderately skilled use of blunt instruments. A diesel traction unit, by comparison, is as a Swiss watch to a sundial. It demands the care of skilled artisans, working to fine limits in conditions of perfect cleanliness. That was not fully appreciated even at some manufacturing plants, which at first tolerated diesel building in the same grimy workshop environment that had adequately served steam construction. Only one or two BR regions made sure that custom-built maintenance depots and trained staff were ready to handle the new traction. Others at the start were tackling the equivalent of wrist-watch repairs in a bicycle-shed. In part, this could be blamed on the 1953 Transport Act. In devolving more authority to the regions, it had weakened the power of BR's mechanical engineering chiefs to control the upkeep and utilization of the new locomotives once they were delivered to the regions.

Other troubles stemmed from over-ambitiousness. The 1955 plan had sketched a dazzling future of 70 mph average and 100 mph maximum express train speeds. That was immediately attainable only with the lightweight Warship diesel-hydraulics of Western Region, and was demonstrated on the Bristolian in the summer of 1959 – but only briefly. Within a few weeks the Warships displayed dangerous instability at high speed, unforeseen because the German type on which they were based had never been run above 80 mph, and their speed had to be reduced until the fault in suspension design had been cured.

BR's first-generation diesel-electrics were limited by the engine output available at that stage of development and by the civil engineer's un-

certainty of the effect the new traction, with its smaller wheels and different weight spread compared with steam, would have on their track. The civil engineers' initial misgivings forced the designers to build very cumbersome machines with undercarriages including idle wheels to allay the fear of excessive tonnage concentration on the powered axles.

After the euphoric promises of the 1955 Plan rail travellers were dumbfounded that BR's first express passenger diesel-electrics (today's Classes 40, 45 and 46) improved so marginally on the inter-city timings of steam. At 2,000–2,500hp the locomotives lacked the power to do better, particularly as so much of the output they did generate was absorbed in moving their own surplus weight, which was the equivalent of one to one and a half coaches.

Above: In the summer of 1957 the LMR tried to revive 'Coronation Scot' traditions with a new lightweight up morning, down afternoon lightweight Glasgow–Euston express, the 'Caledonian'. It is seen in 1962 after take-over by English Electric 2000hp Class 40 diesel-electric.

Below: The rebuilding of Birmingham New Street Station in progress; it was largely financed by commercial development in the air space above – an expedient later taxation measures have probably denied BR.

Above: The latest version of the Southern express electric multiple-unit, a 12-car formation of the stock built for the Waterloo–Southampton–Bournemouth electrification of 1967, speeds past Pirbright, Surrey. For economy, most of these units were manufactured from existing locomotive-hauled Mk1 coaches of the 1950s.

Below: Early in the 1960s the Sulzer-engined, Brush-built Co-Co diesel-electric was adopted as the BR standard high-power locomotive. Originally rated at 2750hp, stresses later enforced derating to 2580hp. No. 47.270 skirts the cliffs near Burnmouth with a Kings Cross–Edinburgh relief in 1977.

Even so, some of the diesel engine ratings had been stretched without adequate endurance testing. Others had been thrust into a BR service totally different from their previous rail traction applications. The Mirrlees-engined, Brush-built Class 31, for instance, was based on a design exported to the Ceylon Government Railways, whose operations were not near as taxing as BR's.

Desperate for economy and higher performance, BR's operators were at once pushing the new diesels to the limit of their capacity for loading, speed and uninterrupted work. For most of every working day the bigger main-line locomotives were on full power; and especially in the traffic conditions of mixed steam/diesel working until the mid-1960s the strain on the power plants was aggravated by constant deceleration and acceleration through signal checks or permanent way work. Only the most rugged engines, like those in the British Electric Class 40s, survived without serious stress flaws that in the first five diesel years reduced more than one type to half operational strength or worse. In winter, moreover, the new diesels were

frequently grounded because of the unreliable performance of their steam train-heating boilers in a vibrating locomotive environment.

The 1955 Plan hopefully envisaged that both the East and West Coast main lines from London Kings Cross and Euston to the north would each be electrified for 200 route miles or more by 1970. That was soon realized to be beyond the capacity of industry and BR's electrical engineering resources. Within a year, furthermore, the BTC had ruled out rapid progress by adopting a new system for further electrification.

25,000V AC electrification

As recently as 1951 the BTC had reaffirmed its faith in the 1,500V DC overhead wire method most recently applied to the former LNER Sheffield-Woodhead Tunnel-Manchester line over the Pennines. However, it was sufficiently impressed by the findings of an expert committee assigned to survey world development to order a test-bed conversion of the Lancaster-Morecambe-Heysham line to a high-voltage AC electrification at the industrial supply 50Hz frequency.

By the mid-1950s the French had been so successful with this method, with its promise of both economy in installation costs and superior traction performance, that the BTC overturned its 1951 judgment and settled on 25,000V 50Hz AC for all future electrification outside Southern Region, where 750V DC third rail was far too securely entrenched to make introduction of a new method sensible.

The Manchester–Crewe section of the London Midland AC electrification was finished in September 1960, giving the new electric locomotives just enough mileage to demonstrate a haulage, acceleration and sustained speed capacity better than that of any other BR traction unit. But at Crewe the work stopped, on government orders.

When the spending had to stop

The railways' mounting deficit had by now become a hot political and public issue. At the BTC's invitation the Parliamentary Select Committee on Nationalized Industries had earlier in 1960 put the railways through a searching investigation. In general the committee endorsed the scale and character of BR's re-equipment and agreed that the problem was to accomplish it more quickly. It also cheered railwaymen by suggesting that there was a corollary to the requirement of BR to break even: BR must then have commercial freedom to fix charges, refuse unprofitable traffic and shut down services as they saw fit. If social or political considerations demanded retention of an unprofitable rail service, subsidy should bridge the gap between reasonable costs and revenue. The committee's most severe criticism was reserved for its discovery, not just that within five years the originally budgeted £118 million cost of the Euston-Manchester/Liverpool electrification had soared beyond £160 million, but that the Treasury had only the vaguest idea of how or why the escalation had occurred.

Inflation and the change to 25,000v AC were factors in an out-turn grossly over budget, the result in particular of the need to rebuild literally hundreds of overbridges with enlarged clearances for the high-voltage overhead wires. Another major avoidable cause was that every department of the railway – operators, civil and signal engineers as well as traction and electrical engineers – had won themselves elaborate projects on the pretext that electrification

demanded as near as possible a new railway. Striking new stations were planned, for instance, at Euston, Manchester Piccadilly, Birmingham, Coventry and Stafford, and others were substantially improved.

Little thought was applied to the economies in track capacity which the superior performance of electric traction might allow. Overhead wires were strung over and the permanent way rebuilt on a great deal of unnecessary mileage – in sidings especially – and the whole thing was elaborately resignalled with multiple-aspect colour-lights remotely controlled from new strategic signalling centres. A lot of this was justifiable renewal of equipment, but it was made to look like an essential component of electrification. The picture was to sour Dr Richard Beeching against electrification throughout his rule of BR.

The Conservative Minister of Transport in 1960, Ernest Marples, not only halted the southward-heading London Midland electrification at Crewe, but also the rebuilding of

Below: English Electric produced its 'Deltic' 3300hp prototype Co-Co as a private venture. After its debut in 1955 it had a lengthy evaluation between London and Liverpool with the down 'Merseyside Express' and up 'Shamrock', on which it is seen here.

Above: Although promised electrification from Kings Cross to Yorkshire in the 1955 Modernization Plan, it was not until 1971 that the Eastern Region got authority for a modest suburban electrification out of London to Hertford North, Hitchin and Royston. The new service was introduced in stages between late 1976 and early 1978. Here, a Class 312 outer suburban emu from Royston to Kings Cross passes Brookmans Park.

Right: One of the East Coast route's 22 production series 'Deltics'. BR Class 55 No. 55.002 Royal Scots Grey heads a rake of MkII air-conditioned coaches near Reston on the 9.00 am Kings Cross–Edinburgh service in September 1978.

Stafford station, which was absurdly left half-demolished in a muddy shanty town of contractors' huts until the following spring. After months of agonizing suspense, the government grudgingly allowed resumption of the Crewe–Liverpool and Crewe–Euston electrification, the latter including both the Trent Valley and Birmingham–Wolverhampton routes, but BR's annual reinvestment rate was now firmly pegged (as it has been ever since), and the BTC had to submit for Ministry vetting and assent every capital project likely to cost more than £250,000. Full electric operation from Euston to the north-west began in the spring of 1966, and to the West Midlands a year later – in both cases with a speed and frequency far beyond what had been offered before.

Problems with AC electric traction

Before that happy day AC electric traction had suffered afflictions as grievous as that of the diesels. Within a month of its inauguration in November 1960, and after boosting the service's previous carryings by nearly 150 per cent, Glasgow's north Clydeside Blue Train electric multiple-units to Helensburgh and Balloch were all withdrawn from service after transformer failures – one setting off an explosion that caused injury to passengers. Right from its opening, also in November 1960, a spate of failures disastrously crippled the Liverpool Street–north-east London multiple-unit service.

On both systems the transformer troubles were largely attributable to current surges set up as the traction gear automatically adjusted from 25,000v to the 6,250v supply which the BTC had thought it wise to use for suburban services in heavily built-up city areas, to avoid a

massive expenditure on bridge and tunnel rebuilding for enlarged overhead clearances. But the effects of the surges were made even worse by serious design faults in some major components supplied by the electric traction industry.

Months elapsed before the flaws were rectified and the Glasgow service could be reliably resumed. Meanwhile the hapless Eastern Region came up against manufacturing faults in the traction motors of multiple-units arriving for its next suburban AC electric scheme, from London Fenchurch Street to Tilbury and Southend. That had to be deferred. So, as a precaution, did the opening of the Liverpool Street-Clacton AC electric service, since its train-sets were equipped by the same traction manufacturer as the north-east London units and it was only sensible to ensure that they had a clean bill of health before they were committed to full public operation. Dual-voltage operation was ultimately perfected, but experience in high-voltage AC electric working gave BR the confidence to begin conversion of all low-voltage sections to the full 25,000v supply in the 1970s.

The diesel-electric triumphs

It was not until the mid-1960s that order and reasonable reliability were extracted from the precipitate dieselization, that the unsuccessful prototype classes had been weeded out and that future construction was standardized on a single electric design in each of four power ranges. The Western had managed to expand its diesel-hydraulic main-line fleet to four types, the biggest and most imposing being the 2,700hp Class 52 Westerns, but all the time in the teeth of opposition from traction chiefs at BR headquarters and of a well-orchestrated campaign against the development of highly German-influenced designs mounted by the British traction industry.

In 1962 the electric alliance won the day. Alleging chronic failure records; high-cost maintenance of intricate lightweight mechanisms compared with the robust medium-speed engines and motors of a diesel-electric; escalating first cost; lack of point in the whole lightweight diesel-hydraulic concept because of failure to brake-fit all freight wagons; and more sophisticated diesel-electric technology – BR headquarters rang down the curtain on diesel-hydraulic construction and began conversion of the Western to diesel-electric operation. The symbol of the developing diesel-electric art was what is now BR's standard high-power diesel, the

six-axle (all-powered) Class 47, introduced that year as a 2,750hp, 95-mph unit with a weight of no more than 114 tons. But the 47, too, was initially rated beyond the practical limit of its engine in a BR traffic environment. A plague of failures was remedied only by rebuilding many engines at great expense, and de-rating of the whole class to its present 2,580hp.

Up to the mid-1960s the only diesel locomotives on BR able to fulfil the 1955 Plan's inter-city speed prospectus were the 22 3,300hp Class 55 Deltics, so named because English Electric conceived them around the triangular-form, 18-cylinder opposed-piston Napier engine originally developed for small, fast naval craft. After demonstrations of almost electric-style speed and power on BR main lines by a prototype which English Electric constructed speculatively, in 1959 the BTC had reluctantly yielded to vigorous East Coast route pressure for a fleet to compensate for their now clearly forfeited hope of electrification. The main objections were the Deltics' high cost and complexity, and having to resort to an engine untried on rail except as a prototype. The Deltics' ultimate triumph – with the London Midland electrics they were the spearhead that ripped through Beeching's gloomy prognosis for BR's inter-city passenger business – was powerfully influenced by a unique contract under which the builders, English Electric, maintained their engines, and did so largely on the basis of replacement from a pool of spare assemblies.

The beginning of the cutbacks

The numerous teething troubles of the new traction frustrated any hope of reversing the downturn of BR's finances in the late 1950s. As yet few were worried about the passenger sector. Fare increases were largely concealing erosion of inter-city business, and drastic petrol rationing following the 1957 Suez crisis artificially inflated passenger carryings to a new post-war peak. As for short-haul commuter and rural services, public opinion was deceived by glowing reports of big traffic increases following the introduction of the new diesel railcars into believing that BR's accounts were miraculously heading for balance. True, there were applications to close services, but not on any scale to cause alarm. The first major shock was the Eastern Region's call in 1958 to abandon the entire e -Midland and Great Northern cross-countr system in East Anglia.

The critical sector was freight, where the railways' staple coal and steel traffics were in recession and BR's only answer to the roads' powerful challenge in the developing merchandise market was to construct automated marshalling yards. The first of those prescribed in the 1955 Plan, at Margam in South Wales, was commissioned in the summer of 1960. As late as 1958 the BTC was still investing in traditional freight working to the extent of planning an expensive outer London freight ring route, from Cambridge via Bletchley, Oxford, Reading and Guildford right round to Ashford in Kent, of which a costly and totally redundant flying junction at Bletchley stands today as a reminder of the blinkered outlook of the period.

On its assurances that modernization would eventually pay off the BTC had been granted extensive loans, not only to fund its investment but also to meet interest charges and what were thought to be temporary deficits. The security for the loans looked very dubious when, in 1958, BR's gross income dipped for the first year since nationalization. Aggravating the railways' financial crisis was a despairing tendency to price inefficient freight working below cost in the hope of offsetting its growing lack of commercial conviction.

By early 1960 Harold Macmillan's Conservative government had decided that a new managerial approach was essential. On 10 March 1960 the prime minister told the House of Commons:

The railway system must be remodelled to meet current needs and the modernization plan must be adapted to this new shape. This will involve certain sacrifices of convenience, for example in the reduction of uneconomic services . . . . The Commission [BTC] must accept a radical alteration of its structure, so as to secure a more effective distribution of functions and a better use of all its assets.

At the same time Minister of Transport Ernest Marples appointed an advisory group of industrialists, headed by Sir Ivan Stedeford, to recommend a role for the railways in the future economic life of Britain and how they should be administered. A member of that group was the Technical Director of ICI, Dr Richard (later Lord) Beeching, at that time a faceless technocrat to the public at large but a man with a brilliant reputation in British industry for his rationalization of ICI's production. His findings particularly impressed the minister. Many suspect that it was he who largely drafted the brief for the first Chairman of the British Railways Board established by the Conservatives' 1963 Transport Act. And that first Chairman was, of course, Beeching.

The
End of an Era

Railways mean different things to all of us but certain
images of its rich history are particularly evocative. These
selected photographs sum up the intangible qualities that
fascinate thousands of railway enthusiasts. To some it is an
A4 gently simmering at Kings Cross, or perhaps flying through
Grantham on 'The Talisman', whistle blowing and shaking
the station to its foundations. To others it could be a Castle
making its way to South Wales or Cornwall on the Great
Western's lovely cross-country main lines; or perhaps on a
quiet country by-way in Kent or on that classic rural railway,
the Somerset and Dorset. Great days, never to be seen again,
but some small consolation – the end of a 140-year era has
at least been recorded for posterity.

Previous page: The last vestiges of a previous century on British railways. Class T9 4-4-0 No. 30715, built by Dugald Drummond for the L&SWR in 1899 meanders along the Camel Estuary with a Bodmin–Padstow train during the final days of steam.

Above: John Hassall's classic railway poster, promoting the then rather obscure Lincolnshire resort of Skegness. The original Great Northern version was first produced in 1908 (advertising an excursion fare from Kings Cross of three shillings) but this example was a much later variation.

Below: A more exoteric effort from the Mersey Railway, also from the Edwardian era. The carriages obviously owed something to American Pullman design. The Mersey service, still free from fogs, gales and tides, has been renovated and extended in recent years to cover a much wider area of Merseyside.

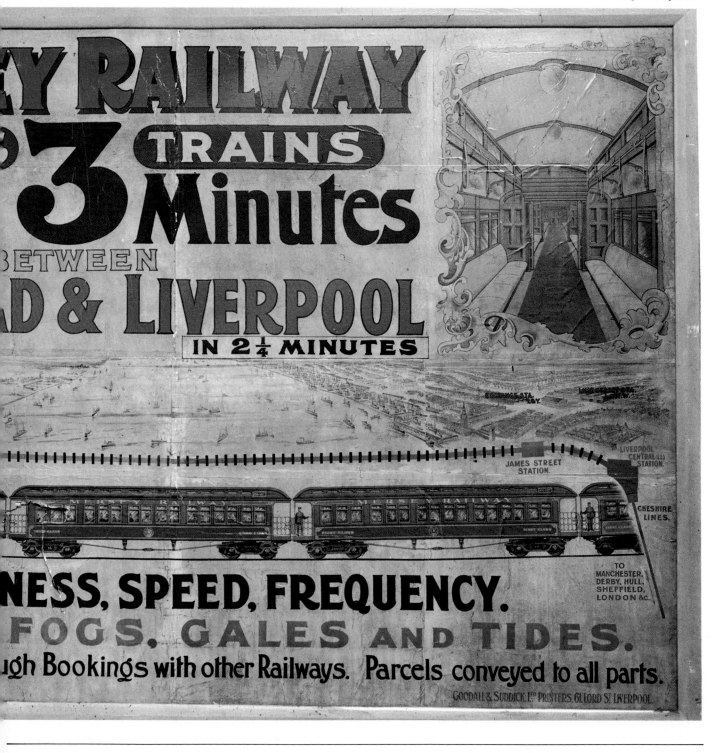

Left: The striking poster which the LNER used to launch their 'Silver Jubilee' with the first of the A4s in 1935. The poster was designed by Frank Newbould, who gave the front of Britain's first streamlined engines a slightly disproportionate width.

ARBOROUGH

32 BOOKLET FREE FROM TOWN CLERK, TOWN HALL OR ANY
L·N·E·R INQUIRY OFFICE OR AGENCY

Above: While all of the major lines produced notable poster campaigns, it was the East Coast efforts which have tended to stand the test of time best. Arthur Cooper's 1932 LNER advertisement for Scarborough is a remarkable period piece – in typography, colour, design and fashion. It was the railways which had created holiday resorts like Scarborough, and a very large proportion of their publicity still exhibited the theme of getting away from the cities to the sea shore.

Right : In 1924 the LMS
commissioned a series of
posters from members of
the Royal Academy,
including this unusually
mundane and sympathetic
scene by Stanhope Forbes.
It was one of the few
posters of the period
which did not attempt to
extol the joys of various
destinations or particular
journeys.

Below : Blackpool before
the Tower – in fact in
the 1890s. This was a
period when resorts and
railway companies pooled
their advertising
resources – in this case
with the Midland, though
it did not actually have
a station in the town.
Blackpool had three
stations, named like its
piers, North, Central and
South. Central, one of the
largest in the land, was
demolished in the 1960s to
make way for a funfair.

LMS **THE PERMANENT WAY**

RELAYING

by Stanhope Forbes R.A.

BLACKPOOL

Health & Pleasure, Glorious Sea

Through Bookings from the Principal Stations on the
MIDLAND ✦ RAILWAY.
Official Guide, with Map, &c., to be had at the RAILWAY BOOKSTALLS throughout England.

This page: The Southern Belles – a designation for named express trains used almost exclusively by the Southern region. The Brighton Belle (top), seen heading south past East *Croydon in the early 1960s was easily the most famous. The Bournemouth Belle (above) was steam-hauled almost to the last on the old London and South Western main line out of* *Waterloo. No. 35011 General Steam Navigation, an unrebuilt Bulleid Merchant Navy, passes Worting Junction.* *Following pages: Old Oak Common Castle No. 5004 Llanstephan Castle with the South Wales Pullman approaching Thingley Junction near Chippenham in the early 1960s.*

Left: The declining days of the British steam train. Among the last locomotives to be built before nationalization were the Ivatt taper boilered tank engines. Delayed because of the War they were introduced on the London Midland in 1946. After nationalization they were thought ideal for the remaining Southern Region non-electric local passenger services: No. 41294 is seen coasting along between Ashford and Canterbury.

Right: Kings Cross arrival: A4 No. 60010 Dominion of Canada at rest after bringing in the Tees-Tyne Pullman.

Below: Midsomer Norton, romantic halt on the Somerset and Dorset, plays host to BR Standard loco No. 73073 on a Bristol–Bournemouth train.

This page: London Midland mainstays: Stanier's Jubilees were mainstays of the old Midland main line from their introduction in 1934 to the end of steam. Here, left, No. 45620 North Borneo waits at St. Pancras with a Nottingham train. On the West Coast route Stanier's Coronation Pacifics took over the major expresses from 1938. In the photograph below, No. 46247 City of Liverpool passes Carstairs on a Crewe–Perth turn.

Left: The East Coast route depended on four separate Pacific 4-6-2 groups – the A1, A2, A3 and A4. One of the A2s, No. 60532. Blue Peter (upper photograph) reverses out of Glasgow Buchanan Street having brought in a train from its home town, Aberdeen, in the early 1960s. The A1s, introduced in 1945 by A. H. Peppercorn, were the last of the East Coast Pacifics to be built. Shown in the lower photograph pulling away from Grantham on a Kings Cross–Hull express is No. 60157 Great Eastern.

Opposite: The last days of steam on Patricroft shed, the old LNWR *stronghold in west Manchester. No. 73050 was one of the all-purpose 4-6-0s built as British Railways Standard locos at Doncaster in the 1950s.*

Right: July 1966 at Birkenhead Woodside, the end of the long and rather roundabout route to Merseyside from Paddington, and shortly before its closure. No. 42942 was one of the small 2-6-0 mixed traffic class introduced by Stanier in 1933.

Below: The ubiquitous Black Five introduced in 1934; eventually over 800 of these all-purpose engines, designed by William Stanier, were to be seen around the British Isles – particularly on weekend specials. Here, in definitive black livery, is No. 45110, which spent much of its life working out of Holyhead.

Right: The sign of things to come: a Euston-bound express, pulled by a Princess Coronation 4-6-2, passes Watford Gap in November 1959, just after the opening of the M1. To its right, a lone motor car approaches the service station. The gauntlet had been thrown down.

Below: The shape of things to come: leaning to the curve, the prototype of the Advanced Passenger Train shows its paces.

Chapter 25

The Beeching years and after

Above: Lord Beeching, appointed to preside over the dissolution of the BTC in 1962 and to chair the newly-formed British Railways Board in 1963. He returned to ICI, whence he had come to railways, in June 1965.

Right: The early 1960s, heyday of Birmingham Snow Hill, when the ex-GW main line was carrying all London traffic during electrification of the Euston route. The 6.30 pm Birkenhead–Paddington, headed by 4-6-0 No. 6002 King William IV finds heavy traffic awaiting its arrival on 18 August 1962.

THE CONSERVATIVE GOVERNMENT'S 1962 Transport Act was intended to check the desperate drift of the railways' finances by focussing more management attention on BR's operations as a commercial enterprise. Thus the all-embracing British Transport Commission was demolished and its London Transport, British Road Services, Docks and Inland Waterways constituents were hived off as independent concerns. The Railway Executive, which had been a subsidiary of the BTC, was superseded by the British Railways Board, directly responsible to the Ministry of Transport.

Most importantly, the new Railways Board was given a substantial measure of freedom to pick and choose the traffic it would carry, and to fix its fares and freight charges according to its own commercial judgment. The historic common carrier obligations were abolished. Another crucial change was that the government shouldered the burden of decision whether to scrap lossmaking services or to keep them going as a social necessity. The BRB could propose for closure any services it argued were irretrievable money-losers. The case would be submitted to a new Transport Users' Consultative Committee (TUCC) investigation procedure through which objectors on grounds of hardship could contest the closure at a public enquiry. The final verdict – and the responsibility for keeping the BRB saddled with the loss if the service were kept – would lie with the Ministry of Transport.

The country relaxed and awaited the first glimmer of financial transformation. But there was never much hope of one, because the cardinal errors of the 1955 modernization had not been faced. A financial reorganization linked with the 1962 Act had written off over £1000 million of BR's accumulated losses and debts,

Above: Diesel-electric No. 40.077 on the East Coast main line near Aycliffe in 1977, returning empty coal wagons from the Bowater mill in Kent to an opencast coal site in Northumberland. These 32-tons capacity air-braked wagons, fitted for automatic discharge, are the basic tool of BR's continuous 'merry-go-round' coal train which feeds from pits and CEGB power stations.

which in effect made the new BRB a present of the railway system as it was in 1954, requiring it only to repay with interest what it had borrowed from 1955 onward. A neatly charted timetable predicted that the BRB would have cleared its slate by 1984.

It might have done if there had been a proper pay-off from every piece of investment in the 1955 Plan. Instead, in its very first year the BRB slumped another £76 million into the red before it had paid a penny of interest. And so suspect were the traditional BR methods of allocating costs to individual traffics – with the result that countless services were undoubtedly being sold below real cost to offset uncompetitive quality – that no one could be quite sure where the money actually was going down the drain.

As a start, the new BRB eagerly attacked the simplest target. In the spring of 1963 it appalled the country by issuing a *Reshaping Report* – very soon and ever since known as the *Beeching Plan* – which advocated closure of over 5000 route miles of railway and 2350 stations as hopelessly uneconomic.

One theme of the whole report was the high cost of having a railway in place. Beeching, who was said to have written much of the document himself, stressed that at least half the BR system

was not earning enough to cover the upkeep of its track, signalling and other structures, let alone the direct running expenses of its trains. At the same time the trunk routes had room for more traffic, the capture of which would justify continuing investment in them.

True enough. But the *Reshaping Report* did not pause to ask whether it was worth simplifying the infrastructure and operation of some marginal services in the hope of justifiably retaining them for the value of the business they fed into the trunk system. So many of the closures subsequently carried out had a domino effect, collapsing the economics of adjoining lines as these lost the feeder business which had switched to road for the whole door-to-door journey. As for the hope of concentrating more traffic on the trunk routes, that hinged on the railways' ability to compete effectively – and, for the improvement of their finances, with assured economy – in terms of service convenience, quality and price.

However, the *Reshaping Report* did squarely confront some key issues which the BTC and Railway Executive never resolutely tackled. Above all, there was BR's dismally inefficient use of wagons. They spent so much of their lives being shunted or lying idle in sidings and depots that the average wagon took on a fresh load only once in 12 days, then spent one and a half or two days completing the average loaded journey of 70 miles from consignor to consignee. The BTC had tolerated this to the point of actually enlarging the wagon fleet to allow for the inefficiency! That trend was now to be abruptly reversed.

The railways' handling of coal, the mainstay of the freight business, had scarcely changed since the horse-and-coal-cart era. The coal left the pits in sensible trainloads. But so much of it ended up shunted into small lots, often just a single wagon, to be dropped off at the wayside station depots of about 4,000 local merchants, nearly half of whom were good for only 20 tons a week – and, what's more, often gratefully hung on to the wagons as free storage bunkers.

In the teeth of furious coal trade opposition, Beeching moved to freeze out most of these local coal yards. The merchants were urged to co-operate in the establishment of fully mechanized, strategically sited concentration depots; BR could then deliver coal in economic trainloads from pitheads to these depots, from which the merchants would serve their customers by road. As for the developing business of bulk coal movement to the big new electricity generating stations, the *Reshaping Report* proposed a conveyor-belt-like operation, feeding the electricity plants with high-capacity trains of new automatic-discharge hopper wagons in continuous 'merry-go-round' circuits between pithead and power station.

New ideas

Much of this rationalization stemmed from a vital tenet of Beeching's thinking. Railwaymen must stop thinking of rail traffic in terms of individual vehicle load. The only efficient unit of movement by rail was a complete train. This maximized the railway's ability to shift huge tonnages at a good speed with a single power unit and a train crew of only two or three men. To overcome its cost disadvantage of having to maintain an elaborately staffed and policed infrastructure out of its own resources, BR must concentrate on trainload movement without intermediate remarshalling in all its business sectors, but in the freight markets especially.

The problem area for the application of this policy was, ironically, the fastest growing freight market – general merchandise, especially consumer goods, from packaged food and detergents to durables like TV sets and washing machines. The main flows parallelled BR's trunk routes, but to a considerable extent they stemmed from

newish factories which were not rail-connected; modern road juggernauts could load these goods much more easily and economically than BR's Victorian short-wheelbase four-wheel wagons.

To penetrate this market Beeching pinned his hopes on combined rail-road door-to-door shipment in containers. A model of what he had in mind had been demonstrated in the London Midland Region's Condor service of the late 1950s. Scheduled far more briskly than any previous British freight trains, Condor was an exclusively container service, twin diesel-hauled, which shuttled nightly between London's Hendon suburb and Glasgow, stopping *en route* only at Carlisle to change train crews. It guaranteed overnight container delivery. Initially it was handicapped by the cramped size of the traditional British rail container, enforced by the skimpy floor area of the period's four-wheel flat wagons. But in the early 1960s the LMR had revolutionized the concept by switching to new, doubled capacity containers in lightweight metal (to maximize payload potential) and long-bogie flat wagons to carry them. This equipment was applied to a new Speedfreight overnight container train service between London and Manchester in 1963.

Condor and Speedfreight were imperfect prototypes, but they taught enough to support another Beeching theory – that intensively used modern equipment could generate service of a quality and convenience and at an economic price that the market would buy, provided the tracks it took were also in incessant use. In other words, the sales effort was to concentrate on filling the trunk routes; and the promised increase of traffic would in turn warrant

Above: In the early 1960s experiments were made with an amphibious merchandize vehicle devised on the US Chesapeake and Ohio RR – the Roadrailer. It was a dual-wheeled chassis easily converted into a rail wagon or a road trailer. A train of 50 was built and subjected to protracted East Coast route tests but never put into commercial service.

substantial investment in the necessary modern equipment.

Thus the pioneer LMR exercise was refined into the more sophisticated and much more costly Freightliner concept. Freightliner would be something of a conveyor belt with fixed-train sets of flatcars shuttling between pairs of strategically sited terminals so fast and so frequently that their intensive use would justify custom-built vehicles with express train performance. The high throughput predicted would also support a massive outlay on new terminals purpose-built for rapid transfer of containers between rail and road transport.

A heavily lossmaking heritage from the pre-motor era and the railways' common carrier status was the so-called Sundries traffic – small-lot consignments of less-than-wagonload volume. Before the 1930s every railway had eagerly competed for it. Consequently the big industrial areas were studded with Sundries depots; on Merseyside alone BR had inherited over 40. But by the 1950s more and more destinations were not attracting enough traffic to fill a single wagon with their packages, so that expensive, time-consuming trans-shipment of parcels from van to van *en route* was making the business an economic disaster area. The BTC had taken some faltering steps to rationalize the Sundries system. Beeching went at it ruthlessly.

The Sundries depot network was cut to a total of only 100 for the whole country; that meant, for example, that Merseyside's depots contracted to just three. Trans-shipment was restricted to seven or eight depots at strategic junctions like Crewe, Reading and York, which enforced some pretty circuitous journeys on packages unable to follow one of the direct depot-to-depot van routes. Such drastic surgery was the only way to eliminate the traffic's high quota of poor van loading and costly intermediate handling – and, moreover, to support desperately needed investment in modernized layouts and mechanization at the reorganized Sundries concentration depots.

The reaction to closures

The reshaping onslaught which provoked the first violent reaction, however, was not one of BR's public services. The publication of the *Reshaping Report* had been preceded by a five-year plan to rationalize and modernize the network of overlapping workshops which dated back to the pre-1923 grouping railways, almost all of which had had their own. A decision to close several of these plants and inflict widespread redundancies was handed to the trades unions virtually as a *fait accompli*.

Such brusque contempt for the BTC's wary – often over-timid, in fact – respect for the railway industry's hallowed tradition of joint consultation and compromise made the unions apoplectic. The one-day strike they promptly ordered was only a minor irritant compared with the souring of management-staff relations which for so long afterwards curdled railwaymen's reaction to any Beeching regime move, whatever its merits. But then Beeching never believed, as BRB chairman, in deferring much to public relations on the issues crucial to a clear definition of the railway's role in the mid-twentieth century. If the country, through its elected government, had voted for a commercially orientated railway rather than an open-ended social service, it must face squarely what, in his view, that entailed.

One of the rare occasions when rationalization plans were tempered before publication came just before publication of *Beeching Part Two*, as the subsequent 1965 proposals to slim down BR's trunk route network became popularly known. By this time the uncompromising 'keep or close' option, which was all the *Reshaping Report* offered on so many branch and secondary main-line passenger services, had been modified. The new document laid out the economic benefits of concentrating the remunerative train-

Opposite, above: Besides acceleration, the East Coast Regions added status to some key merchandize freights by naming them. Class A1 Pacific No. 60140 Balmoral *takes the newly titled 8.10 pm 'Tees-Tyne Freighter' out of Kings Cross goods yard on 1 July 1960.*

Opposite, below: Forerunner of the Freightliner was the LMR's *overnight all-container London (Hendon)– Glasgow overnight 'Condor', inaugurated in 1959. At the start it was headed by a multiple-unit pair of one of the dieselization pilot scheme's least successful types, the Metrovick Type 2 Co-Bo.*

Above: One of BR's biggest Freightliner container transfer depots at Stratford, East London. The gantry container crane spans four road or container standage tracks and four rail trucks. The depot adjoins a train-ferry wagon loading and unloading depot on the right.

load traffics – passenger and freight – on selected main lines, to take up the latter's spare track capacity over routes where duplicate – or even triplicate – lines had been inherited from the private enterprise companies; from London to the West Midlands, for instance, from London to the West Country and across the Pennines between Yorkshire's West Riding and industrial Lancashire. But this time the closing of these routes was not considered essential; single their tracks and simplify their signalling, it was said, then maybe they could still viably support a residual traffic (at the time the first costs of this simplification were underestimated).

Underlying this new rationalization move was the recognition that BR could no longer generate the surplus – or count on government handouts – to keep pace with obsolescence. There was no sense in spreading what re-equipment jam was available very thinly all the way from Penzance to Wick; it must be applied to thoroughgoing

modernization in every department along the lines of main traffic flows.

As published, *Part Two* was set out as a reasonably tentative discussion document, not a firm prescription for more axework. In draft, however, it had bluntly proposed chopping off large chunks of the system, such as the Western Region's main line between Newbury and Taunton (all trunk traffic for Exeter and beyond would have been sent via Bristol) and the entire railway west of Plymouth. Anguished Regional managers protested strongly that these unequivocal threats would further sap their freight customers' confidence. So the Report's teeth were drawn before it was issued.

At the end of the Beeching day the only main line to be shut down was the last into London from the north and from its creation in 1899 the most expendable; that was the Great Central, closed in May 1969 all the way from its border with London Transport at Aylesbury to the outskirts of Sheffield. A number of others, however, were reduced largely to single track: for instance, Salisbury–Exeter, Oxford–Worcester and the ex-GWR route from London to the West Midlands.

The public at large still thinks of Beeching predominantly as the branch passenger train's axeman. The rest of his rationalizing programme, however, had far more impact on the total of BR's human and physical assets, as this comparison between January 1963 and December 1968 shows:

	January 1963	December 1968
Steam locomotives	8,767	3
Diesel locomotives	3,683	4,326
Electric locomotives	178	329
Passenger coaches	33,821	19,544
Freight vehicles	862,640	437,412
Passenger stations	4,306	2,616
Freight depots	5,165	912
Marshalling yards	602	184
Passenger route mileage	12,915	8,471
Total track mileage	47,543	33,976
Rail and workshop staff	476,545	296,274

Cuts in manpower

The traction stock figures – which highlight the pace of steam's extinction in the mid-1960s – need a footnote. The reduction in total number of power units was not so dramatic as it appears from this summary, since diesel multiple-unit railcars which took over many locomotive tasks in the passenger business are lumped in with passenger coaches. The most significant figure in the whole table, of course, is the already swingeing cuts in staff that had been achieved by 1968.

Productivity indices were improving, too, but not to the same extent – there was too much leeway lost in the 1950s to recoup and the transport market was too competitive. Moreover, Beeching still relied on the railway's traditional costing and data-producing techniques; the root causes of continuing financial losses had still to be determined.

The government was not yet closely scrutinizing the way the BRB was spending public money on its progressive re-equipment. Since the railways were unable even to repay their debts, the ongoing modernization had to be funded out of a global deficit grant which the government stumped up annually to balance the BRB's books. With much of the modernization money going on labour-saving equipment and already insidious inflation, the economies were now being rapidly swallowed by annual wage claims. And since the 1962 Act's insistence on public hearings of the case for and against

closures prevented large-scale cost-saving under that head, in one way and another Beeching was unable to leave BR in much better financial state than he found it, though his effect on BR management and method had certainly been decisive. He returned to private industry after Labour ousted the Tories in 1964.

The 1968 Transport Act

His successor, Stanley Raymond (later Sir Stanley), the chief gatherer and analyst of data for the 'Beeching Plan', confronted Barbara Castle, the Transport Minister, who was determined to put BR and its relationship with the state on a new footing. She sponsored Britain's third major postwar piece of transport legislation – to date the most voluminous of all – the Transport Act 1968. Its main aims were twofold: to tackle the social service dilemma by dividing the railway openly into supposedly commercial and non-commercial sectors, in the hope that after more writing-off of debts the BRB could make a viable go of the commercial sector; and to resume the 1945 Labour government's drive for public transport co-ordination.

Only rail passenger services qualified for non-commercial, socially necessary status, and as such for the government's financial support which the 1968 Act allowed. But the BRB was discouraged from overloading its claims. The new support grants were to be made to specific services; there was to be no blanket grant for the whole passenger system. The Ministry of Transport, in fact, was now to get deeply involved in the operational detail of BR. In agreeing to maintain and grant-aid a specific passenger service, it

Below: A sundries merchandize depot at Birmingham in 1948. As yet no fork-lift trucks are in evidence but a slatted conveyor belt offers modest help in sorting packages.

would be the judge not merely of how much cash that service merited – under a complex formula which allowed for likely upkeep and renewal costs as well as day-to-day running expenses – but also of the level and quality of train service, and of the period for which support should be guaranteed wihout reappraisal. The BRB, naturally, was not anxious to submit its key Inter-City passenger services or their feeders – not even lossmakers like Plymouth–Penzance, which Beeching had thought of cutting off – to such interference. They were not put up for grant and constituted, therefore, the main body of the commercial passenger system.

Beeching had fretted publicly and ominously at the serious failure of provincial conurbation rail services to cover their costs. The new government believed there was a chance of

making all public transport in these areas viable if it were locally co-ordinated to better economic effect and to enhance its convenience. Ideally, too, the further evolution of public transport should go hand in hand with highway, housing and industrial planning, and with some restraint of private transport in the inner cities.

So the 1968 Act gave birth to the first four Passenger Transport Executives, or PTEs, in Greater Manchester, Merseyside and the Wirral, the West Midlands, and in the north-east. The PTEs were to take over all municipal bus services in their respective areas and integrate them and the area's local rail services; BR would equip and run the local services under contract as agents of the PTEs, who would fix fare and service levels and meet any operating losses their requirements incurred. Any PTE area service maintained solely

as a BR decision would be BR's entire financial responsibility. At the same time the government offered 75 per cent infrastructure grants towards approved redevelopment of PTE systems – for instance, electrification or new rail links for better integration of existing services. Notable instances of urban transport improvement with this support are the revitalization of Merseyside's electric commuter railways by completion of the underground Loop and Link in the heart of Liverpool, and Newcastle's brand-new Tyne Metro.

There are now seven PTEs, which under the local government reorganization Act of 1973 became agents of, and were made geographically co-terminous with, the reconstituted County Councils. The PTEs cover Greater Manchester, Merseyside, South Yorkshire, West Yorkshire, Tyne and Wear, Greater Glasgow and the West Midlands. By and large the concept has been effective and in most of the conurbations local BR management and the PTEs have gradually built up a harmonious and productive relationship.

On the freight side the 1968 Act was particularly concerned in making more economic sense of the Sundries business and focussing BR's energies on the bulk traffics. A National Freight Corporation (NFC) was set up to take over the entire rail Sundries business and with it all BR's road collection and delivery vehicles, for reconstruction as the National Carriers Limited subsidiary of the NFC. Apart from the parcels carried in passenger or parcels trains, BR were left in full control only of freight originating in full wagonloads from their terminals or from private sidings.

The aim was to bring under the NFC's wing any freight emanating from non-rail-connected premises. That predicated, in the government's logic, the Act's most detestable provision so far as railwaymen were concerned, the rape of BR's Freightliners. They too were handed over to the NFC as a subsidiary company, in which the BRB had a minority – 49 per cent – share. Henceforward the BRB would only be concerned with the running of Freightliner trains to NFC order. For the next ten years railwaymen perennially protested the changeover, complaining with some justice that the NFC's preponderant concern with road transport diminished its incentive to work vigorously for expansion of the Freightliner network. At last, under the next Transport Act but one, the Freightliner company was restored to full BRB control in 1978.

One other 1968 Act provision should be mentioned. Recognizing that the substantial costs of yet more simplification of the rail system, which the government held to be ineluctable, would outstrip the BRB's resources and dissuade it from action, the government put up £50 million towards the expense of eliminating surplus capacity over the ensuing five years. That spurred the BRB to an extensive programme of reduction from double to single track, and of lifting little-used loops and sidings. With all the resignalling involved, the eventual bill was double the sum advanced by the government.

BR entered the 1968 Act era with a new Chairman. Following Sir Stanley Raymond's resignation after a clash with the minister, Sir Henry Johnson, a career railwayman who had risen to the top from operating trains at ground level, took over the BRB. With the financial benefits of the new Act he was actually able to preside over a small financial surplus from the BRB's activity as a whole – that is, including results from its subsidiaries such as shipping – in 1969. But it was an artificial glimmer of dawn which never materialized into natural sunshine. Inflation was now rampant, quickly swallowing up any gains in revenue or from higher productivity.

That redoubled pressure for intensive use of assets and brought into sharp question the disinterest in less-than-trainload traffic which the *Reshaping Report* had induced. True, it lost money. But in 1970 it still represented nearly half BR's annual freight tonnage and helped to spread the costs of the track, signalling, traction and staff which it employed; the more it was diminished the more the overheads would fall on other traffic, prejudicing their viability in turn. To retain the wagonload traffic BR had, let alone increase it to break even, it was imperative to re-equip with high-speed wagons and a modern control system to ensure customers a reliable as well as a faster transit.

Investment and subsidies

Unhappily, the government had become increasingly cautious about investing in railways. A powerful coterie of establishment economists, scientists and officials was now persuaded that BR's modernization purse was a bottomless pit; as fast as one area was updated, another was crying out for cash – the goal of complete re-equipment would forever be out of sight. So, under the guise of a rigorous scrutiny in the national interest, more and more BR investment proposals were interminably stalled or pigeon-holed.

The 1970 general election returned the

Below: Basford Hall marshalling yard, south of Crewe, in the early 1960s. Most of the automated yards built under the 1955 Modernization Plan (this was not one) are now only partially employed.

Conservatives to power on a platform in which curbing of public expenditure was an important issue, given the now inexorable inflation. In 1971 Sir Henry Johnson retired, to be succeeded as BRB Chairman by a former Labour transport minister, Sir Richard Marsh.

The new government promptly lowered the rate of investment – now effectively half what it had been in the late 1950s – in BR and cut the services. In the spring of 1971 the country howled at the inevitable outcome: the most drastic fare increases since nationalization, in which up to 25 per cent more was clapped on at a stroke to passenger charges in the Inter-City and south-eastern England passenger network. Worse still, the Conservatives seemed minded to eliminate grant aid support entirely. With freight volumes and revenue sharply contracting – at constant money values receipts slumped by a horrifying 31.8 per cent between 1967 and 1972 – this was a grave threat.

Back in the Beeching days some BR managers were reluctant to bother with what seemed to be the lost cause of the secondary passenger services. But not now. Beeching's rather withering prognosis for the Inter-City services had been confounded by sensational upsurges of traffic on the accelerated, intensified and re-equipped trains between London and the north-east, the north-west and the west. With coal tonnage declining, iron and steel a prey to chronic

recession and general merchandise difficult to penetrate until the wagonload operation was comprehensively reshaped, BR's passenger sector was registering twice the growth rate of the freight sector. In 1969, for the first time in British rail history, passenger revenue exceeded that from freight. Besides their feeder value, with the benefit of their grant aid the secondary passenger services were contributing very significantly to the costs of 'commercial' rail routes and easing the burden on Inter-City services. If the grant system were abolished, the ripple effects could be traumatic.

In the event, however, the government stopped short at a token cut of the London and south-eastern England sector grant. Like the Churchill administration of the 1950s, it sacrificed BR to the anti-inflation battle by pegging fare rises below the rate of cost increases. The disciplines of the 1968 Act were thrown out of the window as ever bigger sums of state cash were poured into the scales to balance the BRB's disrupted books. By 1975 the shortfall to be made good was topping £300 million a year. Even at constant money values that was three times the amount of support in the false 1969 dawn following the passage of the 1968 Act.

Not only was the financial ceiling imposed on the BRB's investment now so pinched that it covered little but inescapable renewals; it was decided from year to year, which drastically

Above: Development of the 100-tons glw air-braked tank wagon, capable of 60 mph operation, was a prime factor in BR's conclusion of bulk refinery-to-inland-depot haulage contracts with major oil companies, now worth nearly 20 million tons a year. A crucial factor in these deals is the customer's long-term investment in his own rail vehicles. A train of empties from Skinningrove steelworks to Teesport moves along the coast near Brotton behind No. 37.072 in March 1977.

handicapped the BRB's forward planning. Every time an electrification scheme neared completion, for instance, its skilled engineering team was likely to break up because there was no assurance that it could move straight into a fresh project. Nor could the BRB reap the cash benefits of guaranteeing a rolling programme of orders to industry over a cycle of years. To build up a 2000-wagon fleet of standard Freightliner flatcars between 1964 and 1973, for example, involved the laborious and costly organization of 17 successive order schedules and construction programmes.

As the BRB pressed for a fresh appraisal of its remit, a baleful road bias was gaining strength in some echelons of the railways' sponsoring ministry. Why not, argued this faction, slim the railways down to a financially manageable size by attrition? In other words, avoid a Beeching-type confrontation with the public over closures by compelling the BRB to take the initiative; deny the BRB re-equipment funds and that would compel it gradually to shut down more mileage simply because of assets rotting through decrepitude. The basic network these young mandarins had in mind was disclosed in late 1972, when The *Sunday Times* leaked a discussion paper which – to the outrage of the affected public as well as railwaymen – envisaged halving the already mutilated BR system to a mere 6000 route miles, erasing tracks almost completely from the West of England and from great swathes of Wales and of Scotland north of the Forth-Clyde belt.

Re-thinking

A few months earlier the government had requested the BRB to put its past and present policies and the history of modernization under the microscope. In its summer 1973 response the BRB for the first time conceded that despite the massive pruning of staff and assets since 1948 and the attestable improvement of service quality and productivity through modernization, the railways would never pay their way under the existing terms of reference, let alone generate enough surplus to finance a satisfactory level of ongoing re-equipment. What then?

Exhaustive computer analyses of a whole range of network sizes and traffic mixes, the BRB submitted, had simply confirmed experience since the Beeching cuts: that the more you shut down the periphery of the railway system, the more traffic sapped from its hard core, until that too started to drift into the red. Far from making the railways viable, in fact, halving their

route mileage would only worsen the losses, not least because of the huge costs of transition, especially redundancy payments to staff. (These so-called transition costs were at last being fully appreciated: in other words, that it was a long time after a service was abandoned before any money was saved, because, while its revenue was cut off at a stroke, so many of the assets it used took literally years to get rid of or simplify.) Fortified by market analyses predicting sustained growth in the remunerative bulk traffics, both passenger and freight, where new technology and astute marketing techniques were now paying dividends, the BRB stood its ground on system size. By and large, the existing network of some 11,500 route miles should be stabilized.

Almost overnight the Arab-Israeli war and oil sanctions transformed attitudes towards energy-efficient railways. At the end of 1973 the Conservative government not only accepted the case for retaining the rail network virtually untrimmed, but proposed to switch some of the tightly controlled public transport expenditure from urban road development to railways. The grant-aided passenger system would be preserved, commuter railway electrification and improvement would be encouraged, development of BR's new High Speed Diesel Train and 155 mph Advanced Passenger Trains for Inter-City services would be supported, as would a computerized control system for freight and parcels services and the building of modern high-capacity 75 mph freight wagons; finally more money would be ploughed into track reconstruction and modern signalling.

The 1974 Railways Act

Early in 1974 the electorate ejected the Conservatives and it was a Labour government which enshrined the changed policy in yet more major legislation, the Railways Act 1974. A vital modification of the 1968 Act was the abandonment of line-by-line grant support of passenger services for a global Public Service Obligation (PSO), under which the entire passenger system, Inter-City included, received a general grant.

The BRB no longer had to argue a detailed case for each individual service. In effect, it was contracted by the government to run the whole rail passenger service for a figure to be agreed from year to year. Freight services would then have to support only their avoidable costs – that is, the expenses incurred solely in running them in addition to the passenger services. The conurbation PTEs, too, were allowed to exercise more of their own judgement in determining their

Above: The Cartic 4, an articulated four-car double-deck unit of ingenious cantilevered design evolved in conjunction with Ford, which appeared in 1964. Air-braked and capable of 70 mph, each Cartic 4 can carry up to 34 cars of Mini size. With it, BR has made considerable inroads into the movement of new cars from factory to distributor.

forward strategy. Central government support was no longer apportioned under specific heads of expenditure, but provided in a lump sum – the Transport Supplementary Grant (TSG) – against an acceptable four-year projection of its transport plans, called the Transport Policy and Programme (TPP), from each County Council.

But for a worsening national economic plight which culminated in near-collapse of the pound sterling at the end of the summer of 1976, BR's outlook might have been at its brightest since the 1950s. But though the 1974 Act wrote off more of BR's capital debt, the previous Conservative government's commitment to a rising scale of investment in BR over the succeeding five years was repudiated. The now chronic state of economic crisis did not even ensure 12 months' validity for BR's investment programme; one annual plan after another lasted no more than six months before the government had it revised downwards in successive moves to brake public

expenditure. So the BRB was abruptly thrown back on a hand-to-mouth investment existence which allowed it to plan with assurance for renewal only of thoroughly clapped-out assets.

The 1974 Act did include in its Section 8 one sensible gesture to placate those urging measures to get suitable freight off juggernaut road transport and on to under-utilized railways. Wherever it could be shown that the switch of a firm's freight from road to rail would be economically and environmentally beneficial, the government would pay half the cost of laying in private sidings and terminals on the company's premises. The subsequent 1978 Act went further and brought a company's acquisition of its own freight wagons within the scope of this 50 per cent Section 8 grant aid. By mid-1978 the government had endorsed 50 Section 8 applications together worth £12.5 million, and promising BR an extra 10.5 million tonnes of freight annually.

A Channel Tunnel

One enterprise calculated to send substantial and highly remunerative new traffic coursing through BR's arteries was snuffed out by the country's economic sickness. First canvassed abortively in 1802, the concept of an Anglo-French Channel Tunnel had been frequently exhumed and reinterred thereafter. With the post-World War II upsurge in international movement of people and goods, and Britain's faltering steps into the European Economic Community (EEC), the British and French governments finally, in 1973, signed an agreement of principle to build the Tunnel.

To be financed by private enterprise against a share of operating profit, the twin-bore tunnel was to be of outsize diameter so that double-decker transporter trains could operate a fast, intensive shuttle under the sea for road transport of all sizes. But the tracks were also to carry conventional passenger and freight trains between mainland European cities and, chiefly, London. The particularly exhilarating prospect was of wholesale recapture of Paris–London passenger traffic via a $2\frac{3}{4}$-hour transit between city centre terminals. The French were set to build a 160 mph railway between their coastline and Paris; the BRB intended to carve a new railway from the British tunnel mouth to London, with a great deal of tunnelling from around Croydon to a new city centre international terminal, probably near White City.

By late 1974 the prospective bill for this new railway alone had soared to over £370 million. The government baulked. For some time the BRB had unwisely given the impression that the new railway was a *sine qua non* of the 'Chunnel' project, as the existing Southern Region lines between the Kent Coast and London were over-burdened with commuter trains, quite apart from their handicap of tighter clearances than the rest of the BR system. Unprepared with a fully worked-out alternative, they handed the government a ready excuse to pull down the curtain on the Tunnel concept once more on grounds of national economic stringency – notwithstanding solemn pacts with the French, forfeiture of financial guarantees and even the fact that boring had already begun.

The tunnelling machine was left to decay inside the short length of pilot bore which had been excavated outwards from Shakespeare Cliff, Dover, just a thickness of chalk from an earlier machine abandoned when another British government had unilaterally abandoned the only previous Chunnel scheme that had got as far as excavation, in 1887. But within a year the EEC had rekindled ambition by offering hope of aid from EEC funds for transport infrastructure projects considered to benefit communications between Community members in general.

British and French Railways buckled down to drafting a much more spartan scheme for a single-bore, single-track Chunnel, through which conventional trains only could be projected in 'flights' – that is, uni-directional flows alternating roughly each hour. This time new connecting landward railways were eschewed, so that the best London–Paris rail passenger time was expected to be $4\frac{1}{2}$ hours. Moreover, through trains would have to be exclusively of BR-gauge rolling stock until some future British government acceded to French pressure for clearance enlargement on the Southern Region to allow the acceptance of mainland vehicles built to the more generous mainland European cross-section, the so-called Berne loading gauge. In late 1978 this 'economy' scheme, estimated to cost up to £700 million in total – about a third of the final 1975 estimate for its predecessor – and to be capable of completion within a decade, was laid before the British and French governments. But neither showed much inclination to endorse the scheme, a prerequisite for an EEC grant.

The 1976 Consultation Document

To revert to 1975, the year when the country was throttled by recession and rampant inflation, and BR's prospects were at their bleakest since nationalization; that was the year railwaymen extracted a wage rise of 29.8 per cent and the BRB was driven to increase fares three times in twelve months. On the railways, the investment ceiling was cut back 35 per cent to an annual level of £200 million, and the BRB was ordered to plan for no higher rate of capital investment before 1981; this represented a total shortfall of

Above: An impression of one of the drive-on, drive-off, outsize-loading-gauge car ferry trains that might have been built to serve the Channel Tunnel: the building of the latter was agreed in 1973 but abandoned by the British Government in 1974.

£678 million on the BRB's 1972 submission for the same period to the then Conservative government.

Time scales for series production of new rolling stock and installation of more remotely controlled multiple-aspect colour-light signalling had to be still further extended. Potentially more serious still, renovation of trunk route track with continuous welded rail had to be decelerated, threatening a reduction of maximum speed limits and a deterioration of speed and comfort on key Inter-City routes. On the latter, moreover, the draconian fare increases coupled with the purse-pinching of general recession had hit carryings quite savagely, especially on the newly electrified Euston–Glasgow route. As for secondary passenger services, their elderly diesel and electric multiple-unit trains were getting progressively harder to keep in good and comfortable running order, but most stood little chance of early replacement. To cap it all, the government was yet again picking over the railways' role in the national economy, with an eye to fresh transport legislation.

Professing to be in search of the grail of a national transport policy, the government's first move was to issue a Consultation Document for national debate in the spring of 1976. A rambling, badly organized thesis, highly selective in its choice of data, it rejected any long-term strategy of integrally developing the various modes of transport for the tasks each could most economically and practically perform in the national transport markets likely to unfold up to the year 2000 and beyond. It was obsessed with a narrow consideration of what represented the best value from constricted expenditure in the immediate situation of economic crisis. Its short answer to its own remit, therefore, was that the country could not afford a transport policy *per se*.

Even road interests conceded that the Consultation Document, drafted without any canvassing of professional transport operators' opinions, was heavily biased against the railways – 'hysterically' so, in the view of BRB Chairman Sir Richard Marsh, who promptly resigned, to be succeeded by industrialist Peter Parker (later Sir Peter).

Bitterly attacked, in particular, was the Document's reprise of a theme popular with some academic theorists of the period, that state support of rail passenger services primarily benefitted the better off. Plausible statistical backing highlighted greater use of trains by middle-class families in the south-east than elsewhere, the inference being that these households enjoyed an

unfair share of the PSO grant cake. Therefore, the Document advocated, London's outer suburban and long-distance commuters should be self-supporting by 1981; irrespective of any increases necessary to match inflation, that would have imposed on them an annual fare increase of $7\frac{1}{2}$ per cent from 1977 onwards. But of course the argument ignored the fact that central London is the focus of employment opportunity for a far deeper hinterland than any other British conurbation and thus creates travel to work on a much greater scale.

Another instance of the paper's distorted reasoning was the basis for its dismissal of any

Above: A block train of steel products from the BSC plant at Lackenby bypasses the Tees Yard at Thornaby behind No. 31.285 in March 1977. In the background, to the left, is the Newport lifting bridge.

move to persuade more freight from road to rail as of negligible environmental and economic value. It set the loads at issue against the total of all freight movement – in other words, against everything down to local milk delivery and refuse collection. The crux, however, was the long-haul freight carried in environmentally destructive road juggernauts. Their ton-mileage could be cut by a fifth were only 40 million tons a year of their loads coaxed on to rail, with enormous benefit to the economy of under-used BR tracks.

Given such highly prejudiced attitudes, the the Document naturally held that the prevailing levels of investment in BR were about right. It supported that view by arguing that the railways were taking a disproportionate share of national expenditure on transport – a defensible stand-point only if one restricted comparison, as the Document did, to public money and totally discounted the huge sums of private cash laid out on road transport.

The 1977 White Paper

Mercifully the government was dissuaded from founding future policy on this dubious Document. In 1977 it issued a White Paper, the basis of yet another Act which was passed into the Statute Book in 1978, which reaffirmed the existing roles of BR, removed the threat of enforcing viability on south-eastern commuters by 1981, promised new fiscal and other restraints on the heaviest road freight transport to equalize the terms of competition, and held out hope of raising BR's investment ceiling in appropriate step with any brightening of the national economic outlook. Most importantly, so far as the short term was concerned, the BRB was given assurance of government support for five-year programmes of investment in new traction, coaching stock and high-speed, high-capacity wagons, to the immense benefit of its forward planning.

It was also offered a special £50 million annual grant for the renewal of the passenger business assets, which would at least save the BRB some interest charges on money otherwise borrowed for the purpose, even though the investment ceiling could not be raised as yet to make the grant an extra spending allowance. But at least the BRB could now, with reasonable medium-term assurance, plan steady replacement pro-grammes in the most vexed areas of obsolescence – outstandingly in this context the renewal of the Southern Region's electric multiple-unit suburban train sets. They could more confidently reckon on approval for steady production of new

125 mph Inter-City train sets for prime routes and, in turn, for the cascading to neglected routes of the good-quality 100 mph coaches which these new High Speed Diesel Trains and perhaps APT's would supersede.

However, with the continued curb on rates of investment these renewal programmes would still be much too protracted for comfort. In too many departments, south-eastern England's passenger equipment especially, obsolescence would go on outstripping renewal and confront BRB and government with a really critical issue by the early 1980s.

Towards the 1980s

Nevertheless, under the inspiring command of Sir Peter Parker BR was advancing into the 1980s in better heart, probably, than at any time since Sir Henry Johnson's first year in the BRB chair. For one thing the stresses of earlier relationships with the ministerial paymasters, often exacer-bated by the inability of long-service railwaymen and Civil Service mandarins to talk a common language, had relaxed into a refreshing rapport. For another, the energy crisis had lifted the last clouds of Beeching's misgivings about the economics of electrification; at the end of 1977 the government had bidden the BRB to produce a new appreciation of the costs and benefits as a basis for review of 'the general case for further main line electrification'. And above all, making allowances for the still depressed state of the national economy, the railways had not only halted the drift to road of their most remuner-ative traffics, both passenger and freight, but were building up gains.

Particularly encouraging was the impact of 125 mph diesel service on passenger carryings between London and the west and South Wales, and between London, the north-east and eastern Scotland; and of trainload movement with modern vehicles on the bulk movement markets for commodities like earths and stones, chemicals and petroleum products. The effect of the new technology was all the more marked for its support by lively and highly professional marketing techniques. How both are deployed is described later. By the end of the 1970s the best testimony to their efficiency was that the BRB could in both 1977 and 1978 report that the railways were meeting their service specification at a significant saving on the government's annual budget, or contract figure, for BR – and at about an eighth of the total cost to public funds of, for instance, the state railway system of West Germany.

Chapter 26

The new age of Inter-City

AFTER WORLD WAR II Britain's express passenger trains were slow to regain their pre-war quality, let alone achieve any advance. In 1950, for instance, the northbound Royal Scot took ten minutes more over its London–Glasgow journey than the equivalent train needed in 1900, when the schedule included four more intermediate stops. On only two of the 50 most important trunk routes had speed revived to the best pre-war levels. Even by 1955 BR's timetables still showed only 51 start-to-stop runs daily timed at 60 mph or more and aggregating 5510 route miles compared with 116 and 12,016 respectively in 1939. Worse yet, unpunctuality was rife.

The root causes were the formidable arrears of wartime track maintenance and renewal still to be overtaken, and the unpredictable performance of steam locomotives. The latter was caused by their run-down postwar state, the dearth of good-quality steam coal such as was readily available in the 1930s, and mounting difficulties in recruiting both engine crews and maintenance staff of reasonable calibre to work in the dirty environment of steam traction.

A few trains were specially treated to create a focus for publicity, such as Western Region's Bristolian, restored to its best ever 1¾-hour London–Bristol schedule in 1954 after the start of the Swindon works' research which so enhanced the efficiency of the GWR King and Castle 4-6-0s in their final years. And non-stop working between London Kings Cross and Edinburgh was revived in the train first called Capitals Limited, then, from coronation year, 1953, the Elizabethan – though on a timing that was a long way from the overall six hours of the pre-war Coronation streamliner.

Unable to achieve much distinction in performance, BR resorted to a rash of new train names in the hope of attaching some status to the key trains on each main route. The extra-fare Pullman train fleet was enlarged, starting with the short-lived Devon Belle of 1947. The Western Region (which was determined to preserve the image of the Great Western) elaborated the window-dressing by thumbing its nose at standardization and exhuming the old

GWR chocolate and cream coach livery for its growing brood of named trains. The same year the Railway Executive discarded its first choice of crimson and cream as standard Inter-City coach livery for overall maroon, which persisted until the switch to present-day pearl-grey and blue in 1966 (WR gave up its chocolate and cream indulgence in 1962).

Motorail and ferries

In 1956 the passenger management of Eastern Region hit on a new train concept which was to be gratefully adopted, not only by the rest of BR but also by the other major railways of western Europe. It followed the old axiom: 'If you can't beat 'em, join 'em.' The family car was beginning to dominate holiday planning, but as a result summer trunk road congestion – with the first motorways still three years away – was making purgatory of the drive there and back. Motorists seemed a receptive market to an idea which relieved them of that strain. The Eastern's brainchild was the accompanied car-carrying train – a set of sleeping cars, a restaurant car, and a string of transporters for the vehicles – the first of which was inaugurated between London and Perth.

The market quickly responded in a way which justified gradual expansion of these car-carrying services into a network covering most of Britain's long-haul holiday routes, in some cases with day instead of night trains, under the marketing brand-name of Motorail. It took time to balance the books of the Motorail operation; its pricing was a matter of fine judgment between the customer costs of motoring the distance, not necessarily overnight, and the operators' expense in sleeping cars and specialized car-carrying vehicles. It was made a lot easier after the demise of steam, which eliminated most of the risk of carrying cars on open vehicles. The car-carriers could now be created cheaply by stripping life-expired passenger coaches down to their bare floorboards.

French Railways copied the idea with a Boulogne–Lyon train in 1957. This too was an instant success, and was the starting-point of a

Above: Sir Peter Parker, appointed Chairman of the British Railways Board in 1976.

Right: In 1954 the Western Region tried to revive Great Western glories by restoring the 'Bristolian' to its best-ever 1¾-hour London–Bristol timing; a 'Castle' 4-6-0 heads the eastbound train near Westerleigh in November 1959.

Top: Hengist, *a modern passenger-and-car ferry of the Sealink fleet which* BR *operates in association with the French, Belgians and Dutch.* BR *is the biggest short-sea fleet operator in the world.*

Above: Wagons leave a Sealink train-ferry on the Dover–Dunkirk route. On the European mainland they travel as far afield as Italy and Spain.

mainland European network which is marketed under differing national brand-names. The French move helped swell the burgeoning accompanied car traffic between Britain and the mainland which, in the next two decades, was to transform the character of the short-sea shipping fleet that the BTC inherited from the pre-1948 'Big Four' and welded into a single enterprise.

Today the largest of its kind in the world, operating over 50 ships – mostly passenger ones – to the Continent, the Channel Islands, Ireland and the Isle of Wight, the British Rail Shipping and International Services Division fleet is dominated by big, purpose-built road vehicle-and-passenger ferries. On the continental routes it operates in partnership with French Railways, the Belgian line, RTM, and the Dutch Zeeland company, under the brand name of Sealink. Some former railway-owned ports, such as Southampton, were taken out of BR hands in the dismantling of the BTC, but the BRB still exclusively owns and operates Harwich Parkeston

Quay, Folkestone, Newhaven, Fishguard, Holyhead, Heysham and Stranraer.

In 1966 British Railways were selected to pioneer the public service operation of hovercraft. In that year a BRB subsidiary, British Rail Hovercraft, publicly promoted as Seaspeed, was formed to inaugurate a passenger service between Southampton and Cowes with two small SRN6 craft. Two years later the company stepped up to cross-Channel operation with much bigger SRN4s, which in 1978 were 'stretched' to carry over 400 passengers and 60 cars apiece.

Electrification and regular-interval timetables

The first significant postwar year in Inter-City service development was 1959. June saw a major extension of the Southern Region's third-rail electrification, covering both routes to the Kent coast from their previous conductor-rail limits part-way from London. The Southern naturally applied to these lines from the start the same framework of intensive, hourly-patterned working with standard train-sets which had characterized its predecessor's main line electrifications from London to the Sussex coast before the war.

Simultaneously, however, and with equal commercial success Eastern Region completed the first stage of a pioneering application of this repetitive regular-interval timetable principle to a steam locomotive-hauled service on its two routes from London Liverpool Street to Norwich. The tool for this Great Eastern line service transformation was the BR standard Class 7 or Britannia Pacific, which at last gave the GE line enough traction power within the stringent weight limits its historic infrastructure imposed.

The primary commercial aim of the regular-interval timetable was to compete with the flexibility of departure time possible with a private car. On the convenience score alone private motoring was already savaging rail passenger traffic by the mid-1950s. But with the 1958 opening of the Preston bypass inaugurating Britain's motorways, BR's commercial managers were acutely conscious that road speed was about to make much longer-distance motoring attractive. From 1959 onwards all BR's Inter-City route timetables were gradually redrafted on standardized, regular-interval bases – a difficult job over the longest routes, such as London–Edinburgh, where an end-to-end train would be taking perhaps six hours to complete its journey and would have to be interwoven with area services completing a whole cycle of operations in two

Above: The Settle–Carlisle line has been abandoned by BR *as a through route between London and Scotland: this has ended the career of the 'Thames-Clyde Express', here climbing to Ais Gill summit behind* BR *standard Class 7 4-6-2 No. 70051 Firth of Forth.*

hours or less.

Following electrification of the London Midland main lines from London Euston to the West Midlands and north-west this patterned timetabling was taken a very intricate stage further. The new and enlarged Birmingham New Street station was made the nucleus of the whole Inter-City system; and throughout the country the main line passenger timetables were re-orientated step by step so as to set up, via the nodal point of New Street, decent, traceable connections between any main rail-served town in Britain and all the radial interval services out of London.

From BR's point of view patterned train services had an economical justification. The railways could afford to offer the public more trains in the day because a simplified train timetable structure simplified the programming of men and equipment to fulfil it, obtaining more productivity through quicker terminal turnrounds of locomotives, train-sets and train-

crews. Almost everywhere there was certainly spare track capacity to absorb the additional trains.

Rationalization and cutting back

Other changes were inevitable products of this policy, though other influences accelerated some of them. A standardized timetable and the drive for higher-asset productivity demanded standard train-sets. In the old days train-sets would be individually marshalled to suit the traffic mix, not only of one specific route, but of that route at specific seasons or even times of day. A train-set constituted to suit morning peak demand from London to Bristol, Birmingham, Leeds or Liverpool often stood idle at its destination for hours during the middle of the day until it was sensible to re-use it for an evening peak return trip to London.

Now the aim was to turn round as many train-sets as possible in the platform, after essential

Above: In conjunction with electrification of the main line, Euston Station was completely rebuilt in a lengthy operation eventually completed in 1968. An effort to achieve a city station on the Continental model, with a bank and a wide range of shops and catering establishments, was somewhat flawed in execution – one notable inconvenience being the interchange between main-line trains and other transport.

servicing there rather than in sidings, and to go for the highest possible average mileage per day. Not only, therefore, must the make-up of a train be the best possible compromise in terms of accommodation demands throughout a day, but it must also be a compromise between the requirements of different routes; often the high mileage targets would only be attained through complex rostering which sent a train-set out on a different route from that by which it had arrived and might not get it back to its starting point until 48 hours and perhaps half-a-dozen varied journeys later.

Another factor dictating standardization of train formations, of course, was the patterned timetable's need of standard train performance. This predicated standard train weights – a still more important requirement in the diesel and electric traction era. Extra haulage effort could be coaxed from a steam locomotive in good order, but the output of a diesel or electric unit in good health was precisely predictable, so that before long timetabling would be founded on a computerized relation of each traction type's characteristics and given train loadings to the parameters of each Inter-City route – its intermediate stops, its gradients, speed restrictions and so on.

All this enforced a steady and widespread reduction of sectional train working. There was no place in the new system for a train like the Southern's Atlantic Coast Express, which *en route* from London Waterloo shed a coach at Salisbury, one each for Sidmouth and Exmouth at Sidmouth Junction, restaurant cars and a

coach at Exeter, then finished up as one part-train of through coaches for Plymouth, Padstow and Bude, separated at Okehampton, and another part-train for Ilfracombe which also carried a through coach for Torrington.

Obviously outdated, too, was the slipping of coaches from the tail ends of speeding through trains to serve stations where a full-scale call by the main train was not commercially or operationally practicable. Only the GWR was operating slip coaches by 1939 and its resumption of the practice in 1950 had surprised everyone. Apart from anything else, the operation demanded specialized vehicles and extra train staff, but as late as 1958 the WR was adapting postwar coaches for that purpose. That same year, however, the progressive elimination of slip-coach working was ordered; the practice died out with its sole survivor, the Bicester slip off the 17.10 Paddington–Birmingham, on 9 September 1960.

Naturally, this process eventually stripped some major towns of through London services they had taken for granted. Typically affected was West Wales. In 1963 Western Region decided that the utilization of train-sets covering its Paddington–Bristol/South Wales services would be maximized if none went further than Swansea, because so much time was necessarily drawn out over comparatively little mileage on the speed-restricted route after Swansea in West Wales. For decades Paddington trains, or at least part of them, had continued to Pembroke Dock, Neyland and Milford Haven; now, while a Fishguard boat train was retained for the Irish traffic, any other travel between these western Welsh towns and points east of Swansea could only be by diesel multiple-unit to Swansea and a change there into a main line train.

More population centres suffered, of course, as the duplicate main line services were rationalized. The West Country howled in 1964 when decades of Southern route express service between London, Salisbury, Exeter, North Devon and Cornwall were ended by a BRB decision to concentrate long-distance business on the ex-GWR main line and relegate the parallel route to the status of a Waterloo–Salisbury–Exeter semi-fast service.

Three years later Shrewsbury protested with equal bitterness when the downgrading of the ex-GWR route from Paddington to the West Midlands in favour of the newly electrified LMR line from Euston deprived the city of almost all its through London trains. But it was unarguable economic sense for BR to run the patterned electric service from Euston on from the West Midlands to Liverpool or Manchester, and require Salopians to make contact with it at Wolverhampton via a connecting diesel multiple-unit.

Pressure for intensive use of coaching stock, on top of competitive pressure from the motor car, gradually changed the summer face of BR. On pre-Beeching summer weekends the routes to the popular coastal areas of Devon, Cornwall, the east and north-west were crowded with extra trains from originating points far and wide. Enthusiasts lined the tracks to revel in the unlikeliest matches of locomotives and coaches when every kind of locomotive, freight as well as passenger, invalid – as well as fighting fit – was mobilized to head train-sets that scraped the recesses of the coaching pool.

The trouble was that recesses needed exploring only at the peak of the summer. Beeching's *Reshaping Report* calculated that, of 6000 coaches forming a third of the total main line stock at the time the report's data was compiled, 2000 made a mere 10 revenue earning journeys a year, another 2000 only 14 and the remaining 2000 not more than 18. At best those 6000 coaches, the document asserted, were earning only 15 per cent of their upkeep costs, after setting off revenue when they were actually in use against their train operating costs. Less than a third of BR's entire coaching stock was in effective all-year-round revenue-earning employment. These statistics, inevitably, were the starting-gun for a drastic reduction of the coaching stock pool and of BR's ability to produce spare train-sets for seasonal extra trains and excursion workings.

A natural side-effect of the rationalization of express-train working was the gradual reduction of individual train names. Titling a train lost point when its set of coaches would see other use the same day on less distinguished services, possibly on a different route altogether. From 79 in 1958 the roll of BR's named trains had shrunk to 34 by 1968 and a decade later it was down to only 22, many of which were retained only for their historic value in promotion abroad as well as at home – Flying Scotsman and Royal Scot, for instance – since other trains on the same route were just as fast and had the same equipment.

The Pullmans

For a time Pullman trains were retained as conspicuous exceptions to standardization. BR was especially anxious to court the business travel market in the 1950s and 1960s because of its preponderance – in those days – of regular first-class travellers paying premium fares. With end-to-end rail speed not yet competitively invincible, a luxury option in the peak periods on each main business route was reckoned to be the next best selling-point. In July 1954 the BTC bought out the entire ordinary share capital of the Pullman company; then, after acquiring its preference shares in 1962, the succeeding BRB made the Pullman business a wholly-owned subsidiary.

Besides setting up a number of new Pullman services with pre-war locomotive-hauled cars on the East Coast and Western Region routes, such as the Kings Cross–Sheffield Master Cutler and the Paddington–Swansea South Wales Pullman, the BTC ordered brand-new diesel-electric Pullman trains in a controversial format. There was nothing to complain of in the appointments of the new Blue Pullmans, as they were popularly dubbed because they featured a new blue-and-white livery instead of the dark brown and

Below: The 'Midland Pullman' leaves St Pancras for Manchester. The air-conditioned, so-called 'Blue Pullman' diesel multiple-units were elegantly furnished but were disappointing in their ride quality.

cream which British Pullmans had worn since 1906. Lavishly furnished, with all the traditional Pullman flourishes of internal decor brought up to date, they were also the first British train-sets to be fully air-conditioned.

The creature comforts were enough to pull in good business – despite the trains' rather unadventurous timings – when the Blue Pullmans were put into service in 1960–1 between London St Pancras and Manchester (this operation, the Midland Pullman, terminated with the completion of the London Euston–Liverpool and Manchester electrification in 1966), and London Paddington and Birmingham, Bristol and South Wales.

The debatable feature of the Blue Pullmans was that they had been made double-ended multiple-unit train-sets. In the first two post-war decades many railwaymen on both sides of the English Channel were backing this format for diesel- or electric-powered express train-sets, either because it made for quick turnrounds at terminal stations (an important consideration on some continental routes, which involved reversals *en route*), or because it enabled the power

plant to be distributed throughout the set, reducing axle-loads and wear and tear on the track. In Britain Western Region embarked on modernization with the aim of working almost all its express services bar the West Country, South Wales and West Midlands trains from London with fixed formation and multiple units.

Very early in its diesel multiple-unit railcar building programme, in 1957, the BTC ordered, besides short-distance and commuter sets, the first of two series of Inter-City multiple units, including buffet accommodation, largely for the Trans-Pennine services between Liverpool and Hull or Newcastle. But like the far more numerous short-haul and suburban units, they rode badly and noisily and disenchanted the Inter-City public. As yet no one in Europe, least of all BR, had really mastered the design of powered multiple-unit bogie and suspension, and nowhere did a train of such vehicles ride as smoothly as the coaches of a locomotive-hauled train.

That was the Achilles heel of the Blue Pullmans. Although BR fitted them with Swiss-designed Schlieren bogies which were highly

Below: Since the spring of 1979 the interval express service between Kings Cross and Newcastle, Edinburgh and the West Riding has been monopolized by 125 mph HST *diesel units, one of which is seen at speed between Darlington and York. The two fastest trains in the timetable cover the 48.7 miles between Stevenage and Peterborough in 27.5 minutes for a start to stop average speed of 106.25 mph. The* HSTs *are the world's fastest diesel trains.*

regarded on the Continent, the imported running gear did not suit necessarily shorter British coach bodies (necessarily so, because lineside clearances on curves, at platforms especially, would be violated by the continental length) or British track. It was BR engineers' sharpest lesson to date that good riding at high speed is not the natural product of a combination of individually proven components, but heavily influenced by their interaction; that prompted the exhaustive research at the BRB's Derby research centre which eventually evolved the Advanced Passenger Train.

The Blue Pullmans, which from the spring of 1967 were concentrated on the Western Region, were withdrawn after only a dozen or so years of life in the spring of 1973, when the mass production of air-conditioned and far better-riding BR Mk IId standard coaches for ordinary Inter-City services was stripping Pullmans of their sales point. They were BR's last attempt at high-speed train-sets with motored bogies dispersed among several coaches.

The double-ended, quickly reversible train-set is still vital to the high productivity the BRB seeks from its assets, but nowadays it is achieved by locomotive push-and-pull – with a locomotive or power car at each end of the train-set, as on the Glasgow-Edinburgh route and in the Inter-City 125 High Speed Diesel Trains; or with powered bogies concentrated beneath a power car at one end of, or in the middle of, a unit, as in the Advanced Passenger Train or the most recent Southern Region express electric multiple units.

New locomotive-hauled Pullmans were built for the East Coast route services in 1960–1 and to equip new London–Manchester and London–Liverpool Pullman trains when the main line from London Euston to the north-west was electrified in 1966. In the mid-1960s the BRB's passenger service managers were still intent on developing Pullman services, but were soon dissuaded by the commercial impact of higher speed and the enhanced comfort (in second class especially) of new air-conditioned standard coaches on every sector of the Inter-City passenger market. Moreover, as railwaymen's wages rapidly inflated, the crew cost per passenger of a Pullman train's traditionally lavish staffing, with its spread of kitchens throughout the formation, started to knit brows.

In the later 1960s some Pullman trains were abandoned and others cut back to part-Pullman trains; on the inception of the Inter-City 125 service with High Speed Diesel Trains in 1978 the last of the East Coast route Pullman trains,

the Yorkshire Pullman and Hull Pullman, were discarded, and only the LMR Manchester Pullman survived.

The Deltics

The Blue Pullmans had made their debut just before the first light of BR's new Inter-City era, in 1962. After its commercial success with a regular-interval service of fast, comparatively lightweight trains between London and East Anglia, the Eastern Region clamoured for traction with capability to reproduce the achievement on its main lines from London Kings Cross to the West Riding, north-east and Scotland. **The imminent motorway age predicted machines which could average 75 mph from end to end, inclusive of intermediate stops.**

Providentially English Electric had just come up with the answer in the Deltic, a prototype six-axle diesel-electric locomotive, constructed as a speculation, which exploited an unusual triangular-shaped, opposed-piston Napier engine developed originally for fast naval patrol craft. It was a 103-ton unit with an output of 3300 horsepower and a top speed of 105 mph. A production series of 22 was acquired.

The first full Deltic-operated East Coast timetable of 1962 cut the London–Edinburgh journey time overnight by as much as an hour, down to a best end-to-end schedule of six hours by the Flying Scotsman, and trimmed other timings proportionately. For the first time stretches of the East Coast route were opened up to daily 100 mph running. Moreover, frequency of working to each main centre in the north was intensified, but with remarkable economy in resources, since the faster journeys and quick

Above: A Euston–Glasgow Inter-City express of British Rail's latest MkIII coaches soars up to Shap summit behind 25kV AC electric locomotive No. 86.206. In the mid-1980s the locomotive-hauled trains of this route will give place to squadrons of APTs (Advanced Passenger Trains).

terminal turnrounds allowed the operators to programme the Deltics for an unprecedented average of over 200,000 revenue-earning miles a year per locomotive, and their train-sets to cover a return London–Edinburgh trip daily as a commonplace.

Further electrification and reduced fares

The traffic gains registered by the accelerated East Coast service were heartening enough, but within a few years they were outclassed by the startling results from LMR's London–Liverpool and Manchester electrification. Given electric traction's accelerative power, longer spells of sustained 100-mph running were possible on this route and consequently start-to-stop averages of up to 80 mph could be timetabled between Euston and Crewe. Inaugurated in 1966 and followed a year later by full electric operation from Euston to the West Midlands, the LMR's intensive regular-interval main line electric service had by the end of the decade doubled rail passenger journeys between London and the north-west, built rail's share of the total travel market on the route up to 75 per cent, and compelled the domestic airlines to thin out their flights between London and both Liverpool and Manchester.

This commercial coup was not entirely the product of technical advance. The LMR's new electric service was the first BR passenger operation to be backed by a grand scale deployment of modern promotional and marketing techniques. Exploiting the pricing freedom afforded by recent legislation, the LMR's passenger management boldly courted new off-peak optional travel business with a range of reduced fares. Full economic benefit from electric working hinged on maximizing the system's prime advantage of continuous availability for work, which in turn makes the case for as intensive a service as possible; and above a defined passenger load factor, it is justifiable to fill the extra passenger space by pricing on a marginal long-run cost basis.

Confident of capacity business for its peak-period trains the LMR passenger management bid for new optional travellers to fill the balancing off-peak trains with a bold range of reduced fares. At the time the policy had its virulent critics elsewhere on BR, but its unquestioned success in pulling in new custom eventually converted most of the cynics. Today, refined and elaborated, market pricing is one of the cornerstones of the BRB's passenger policy throughout the network.

Further improvements in speed

The commercial magnetism of the East Coast Deltic and LMR electric services made nonsense

Right: After the most exhaustive research ever conducted into rail vehicle riding, BR in 1967 unveiled its Advanced Passenger Train (APT) concept, in which a combination of lightweight body, innovatory suspension and running gear, and automatic body-tilting were forecast to make 155 mph possible on existing track. A gas turbine-powered prototype eventually appeared in 1973 and in August 1975 was tested at up to 152 mph between Swindon and Reading, as seen here. It is now in the National Railway Museum.

of the Beeching era's trunk route reshaping prognosis of 1965, that long-haul rail passenger services could not hope to hold the pass for ever against motorways and the air. Given that conviction, the document had held 70 mph to be an adequate end-to-end average speed at which to aim well into the 1980s. Now eager passenger managers in every BR region were badgering the engineers for equipment capable of 100 mph-plus maximum speeds and end-to-end averages of 80 mph or better.

Some advance was attainable by comparatively modest expenditure on infrastructure improvements to eliminate historic speed-restricting features. In the early 1970s, for an outlay of some £60 million Eastern Region made the East Coast main line fit for continuous 100-mph running practically the whole way from London Kings Cross to Doncaster and for 85 of the 112 miles on to Newcastle. That done, the Flying Scotsman could be accelerated in 1976 to a 5 hrs-27 mins timing from Kings Cross to Edinburgh, end-to-end average 72.1 mph, and a best schedule for the route of 80.8 mph. Other Regions took similar steps.

Meanwhile the government had at last conceded projection of the LMR 25kV AC electrification to Glasgow from Weaver Junction, north of Crewe, where the Liverpool route diverged from the West Coast main line. That completed in the spring of 1974, the celebrated climbs of England's northern fells and the Scottish lowlands, Shap and Beattock banks with their long grinds at 1 in 74–5, were tamed, and the Royal Scot could be speeded up to a five-hour overall timing between London and Glasgow, for an average of 80.3 mph despite an intermediate stop at Preston. Yet again the 'sparks effect' on passenger business was marked: that autumn the route's carryings were more than 50 per cent up on 1973. By 1978 the LMR electric main line timetable as a whole was studded with 165 daily start-to-stop runs averaging 80 mph or better, up to a peak of 88.8 mph between Rugby and Watford Junction.

This might have been the limit of advance until the mid-1980s, had the BRB been staking the Inter-City future entirely on a major advance in technology, as both its own and the government's scientific advisers were urging in the late 1960s. At the start of the 1960s BR had recruited a number of young brains from the shrinking British aerospace industry to help found, in 1962, its Derby research and development centre, which was to become the most comprehensive and best-equipped railway establishment of the kind in the western world.

Given a priority mandate to improve vehicle riding, the Derby team set up an exhaustive study of wheel and rail interaction from first principles. This yielded volumes of invaluable new data on the integrated design of running gear and track essential for a stable quality of ride both of the vehicle and of the permanent way in all likely conditions; the findings were applied, with palpably impressive results, to new bogie designs for BR's Mk II and subsequent longer-bodied (70-ft) Mk III standard Inter-City coaches. But the new science was also extrapolated to the concept of an Advanced Passenger Train, or APT, which it claimed would ride immaculately at up to 155 mph on the straight and 40 per cent faster round curves than a conventional train, all without any further modification of existing main line routes.

Briefly summarized, APT theory was based on the application to a lightweight coach, embodying aerospace constructional techniques, of a patent suspension system that positively 'steered' wheels into and through curves; allied to this system was an automatic body-tilting system, which was to increase the vehicle's inward cant

Above: On test in the Western Region in the mid-1970s the prototype diesel HST train-set, No. 252.001 (since retired from commercial service) passes Filton, Bristol, as a Concorde takes off from the nearby BAC airfield.

Above: The operating floor of Saltley signalbox in the West Midlands. It is typical of the modern electronic installations from which, thanks to miniaturization of components, over 100 route-miles and 250 track-miles can be controlled from a single centre. On the operating panel the controls are all push-button and the signalmen have a continuous illuminated display of the location and identification of every train and of individual point and signal settings.

on a curve and counteract the excessive centrifugal force which would otherwise discomfort passengers when curves were taken faster.

When the APT project was unveiled in 1967 the BRB claimed that, given enough resources to complete research and development, and then to launch series production, the first squadron of trains could be running by 1972. Backed by their counterparts in government backrooms, the researchers at Derby urged exclusive concentration on the APT for future Inter-City equipment, and in 1968 the government agreed to put up half the estimated APT research and development cost.

But the APT was to be no short story, rather a long-running serial of increasingly unpredictable duration. With the railways yet again sliding into a financial mire, the government was reluctant to increase investment in unproven technology. Moreover, there was another contender for high-speed surface transportation money in the linear motor-powered tracked hovercraft, which was not conclusively written out of the lists until 1973. Even if the government had laid more cash on the BR table, the APT, as it turned out, was more theory than fully warranted specification. There were some radical changes in design before a prototype eventually took the rails in 1972.

The old hands in BR mechanical engineering had resented the aerospace engineers' invasion of their territory from the start. The APT's halting progress gained them the growing support of impatient passenger managers up and

down the system, and in 1970 the BRB agreed to hedge its Inter-City bets by ordering a fresh development of orthodox design, the 125-mph High Speed Diesel Train or HST.

The prototype HST, a double-ended set enclosing seven of the new Mk III coaches between a pair of 2500-horsepower diesel-electric power cars, emerged in 1972 almost simultaneously with a four-car APT prototype. The latter was gas turbine-electric powered. In the early stages of APT development, the range of very lightweight and compact turbines coming on to the market for helicopters and heavy road vehicles held high promise for high-speed lightweight train power, but the oil price explosion after the 1973 Arab-Israeli War abruptly cancelled many of their economic advantages and wrote *finis* to any further exploration of turbine traction for railways around the world. During their evaluation both prototype train-sets were to set new British speed records: on 11 June 1973 the HST was worked up to 143 mph on near-level track between Darlington and York, and in August 1975 the APT touched 151 mph on test between Reading and Swindon.

It was the HST which was first accepted for mass production. The first batch went to work on Western Region's London Paddington–Bristol/South Wales routes in the spring of 1977. Track and signalling improvements had fettled up nearly 100 miles of these lines for the new units' 125-mph top speed. As a result, by clever timetabling and very intensive equipment utilization, Western could launch a passenger service equalled for end-to-end speed and frequency only by the Japanese Shinkansen; but while the latter were brand-new railways tailored for and dedicated exclusively to high-speed electric trains, the Western in BR's first Inter-City 125 exercise, had superimposed 48 125-mph diesel trains each way every weekday on all the existing traffic of a historic infrastructure. City-to-city start-to-stop average speeds were as high as 93.1 mph between London and Newport, but the impressive acceleration of the APT enabled a few short sprints between intermediate calls to be timed up to a peak average speed of 103.3 mph. In the first two years of Inter-City 125, passenger carryings on the Western routes affected climbed by a third.

In 1978 Inter-City 125 came to the East Coast route with the second series of HSTs. In a first-stage acceleration the Flying Scotsman was to be brought down to a 4 hrs-37 mins London–Edinburgh journey time, and an average of 92.1 mph from Kings Cross to its first stop at

Newcastle, but the unlucky collapse of a tunnel in Scotland deferred through service for a time. However, the new and intensive timetable to North-East England and the West Riding featured start-to-stop timings which were as fast as 106.3 mph. In 1979 HSTs were to take over the London–Plymouth route and after that the complex of cross-country routes linking Newcastle, Leeds, Manchester, Sheffield and Liverpool, via the pivotal centre of Birmingham New Street, with South Wales and south-west England.

The APT took revenue-earning shape as a 25kV AC electric unit for use on the LMR lines from London Euston, where the route characteristics would extract the maximum advantage from its ability to curve faster with superb passenger comfort than an orthodox train like the HST. Extended experience was thought to be a wise move before mass production was started, so initially three sets only were manufactured, designated APT-P.

Each comprising two power cars and 12 trailers, they were to begin Euston–Glasgow service to existing schedules in 1979, then in 1980 to attempt a 96.4-mph average schedule of 4 hrs-10 mins between the two cities – but without exceeding 125 mph. It had by now been realized that regular 150-mph operation would not only make heavy investment in continuous cab signalling imperative – since at that speed drivers cannot be expected to rely on observing intermittent lineside signals – but also demand costly modification of the current supply system to cope with the high power demands of several 150-mph APTs passing through a single sub-station area simultaneously. At the time of writing a general takeover of the LMR's electric Inter-City services by the APT and the prospect of it superseding, in diesel- or electric-powered form, the HST as BR's standard Inter-City equipment, looks improbable before the mid-1980s. And even that assumes a more favourable ministerial attitude to investment in APT series production than was evident in the first months of 1979.

Below: New look at Kings Cross—a class 254 HST power car at the buffer-stops after its arrival from Newcastle. The photograph was taken in November 1978.

Above: The end of the line, figuratively and physically: the terminus of the Northumbrian Alston branch, a loss-making line which clung to a heavily subsidized existence for many years because of the inadequacy of local roads in an area where winter conditions are severe. This photograph was taken shortly before closure.

·INDEX·

Numbers in italics refer to illustrations and captions

Acknowledgement

Colourviews would like to thank the following

for their help and advice in the selection of pictures:

John Edgington (National Railway Museum), Anthony Lambert, H. G. W. Household, Jeoffrey Spence and John Marshall.